MAKING SCHOOLS BETTER FOR DISADVANTAGED STUDENTS

Around the world, governments, charities, and other bodies are concerned with improving education, especially for the lowest-attaining and most disadvantaged students. *Making Schools Better for Disadvantaged Students* presents detailed research into how poverty affects student segregation and underachievement in schools. It contains the first ever large-scale evaluation of how funding can best be used to lower the poverty attainment gap for disadvantaged students.

Drawing on a wealth of empirical research from England, India, and Pakistan as well as worldwide reviews of relevant studies, the book presents high-quality evidence on the impact of funding policy initiatives, such as the Pupil Premium funding in England, and the many variations of similar schemes worldwide. It analyses education measures which have been put in place and discusses ways in which these can be used efficiently and fairly to allocate funding to students who are persistently at risk of underachievement. The book is unique in synthesising many forms of evidence from around the world and finding a definition of educational disadvantage that can be used fairly across different contexts.

Offering significant implications for ways to improve educational outcomes for disadvantaged students, the book will be essential reading for students of education policy, sociology of education and educational practices, and all researchers, school leaders, and policy-makers working in this area.

Stephen Gorard is Professor of Education and Public Policy at Durham University, UK.

Beng Huat See is Professor of Education Research at Durham University, UK.

Nadia Siddiqui is Associate Professor of Education at Durham University, UK.

Together they form the Directorial team for the Durham University Evidence Centre for Education (DECE).

MAKING SCHOOLS BETTER FOR DISADVANTAGED STUDENTS

The International Implications of Evidence on Effective School Funding

Stephen Gorard, Beng Huat See, and Nadia Siddiqui

Routledge
Taylor & Francis Group

LONDON AND NEW YORK

Cover image: © Getty Images

First published 2023
by Routledge
4 Park Square, Milton Park, Abingdon, Oxon OX14 4RN

and by Routledge
605 Third Avenue, New York, NY 10158

Routledge is an imprint of the Taylor & Francis Group, an informa business

© 2023 Stephen Gorard, Beng Huat See, and Nadia Siddiqui

British Library Cataloguing-in-Publication Data
A catalogue record for this book is available from the British Library

Library of Congress Cataloging-in-Publication Data
Names: Gorard, Stephen, author. | See, Beng Huat, author. | Siddiqui, Nadia, author.
Title: Making schools better for disadvantaged students : the international implications of evidence on effective school funding / Stephen Gorard, Beng Huat See, Nadia Siddiqui.
Description: London ; New York : Routledge, 2023. | Includes bibliographical references and index. | Identifiers: LCCN 2022023908 | ISBN 9781032231372 (hardback) | ISBN 9781032262499 (paperback) | ISBN 9781003287353 (ebook)
Subjects: LCSH: Children with social disabilities--Education--Finance. | Education--Finance--Social aspects. | Educational equalization. | Children with social disabilities--Education--Great Britain--Finance. | Education--Great Britain--Finance--Social aspects. | Educational equalization--Great Britain.
Classification: LCC LC4069 .G67 2023 | DDC 371.826/940941--dc23/eng/20220629
LC record available at https://lccn.loc.gov/2022023908

ISBN: 978-1-032-23137-2 (hbk)
ISBN: 978-1-032-26249-9 (pbk)
ISBN: 978-1-003-28735-3 (ebk)

DOI: 10.4324/9781003287353

Typeset in Bembo
by SPi Technologies India Pvt Ltd (Straive)

CONTENTS

FIGURES

TABLES

PREFACE

This book arose from our research on the kinds of poverty and their role in schooling. Our interest in funding initiatives in education has led us to conduct reviews
of the international evidence, which provide key findings on the most effective
measures and practices for adopting direct funding or using cash transfers to overcome disadvantage in education. We have conducted an in-depth investigation of
the importance of schooling for young children. We have conducted large-scale and
longitudinal analyses of poverty-related indicators and investigated the measures
most suitable and robust for identifying disadvantage in education.

The book is unique in melding so many of these sources of information – conceptual work, systematic reviews of international evidence, a huge analysis of linked
data on 8 million pupils' lives in England over 16 years, a longitudinal study of
school attendance in India and Pakistan, and richer data from observation and interviews. By creating a definition of educational disadvantage that can be used fairly
over time and place, the book contains the first ever appropriate evaluation of how
funding can best be used to reduce socio-economic segregation between school
intakes, and lower the poverty attainment gap. In combination, these datasets and
stories create the most powerful evidence that exists on the impact of targeted funding to address educational disadvantage.

Our innovative approach of identifying the truly disadvantaged in education has
implications for who should receive the benefits of funding, as well as lessons for
developing and selecting targeted interventions for pupils who struggle to achieve
expected educational outcomes. This will be especially valuable for school systems
worldwide struggling to reduce any educational deficit created by Covid-19 lock-
downs. The issue of poverty attainment gaps and educational opportunities is of
worldwide interest – for more and less developed school systems – and the problem

of how best to recover from the deficits to schooling caused by Covid-19 lockdown is also universal.

Some of the research described here was funded by a British Academy (grant code ECE190026) and the ESRC (grant number ES/N012046/1). However, most of the work was completed as an unfunded "labour of love". The authors would like to thank colleagues, including Smruti Bulsari, Keeran Pandy, Sahar Saeed, Saba Saeed, Hamza Sarfaraz and Pauline Dixon, for their crucial fieldwork in India and Pakistan, and Binwei Lu, Nada El-Soufi, and Lorraine Hitt for their help with parts of the reviews.

GLOSSARY OF ACRONYMS AND KEY TERMS USED IN THE BOOK

DfE Department for Education, the government department in England responsible for schools.

EAL English as an additional language. The official designation in NPD for students who do not have English as their home or main language.

EEF Education Endowment Foundation. A charity set up by the DfE in 2010 to provide evidence and summaries of evidence on how Pupil Premium money might best be spent.

FSM Free school meal. A meal provided for infants, and for older pupils who are eligible due to low household income or similar disadvantage. Eligibility for Pupil Premium funding is largely based on FSM-eligibility.

GCSE General Certificate of Secondary Education. This is the most common form of qualification obtained in England for students at age 16 (KS4). GCSEs are available in every subject.

GDP Gross Domestic Product. A standard economic measure of the size and health of a nation's economy. Usually assessed as a quarterly trend.

GDPR General Data Protection Regulation. The UK (and EU) regulation on data protection for identifiable individuals.

GS The Gorard Segregation Index. A measure of unevenness in the distribution between schools of pupils with certain characteristics between schools.

IDELA International Development and Early Learning Assessment. An instrument to measure early childhood development, created by Save the Children.

KS1 Key Stage 1. Standard assessment for children in England, usually a teacher assessment in literacy and maths.

KS2 Key Stage 2. Standard assessment for children in England, usually a mixture of teacher assessment and more formal test in aspects of literacy, maths, and science.

KS4 Key Stage 4. Standard assessment for young people in England, coming at the end of compulsory schooling at age 16 (see GCSE). KS5 post-16 is optional, although some kind of education or training is required for all students.

LA Local Authority area in England. Run by a locally elected council, authorities used to control all local schools. However, an increasing number of schools (Academies) are now independent of local control.

NPD National Pupil Database, held by DfE. A dataset with records for all pupils in state-funded schools in England, containing assessment entries and outcomes, linked to details of pupil background and characteristics.

Pupil Premium a policy of additional funding for schools, proportionate to each school's intake of disadvantaged students. Introduced in England in 2011.

RCT Randomised control (or controlled) trial. A research design attempting to make a fair comparison between cases experiencing an intervention and cases not experiencing it.

SEN Special Educational Need. This is the official designation used by DfE for students with clear individual challenges for their learning. These challenges could be cognitive, behavioural, or physical. Often includes "disability", SEND.

SLASC School level annual school census, held by DfE (see NPD). A record of the characteristics of and intakes to all state-funded schools in England.

VA Value-added. Intended to be a measure of progress made at school, independent of the actual level of attainment of each student.

INTRODUCTION

1

GLOBAL INTEREST IN NARROWING THE ATTAINMENT GAP

Introduction

Around the world, governments, charities and other bodies are concerned with improving education, especially for the lowest attaining and most disadvantaged students. This concern has been magnified recently as such organisations try to help their schooling systems recover from a global pandemic that has reportedly affected the education of disadvantaged students more than the others, on average. This book presents the strongest and most up-to-date evidence so far on how funding can be best deployed to improve schooling and narrow the disadvantage attainment gap.

This book is about several linked problems in compulsory education, which have potentially lifelong impacts. The main policy problem is the gap, gradient or unfairness in educational opportunities, treatment and outcomes when comparing students from high- and low socio-economic status (SES) backgrounds. These appear in some form in all education systems worldwide, and to some extent unfairness and inequalities due to socio-economic poverty are becoming more visible as more and better data is available for understanding and comparisons (Krafft 2019, Chmielewskia 2019). There have been developments in the expansion of school education systems, but inequalities still persist in access to high quality education and more so in developing countries that have had incomplete enrolment to schools (Wagner et al. 2022). More developed countries have generally achieved the targets of access to free and universal education, enrolment of all children, and completion of compulsory school up to a certain age.

Improving enrolment by expanding access to schools can then lay bare the educational inequalities that had been hidden at home until then. However, the attainment gap is wide and even growing in some countries with full school enrolment. This is a point that we will return to many times in this book.

DOI: 10.4324/9781003287353-2

Overcoming the impact of socio-economic disadvantage in education has been an important policy area in which international and local governments have made huge investments over the last two decades. Direct financial investment to overcome educational challenges has been implemented in many countries, but the impact of such costly policy initiatives remains unclear due to the varied formats of implementation, and differences in the selection of measures for identifying disadvantaged students.

Government education funding to address persistent achievement gaps due to childhood poverty is costly for the public purse, whether the funding is given to areas, schools, or teachers, or to students or their families. This book presents findings on the implementation, success, failure and impact of government funding initiatives of all of these kinds in helping to overcome educational disadvantage. These policy initiatives are unlikely to be sustained if their impact remains unclear, or if they are criticised on grounds that are not supported by high quality evidence. The danger of sustaining or abolishing any education policy initiative has a direct impact on education stakeholders, both in terms of opportunity costs, and the damage that may be done to young peoples' one chance at childhood education. Therefore, evidence is essential on progressive and beneficial policy initiatives and implementation.

In the UK, inequality in educational outcomes and occupations has generally been declining over historical time. This is true for all four home countries, and as such is not apparently linked to specific policies, certainly not in education (Paterson 2022). In richer countries like the UK it is therefore sometimes harder to see what difference specific government policies on education actually make (Gorard 2006). To address this, throughout this book we look at educational policies and practices worldwide, and several chapters focus on poorer or less uniformly developed countries, including India and Pakistan, while others focus on changes occurring in England that have relevance for all education systems.

What is this book about?

The book has six main parts. This first section provides an introduction to the key issues covered in the book (Chapter 2). It establishes the importance of addressing the poorer educational outcomes of disadvantaged students, and why this is a matter of worldwide justice as well as efficacy. The second section on improving school enrolment and attendance worldwide presents the results of structured reviews of existing evidence on the use of financial and other incentives (Chapters 3 and 4). It then summarises our new work on the impact of early school attendance in India and Pakistan (Chapter 5). The third section covers more evidence from structured reviews of existing evidence on the use of financial and other incentives, now in the context of improving attainment at school, and encouraging qualified teachers to work in hard to staff schools and areas (Chapters 6 and 7).

Much of the rest of the book then focuses on a specific cash transfer policy in England – Pupil Premium funding. The fourth section outlines this policy, its background and implementation (Chapter 8), the difficulties faced in evaluating its impact, and the solutions we used in the rest of the book, including datasets and methods, (Chapters 9 and 10). Section 5 then presents key consolidated findings from our Pupil Premium policy evaluation. Chapter 11 looks at changes in socio-economic segregation between schools, and the extent of clustering of poorer children in specific schools since 1989. Chapter 12 looks at changes in the poverty attainment gap since 2006. Chapter 13 looks at the background and other characteristics of long-term disadvantaged students in England. And Chapter 14 shows how the segregation and attainment gaps are related, and considers what the overall impact of Pupil Premium funding has been.

In the final section, the book concludes by considering and consolidating the evidence on which ameliorating interventions seem to work and which do not, and summarising the implications from all of the foregoing material for addressing educational disadvantage worldwide (Chapter 15).

References

Chmielewskia, A. (2019) The Global Increase in the Socioeconomic Achievement Gap, 1964 to 2015, *American Sociological Review*, https://journals.sagepub.com/doi/pdf/10.1177/0003122419847165

Gorard, S. (2006) Does policy matter in education? *International Journal of Research and Method in Education*, 29, 1, 5–21.

Krafft, C. (2019) *Economics for the greater good: An introduction to economic thinking for public policy*, USA, Press Books.

Paterson, L. (2022) Education and high-status occupations in the UK since the middle of the twentieth century, *British Journal of Sociology of Education*, http://dx.doi.org/10.1080/01425692.2022.2026763

Wagner, D., Castillo, N. and Lewis, S. (Eds.) (2022) *Learning, marginalization, and improving the quality of education in low-income countries*, Cambridge: Open Book Publishers.

2

WHY DO WE CARE ABOUT EDUCATIONAL GAPS?

Introduction

This chapter is about the "gaps" within any educational system, in terms of educational opportunities, treatment, and outcomes, between economically disadvantaged students and their peers. In later chapters, we also discuss the differences in educational systems between richer and poor countries.

On average, socio-economically less advantaged students have lower attainment outcomes at school and poorer opportunities for continued education, once they have left school (Gorard and See 2008, Lessof et al. 2018, Hanushek et al. 2019). On average (and only on average), disadvantaged pupils can present the schools they attend with greater challenges to successful teaching. This may be due to a variety of factors (see below) including health, learning difficulties, having other priorities, and having fewer relevant resources at home.

In England, relative poverty, as represented by eligibility for free school meals (FSM), and being registered as having a special educational need or disability are the most important known challenges facing pupils when they start school (Gorard and Siddiqui 2019). And attainment at school and continuation in education after school are heavily patterned by similar indicators of disadvantage both in the UK and elsewhere (Rutkowski et al. 2018, Hanushek et al. 2019). These attainment and participation gaps suggest that there is an underlying unfairness in the education system. Of course, such "effect" sizes do not imply that relative poverty is their sole cause – and the term "effect" size is really a misnomer here, actually representing just a standardised difference between two mean scores. Many other factors such as talent, motivation, and a "learner identity" may play a role in creating these gaps (Gorard 2018). Moreover, there is always a proportion of disadvantaged students who "succeed against the odds" (OECD 2011, Borman and Overman 2004).

DOI: 10.4324/9781003287353-3

The permanence of child poverty, the timing of its onset, and higher concentrations of poverty in the community, all appear to matter for children's outcomes. Early, long-term family poverty generally leads to worse outcomes later. Living in poverty is a key determinant of child's well-being, and cognitive and educational outcomes (Chaudry and Wimer 2016). Poverty and low income are related to worse child development outcomes, particularly cognitive developmental and educational outcomes (Treanor 2020, Knowles et al. 2016). Mechanisms through which poverty can affect these outcomes include material hardship, family stress, parental and cognitive inputs, and the developmental context to which children are exposed.

Of course, this well-known average relationship between socio-economic status (SES) and student attainment at schools is not a fully causal one (Marks 2021). We recognise that there are almost certainly genetic, hereditary, or related reasons for part of the systematic gaps between social groups in terms of educational outcomes (Zeeuw 2019). Children from high SES families appear better at solving problems from a very young age (Ginsburg and Pappas 2004), suggesting a role for inherited "talent" in the link between SES and school attainment (Selzam et al. 2016). We need to acknowledge these lucky genetic differences if we are to overcome the idea of a simple meritocracy of results in education, and so help fairer outcomes to emerge (Harden 2021). The gaps in education between social groups may never disappear entirely.

Nevertheless, the observed educational gaps between social groups around the world are to do with more than any hereditary talent, and things can be improved, even if only partially. Giving poorer families substantially higher incomes, irrespective of their behaviours, can improve their children's outcomes at schools (Cooper and Stewart 2020). This creates the kind of society that most of us would want if we had to decide before knowing where we would be born into it – Rawl's notion of a veil of ignorance (Cameron et al. 2018).

Talent flourishes more in certain environmental conditions than in others, and this can be affected by education (Ritchie and Tucker-Drob 2017). So, for the remainder of this book we focus on what can be done to reduce the SES gap in school outcomes, and most especially what can be done within education. We start by considering in more detail a reasonably wide range of possible influences on educational outcomes, of the kind that could help explain why poorer students are also educationally disadvantaged in most school systems around the world.

A classification of possible influences in biographical order

There are many ways to classify the possible influences on educational outcomes at school, including structurally, geographically, socially, individually, or in/out of school factors. Here a range of candidate influences are listed first in approximate life order. However, most factors (such as nutrition) run across school phases and operate both inside and outside of schools.

The following tables are divided into the phases of birth, infancy, primary and secondary schooling. The factors are listed in the phase to which they might be most relevant, but in reality most will continue to be an influence throughout. The factors also linked to a "level" at which they operate – such as individual, family, or school. But again these factors might operate in more than one way. For example, the decision to breastfeed a child or not could be health related or cultural. The tables merely suggest a preliminary tentative classification in terms of the extent to which each factor is clearly malleable or not. We have tried to exclude factors that cannot be easily changed. So our classification here labels factors as clearly within the remit of education ("Y" in the final column), malleable but less obviously within the remit of education ("y"), or not easily malleable in the short-to-medium term, and anyway not really addressed by education ("N"). It is important to recall that even the factors labelled "N" are changeable and many should indeed be addressed by policy. They are not necessarily either genetic or inevitable. But they require wider societal or much longer-term investments than those we consider further in this book.

Other than parental education, dealt with later, none of the factors listed in Table 2.1 are really addressable through traditional school education. Programmes to improve the health of parents (carers or guardians), especially mothers, are covered in the subsequent chapters.

There are a substantial number of issues in Table 2.2 that might be addressed through investment and improvement in education. Chapter 3, in particular, looks at the impact of providing more pre-school facilities and places, and its relationship to subsequent school readiness. Chapter 6 discusses the summary evidence on parental involvement in their children's education. And Chapter 13 looks at the intersection of economic disadvantage and educational challenges like disability and special educational needs (SEN).

Tables 2.3 and 2.4 relate to the years of formal and usually compulsory schooling for children and young people. Unsurprisingly, they contain a larger group of education-relevant issues, that underlie the emergence of poverty attainment gaps, and which could be improved through policy or practice. Some of these

TABLE 2.1 Examples of birth issues stratified by advantage and linked to cognitive development

Element potentially stratified by poverty	Level	Malleable?
Health and nutrition of mother	Family	y
Smoking and birth weight		y
Breast feeding or not		y
Stress for mother from challenging life conditions		N
Antenatal depression/anxiety		N
Poor-quality or overcrowded housing	Economic	N
Parental investments of time and childcare		N
Differences in hierarchy of needs		N

Sources include: Crenna-Jennings (2018), Gershoff et al. (2007)

TABLE 2.2 Examples of issues in infancy and early years stratified by advantage and linked to cognitive development

Element potentially stratified by poverty	Level	Malleable?
Early language development and school readiness	Individual	Y
Attentiveness, curiosity and motivation		y
Having a special educational need, challenge, or disability		N
Poor physical health and motor skills		N
Ability to concentrate and recall		N
Living in care		N
Sex, gender		N
Numbers games with parents	Family	Y
Early reading experiences		Y
Toys and books to stimulate cognitive development		Y
Singing and rhymes, artistic activities, with parents		Y
Outdoor physical activity		Y
Play dates		y
Adult talk and range of vocabulary		y
Early life neglect and abuse		N
Inter-parental conflict and mental health		N
Insecure attachment to caregiver		N
Other priorities than education		N
Family structure		N
Richness of home learning environment, place to study at home	Economic	y
Other material deprivation – access to heating, clothing, transport		y
Nutrition		y
Childcare and benefits policies		y
SES segregation by area of residence		N
Place and community disadvantage		N
Misdiagnosis or differential diagnosis of SEND, in either direction	Social	Y
Access to, and quality of, early years and nursery experiences	School	Y

Sources include: ChildFund (2021), Goodman and Gregg (2010), Gorard et al. (2017), Sammons et al. (2008)

are psychometric characteristics such as attitudes. We have previously shown that although these characteristics may indeed be stratified across social groups, there is little evidence that changing the attitudes in themselves does anything to address the achievement gap (Gorard 2012, Siddiqui et al. 2019). These differences in attitudes between students do not appear to be causal factors for attainment, but are the outcomes and correlates of other determinants, and the success or failure in achievement that they bring (Easterbrook et al. 2022). These factors are not addressed much further in this book, but it might be assumed that they would improve as a consequence of the recommendations made there. We discuss the role of assessment in Chapter 9.

As noted above, parental involvement is dealt with in a later chapter (and in See and Gorard 2015, See et al. 2021). The impact of disadvantaged settings on teacher and student interaction is dealt with later in this chapter, as part of a consideration of the damage that SES segregation does. Pupil Premium funding in England, and the ways in which it can be deployed by schools to improve teaching and the curriculum is covered in detail in later sections of this book. Access to tutoring is addressed in Chapter 6.

There are, of course, many other possible issues linked to inequalities and attainment in education. Where countries have a clear cut-off date for entry to each school year, then the youngest children in each year are at a serious disadvantage. They may be nearly a year younger than their peers. And this shows up in their development, participation in sports, misdiagnoses as having learning challenges (Gorard 2018), and attainment and progression (Marcenaro-Gutierrez and Lopez-Agudo 2021). However, this issue like several others is not really patterned by poverty.

The rest of the book considers a range of the issues in Tables 2.1 to 2.4, focusing on those that can be addressed by schools, mostly labelled "Y" above, and mostly from Tables 2.3 and 2.4, ignoring attitudes, aspirations and expectations, for the reasons already given. The book goes into more detail about the factors that we think could be the most important, and that could be relatively easily addressed by school systems alone. These include:

- Having access to schools, enrolling in and attending them
- The challenges of attending a disadvantaged area or school such as
  - the provision of good teachers
  - differing classroom practices
  - how behaviour is dealt with
  - possible teacher bias, and deficit thinking
  - teacher:student relationships
  - breadth of curriculum, and access to other activities
  - the damage caused by socio-economic, ethnic and other segregation between schools
- And the best bets in the deployment of cash transfers to schools and related interventions to improve attendance and attainment

These issues are what the rest of the book is about. The book provides the most up to date (at time of writing) evidence, especially concerning attendance and enrolment at school, socially segregated settings at school, and how best to reduce the poverty attainment gap. We have conducted new research in all three areas, and we also present the findings of our structured reviews of existing evidence on attendance (Chapters 3 and 4), and improving attainment (Chapters 6 and 7). However, we did not find any credible body of prior robust evidence on how to address between-school segregation. The literature, on this clustering of poor pupils

TABLE 2.3 Examples of issues during primary school years stratified by advantage and linked to cognitive development

Element potentially stratified by poverty	Level	Malleable?
Perceived locus of control	Individual	Y
Deficit thinking by pupils		Y
Self-esteem		Y
Aspirations and expectations		Y
Resilience, success against odds		Y
Behavioural difficulties		y
Mental health, social, emotional difficulties		y
Adverse child event, distressing experiences		N
English as a first language or not		N
Parental aspirations for child	Family	Y
Access to space and suitable technology for learning		Y
Time spent with parents		Y
Parental involvement in child's education		Y
Access to enrichment activities and sports at home		Y
Parenting styles, child-rearing practices		y
Cultural and social capital		y
Home learning environment		y
Parental substance abuse		y
Parental physical and mental health		N
Parental cognitive abilities		N
House moves, pupil mobility, immigration		N
Loss of parent through incarceration, divorce or death		N
Teacher quality and experience	School	Y
Challenges faced by schools in disadvantaged settings		Y
Classroom practices in disadvantaged settings		Y
Teacher unconscious bias, teacher assessment, grading		Y
Deficit thinking by teachers, stereotype threats, labelling		Y
Pupil:teacher interactions		Y
Deployment of Pupil Premium or similar cash transfers		Y
Breadth of curriculum		Y
Access to enrichment activities and sports at school		Y
Attending schools with high disadvantage intakes – SES segregation		Y
Use of elaborated code in schools and assessments		N
Conflicting policies, such as making KS2 harder	Social	y

Sources include: Bernstein (1971), Coughlan (2021), Crenna-Jennings (2018), Goodman and Gregg (2010), Gorard and Smith (2010), Gorard (2018), Gorard and Siddiqui (2019), West (2007)

TABLE 2.4 Examples of issues during secondary school years stratified by advantage and linked to cognitive development

Element potentially stratified by poverty	Level	Malleable?
Pupil expectations	Individual	Y
Experience of transition to secondary school		Y
Summer learning loss		Y
Attendance, long-term absences		Y
Anti-social behaviour/alienation		y
Insecurities, fearing consequences of poverty		y
Feelings of powerlessness/anger at unfairness in society		y
Experience of education as failure		y
Deferred gratification, especially concerning leaving school		y
Sense of worth and belonging		y
Permanent learner identity built up from all other factors		y
Parental expectation	Family	Y
Attendance at parents' evenings		Y
Focus on goals outside education		y
Additional academic support and private tutoring	Economic	Y
Activities that require parental contributions to fund		Y
Need for students to take paid work		y
Pupils treated differently in high disadvantage schools	School	Y
Use of setting/streaming, quality of teaching and opportunities		Y
Less careers advice/work experience, without networks to make good		Y
Interactions between pupils		Y
Predicted grades, allocation to sets		Y
School exclusions		Y
Academic and other forms of selection to school		y
Access to popular, deemed high performing, schools		y
Availability of role models, among students and adults at school		y
Teaching experience, qualification, subject expertise		y
Teacher turnover		y
Inspection bias causes higher SES families to avoid specific schools		y
Anti-school sub-cultures	Social	y

Source include: ChildFund (2021), Crenna-Jennings (2018), Goodman and Gregg (2010), Gorard and Rees (2002), Sugarman (1970)

with others like them in specific schools, has largely been concerned with how strong the pattern is, why it arises, and what damage this causes. Internationally, we have found no prior studies looking at the effectiveness of additional funding, in itself, for reducing socio-economic segregation between schools. So we offer no full review on segregation, unlike attendance and attainment. Instead, the next section of this chapter summarises what we do know about segregation, in a standard narrative format.

What is socio-economic segregation?

When poorer children are disproportionately clustered in particular schools with others like them, we call this phenomenon socio-economic segregation between schools (Gorard et al. 2003). Segregation here is the opposite of evenness in the distribution of student characteristics across the schools in any area or system. If, for example, 10% of students in an area were from black ethnic backgrounds, and each school in that area had around 10% black origin students, then we could say that this particular characteristic was evenly distributed between school intakes. If, at the other extreme, black students only went to schools with other black students, so that perhaps 10% of schools consisted of all black intakes, and 90% had no black students, then we could say that the system was totally segregated. The index we use for assessing the level of segregation for any student characteristics is a measure of this uneven spread between schools, and is described in Chapter 10. Segregation can be of any individual student characteristic. But we are concerned here only with characteristics that could be considered as an indicator of potential disadvantage in education.

Our main focus is on economic poverty. In any school system, poorer children tend to be clustered to some extent in particular economic regions, areas of housing, and schools (Jenkins et al., 2008, Gorard 2015, Roew and Lubienski 2017). Of course, disadvantaged students may also be segregated in a number of ways within the school that they attend. The damage caused by segregation between schools could also arise from segregation within schools, and schools should act to reduce it (Dalane and Marcotte 2022). We do address this in the book, but how students are deployed <u>within</u> schools is not the main focus.

Why does segregation matter?

We have previously presented evidence that clustering disadvantaged students into specific schools has potentially very damaging impacts for the students, the school system and society more generally (e.g. Gorard et al. 2003, Gorard and See 2013). This kind of damage can happen as early as pre-school (Stewart et al. 2019).

Exposure to a more varied set of possible friends at school leads to improved role models for lower attaining pupils (Gorard 2018), and more tolerant wider pupil attitudes such as trust in others (Bhattacharya 2021). Socio-economic segregation between schools, on the other hand, is strongly associated with higher degrees of social reproduction (Reichelt et al. 2019). In heavily selective school entry systems, such as grammar and secondary modern schools in England, or early-age tracking as used in Germany and elsewhere, the social origin of students has a stronger link to their later social status. Such systems create a kind of social stagnation rather than mobility. This may be due to a peer effect whereby young people adapt their expectations towards the average outcome expectations of their friends (Lorenz et al. 2020). According to an analysis of longitudinal data for England by Dickerson et al. (2018), this peer effect is more serious for lower-attaining and more disadvantaged pupils. By disproportionately denying poorer students access to more academic schools, tracked schooling systems tend to concentrate social disadvantage into schools with lower academic expectations of students by their teachers.

The same kind of damage can also occur in non-selective (or ostensibly non-selective) systems, such as those where school places are influenced by religion or the cost of local housing. Any reason for segregation will do.

There is a long-standing body of evidence showing that equivalent student behaviours, interactions and achievements are interpreted differently in different settings as defined by the peer group. Indeed, the peer group can actually induce different behaviours, interactions and achievements. For example, children clustered in low ability groups tend to demonstrate more hyperactivity and emotional problems (Papachristou et al. 2021). In the US, racial segregation between schools is linked to lowered life expectancy, with segregated students more likely to adopt negative behaviour and practices.

Going to school in segregated settings is therefore potentially damaging in a variety of ways (Horgan 2007) – such as lowering aspiration, expectations, and participation for individuals. It reduces national and regional social and ethnic cohesion (Danhier 2018, Hewstone et al. 2018). SES-segregated schools are also linked to students' decreased trust in public and private institutions (Molina and Lamb 2021), and to different experiences of fairness at school (Gorard and Smith 2010, Gorard 2012b). SES segregation between schools can act to deter more qualified teachers from working in heavily disadvantaged schools (Copeland 2019).

Perhaps most importantly for this book, there have long been accounts of a peer or compositional effect on attainment. Research has relatively consistently reported that socio-economic segregation between schools leads to worse inequalities in schooling outcomes (Sciffer et al. 2020). Whether this is so or not, trying to improve average attainment, the attainment of all students, and to reduce the poverty achievement gap, are complementary activities. Acting on one of these can easily help with the others (Kyriakides et al. 2019, 2021). In Chapter 14, we present further important evidence on this issue, based on data from around 8 million pupils in England.

What causes segregation?

The reasons why segregation occurs also form part of our previous explanatory work (Gorard et al. 2013, Gorard 2015, 2022). The acknowledged determinants of segregation between schools start with residential/household segregation, and these two patterns are mutually reinforcing. Where areas or blocks of housing are either rich or poor, then the schools that their neighbourhood serve will tend to reflect those students who are rich or poor. The same would be true of areas with particular concentrations of any ethnic groups. Schools mostly reflect the population of the areas they serve (Taylor et al. 2003).

In some countries, including China and the US, schools are funded partly by local taxation. This means that schools in richer areas or provinces will have greater funding and so more resources, and schools in poorer areas will have less. This is absurd in a national school system. In China the situation is made worse by the *hukou* registration system that prevents access to schools in urban areas to migrants and those moving from rural areas. Instead, migrants are forced into lower quality, poorer-funded schools (Xu and Wu 2022).

Even when the funding of schools is flatter, as it is in England, schools in richer areas with more expensive houses will still have better average outcomes because of the link between average attainment and student SES. These schools might then be seen as more desirable by parents, and families may be willing to pay more for housing near them – the so-called estate agents' premium. If this happens, the cost of housing near desirable schools rises, thereby exacerbating the difference in raw-score school outcomes compared to poorer areas – the "Belfast" model (Gorard et al. 2003).

The way in which school places are allocated is then a further possible driver of segregation. Any system which creates school intakes of students largely based on where they live, will reproduce any existing residential segregation, or make it worse. This is so whether over-subscribed places are decided on the basis of local feeder schools, catchment areas, or distance to travel from home. Moving to open enrolment instead, whether via parental choice or admission lotteries, permits families to use schools further from their homes or outside of their catchment zone. This may involve students travelling further to school, and this is more likely to be undertaken by children from more advantaged families (Scandurra et al. 2021). But, overall the evidence is that open enrolment is usually linked to a decline in segregation by weakening the link between school intakes and residential segregation (Gorard et al. 2003, Bonal et al. 2021).

Other elements of school placement that drive up segregation include selection by "ability" (as above) which also inadvertently (perhaps) sorts them out by family background to some extent (Gorard and Siddiqui 2018), and tracking by ability (Strello et al. 2022), as widely used in countries in central Europe, and in some subjects in the US (Loveless 2021). The younger the students are when this tracking takes place, the worse the situation generally is, as it is in Austria, Hungary and Germany where selection occurs at the age of 10 (Sciffer et al. 2020). Tracking also interacts with the proportion of privately educated students in any population. Any kind of selective intake, including by the faith of the family, leads to segregation. In fact, almost any kind of diversity of schooling, even just a curriculum speciality and even if not ostensibly selective, leads to higher SES segregation (Gorard 2018). This has happened in the US with charter schools, according to most accounts (Marcotte and Dalane 2019).

Conclusions

Many of the problems introduced in this chapter, and discussed in the following chapters, will presumably have long-term solutions beyond education, such as reducing the economic and other differences between regions or social groups. However, given that there is no strong evidence that deliberate segregation leads to any better educational or societal outcomes, in the shorter term we will recommend desegregation of school systems – in terms of student indicators of potential disadvantage such as poverty. This involves not using selection of any kind, not having diverse types of school, and not allocating school places in any way that will reproduce or worsen existing residential segregation. Further measures are discussed in Chapters 11 and 15.

References

Bernstein, B. (1971) *Class, Codes and Control*, London: Routledge.

Bhattacharya, S. (2021) *Intergroup contact and its effects on discriminatory attitudes Evidence from India*, WIDER Working Paper 2021/42, WIDER Working Paper 2021/42-Intergroup contact and its effects on discriminatory attitudes: evidence from India (unu.edu).

Bonal, X., Zancajo, A. and Scandurra, R. (2021) Student mobility and school segregation in an (un)controlled choice system: A counterfactual approach, *British Educational Research Journal*, 47, 1, 42–64.

Borman, G. and Overman, L. (2004) Academic resilience in mathematics among poor and minority students, *The Elementary School Journal*, 104, 3, 177–195.

Cameron, S., Daga, R. and Outhred, R. (2018) Setting out a conceptual framework for measuring equity in learning, Chapter 2 in *Handbook on measuring equity in education*, UNESCO, http://uis.unesco.org/sites/default/files/documents/handbook-measuring-equity-education-2018-en.pdf

Chaudry, A. and Wimer, C. (2016) Poverty is not just an indicator: The relationship between income, poverty, and child well-being, *Academic Pediatrics*, 16, 3, Supplement, S23–S29.

ChildFund (2021) *Statistics on underprivileged children in the world*, Underprivileged Children Statistics and Facts | ChildFund.

Cooper, K. and Stewart, K. (2020) Does household income affect children's outcomes? *Child Indicators Research*, Does Household Income Affect children's Outcomes? *A Systematic Review of the Evidence*, 14, 981–1005 (springer.com).

Copeland, J. (2019) A critical reflection on the reasoning behind, and effectiveness of, the application of the Pupil Premium Grant within primary schools, *Management in Education*, 33, 2, 70–76.

Coughlan, S. (2021) Teachers' grades biased to more 'agreeable' pupils, BBC News 20/5/21, Teachers' grades biased to more 'agreeable' pupils, claim psychologists - BBC News.

Crenna-Jennings, W. (2018) *Key drivers of the disadvantage gap*, Education Policy Institute, EPI-Annual-Report-2018-Lit-review.pdf.

Dalane, K. and Marcotte, D. (2022) The segregation of students by income in public schools, *Educational Researcher*, https://doi.org/10.3102/0013189X221081853

Danhier, J. (2018) How big is the handicap for disadvantaged pupils in segregated school settings?, *British Journal of Educational Studies*, 66, 3, 341–364.

Dickerson, A. Maragkou, K. and McIntosh, S. (October 2018) *The causal effect of secondary school peers on educational aspirations*, CVER Discussion Paper Series - ISSN 2398-7553, http://cver.lse.ac.uk/textonly/cver/pubs/cverdp017.pdf

Easterbrook, M., Nieuwenhuis, M., Fox, K., Harris, P. and Banerjee, R. (2022) 'People like me don't do well at school': The roles of identity compatibility and school context in explaining the socioeconomic attainment gap, *British Journal of Educational Psychology*, https://bpspsychub.onlinelibrary.wiley.com/doi/full/10.1111/bjep.12494

Gershoff, E., Aber, L., Raver, C. and Lennon, M. (2007) Income is not enough, *Child Development*, 78, 1, 70–95.

Ginsburg, H. and Pappas, S. (2004) SES, ethnic, and gender differences in young children's informal addition and subtraction: A Clinical Interview Investigation. *Journal of Applied Developmental Psychology*, 25, 2, 171–192.

Goodman, A. and Gregg, P. (2010) *Poorer children's educational attainment: How important are attitudes and behaviour?* York: Joseph Rowntree, Poorer children's educational attainment: How important are attitudes and behaviour? (jrf.org.uk).

Gorard, S. (2012) Experiencing fairness at school: an international study in five countries, *International Journal of Educational Research*, 3, 3, 127–137.

Gorard, S. (2015) The complex determinants of school intake characteristics, England 1989 to 2014, *Cambridge Journal of Education*, 46, 1, 131–146.

Gorard, S. (2018) *Education policy: Evidence of equity and effectiveness*, Bristol: Policy Press.

Gorard, S. and Rees, G. (2002) *Creating a learning society?* Bristol: Policy Press.

Gorard, S. and See, BH (2008) Is science a middle-class phenomenon? The SES determinants of 16–19 participation, *Research in Post-Compulsory Education*, 13, 2, 217–226.

Gorard, S. (2022) Segregation and the attainment gap for permanently disadvantaged pupils in England, *Educational Review*, https://doi.org/10.1080/00131911.2021.2007055

Gorard, S. and See, BH. (2013) *Overcoming disadvantage in education*, London: Routledge.

Gorard, S. and Siddiqui, N. (2018) Grammar schools in England: a new analysis of social segregation and academic outcomes, *British Journal of Sociology of Education*, 39, 7, 909–924.

Gorard, S. and Siddiqui, N. (2019) How trajectories of disadvantage help explain school attainment, *SAGE Open*, https://doi.org/10.1177/2158244018825171

Gorard, S. and Smith, E. (2010) *Equity in Education: an international comparison of pupil perspectives*, London: Palgrave.

Gorard, S., Taylor, C. and Fitz, J. (2003) *Schools, markets and choice policies*, London: RoutledgeFalmer.

Gorard, S., Hordosy, R. and See, BH. (2013) Narrowing the determinants of segregation between schools 1996–2011, *Journal of School Choice*, 7, 2, 182–195.

Gorard, S., See, BH and Siddiqui, N. (2017) *The trials of evidence-based education: The promises, opportunities and problems of trials in education.* London: Routledge.

Hanushek, E., Peterson, P., Talpey, L. and Woessmann, L. (2019) The Achievement Gap fails to close: Half century of testing shows persistent divide between haves and have-nots, *Education Next*, 19, 3, 8–17.

Harden, K. (2021) *The genetic lottery: Why DNA matters for social equality*, Princeton: Princeton University Press.

Hewstone, M., Ramiah, A., Schmid, K., Floe, C. Zalk, M., Wolfer, R. and New, R. (2018) Influence of segregation versus mixing: Intergroup contact and attitudes among White-British and Asian-British students in high schools in Oldham: England, *Theory and Research in Education*, https://doi.org/10.1177/1477878518779879

Horgan, G. (2007) *The impact of poverty on young children's experience of school*, York: Joseph Rowntree Foundation, https://www.jrf.org.uk/report/impact-poverty-young-childrens-experience-school

Jenkins, S., Micklewright, J. and Schnepf, S. (2008) Social segregation in secondary schools: how does England compare with other countries? *Oxford Review of Education*, 34, 1, 21–37.

Knowles, M., Rabinowich, J., Ettinger de Cuba, S., Cutts, D. and Chilton, M. (2016) "Do you wanna breathe or eat?": Parent perspectives on child health consequences of food insecurity, trade-offs, and toxic stress, *Maternal and Child Health Journal*, 20, 1, 25–32.

Kyriakides, L., Charalambous, E., Creemers, B. and Dimosthenous, A. (2019) Improving quality and equity in schools in socially disadvantaged areas, *Educational Research*, 61, 3, 274–301 (tandfonline.com).

Kyriakides, L., Creemers, B., Panayiotou, A. and Charalambous, E. (2021) *Quality and equity in education: Revisiting theory and research on educational effectiveness and improvement*, London: Routledge.

Lessof, C., Ross, A., Brind, R., Harding, C., Bell, E. and Kyriakopoulos, G. (2018) *Understanding KS4 attainment and progress: evidence from LSYPE2*, Research report, DFE, https:// assets.publishing.service.gov.uk/government/uploads/system/uploads/attachment_ data/file/748514/Understanding_KS4_LSYPE2_research-report.pdf

Lorenz, G., Boda, Z., Salikutluk, Z. and Jansen, M. (2020) Social influence or selection? Peer effects on the development of adolescents' educational expectations in Germany, *British Journal of Sociology of Education*, https://doi.org/10.1080/01425692.2020.1763163

Loveless, T (2021) Does detracking promote education equity? Brown Centre Chalkboard, Does detracking promote educational equity? (brookings.edu).

Marcenaro-Gutierrez, O. and Lopez-Agudo, L. (2021) Too late or too soon for school? *Journal of Research on Educational Effectiveness*, https://doi.org/10.1080/19345747.2020. 1849479

Marcotte, D. and Dalane, K. (2019) Socioeconomic segregation and school choice in American public schools, *Educational Researcher*, https://doi.org/10.3102/0013189X19879714

Marks, G. (2021) Is the relationship between socioeconomic status (SES) and student achievement causal? Considering student and parent abilities. *Educational Research and Evaluation*, http://dx.doi.org/10.1080/13803611.2021.1968442

Molina, A. and Lamb, S. (2021) School segregation, inequality and trust in institutions: Evidence from Santiago, *Comparative Education*, 58, 1, 72–90.

OECD (2011) Against the odds: Disadvantaged students who succeed in school, *OECD Publishing*, http://dx.doi.org/10.1787/9789264090873-en

Papachristou, E., Flouri, E., Joshi, H., Midouhas, E. and Lewis, G. (2021) Ability-grouping and problem behavior trajectories in childhood and adolescence, *Child Development*, https://doi.org/10.1111/cdev.13674

Reichelt, M., Collischon M. and Eberl, A. (2019) School tracking and its role in social reproduction: Reinforcing educational inheritance and the direct effects of social origin, *The British Journal of Sociology*, 70, 4.

Ritchie, S. and Tucker-Drob, E. (2017) How much does education improve intelligence?, *Psyarxiv Preprints*, https://psyarxiv.com/kymhp

Roew, E. and Lubienski, C. (2017) Shopping for schools or shopping for peers, *Journal of Education Policy*, 32, 3, 340–356.

Rutkowski, D., Rutkowski, L., Wild, J. and Burroughs, N. (2018) Poverty and educational achievement in the US, *Journal of Children and Poverty*, 24, 1, 47–67.

Sammons, P., Sylva, K., Melhuish, E., Iram, S., Taggart, B., Hunt, S. and Helena, J. (2008) *Effective pre-school and primary education 3-11 project (EPPE 3-11): influences on children's cognitive and social development in year 6*, (PDF) Effective pre-school and primary education 3-11 project (EPPE 3–11): influences on children's cognitive and social development in year 6 (researchgate.net).

Scandurra, R., Zancajo, A. and Bonal, X. (2021) Opting out of neighbourhood schools: The role of local education markets in student mobility, *Population, Space and Place*, https:// doi.org/10.1002/psp.2542

Sciffer, M., Perry, L. and McConney, A. (2020) Critiques of socio-economic school compositional effects: Are they valid, *British Journal of Sociology of Education* 41, 4, 462–475.

See, BH and Gorard, S. (2015) Does intervening to enhance parental involvement in education lead to better academic results for children? An extended review, *Journal of Children's Services*, 10, 3, 252–264. http://dx.doi.org/10.1108/JCS-02-2015-0008

See, BH, Gorard, S., Siddiqui, N., El Soufi, N., Lu, B. and Dong, L. (2021) A systematic review of technology-mediated parental engagement on student outcomes, *Educational Research and Evaluation*, Full article: A systematic review of the impact of technology-mediated parental engagement on student outcomes (tandfonline.com)

Selzam, S., Krapohl, E., von Stumm, S., Rimfield, K., Kovas, T., Dale, P., Lee, J. and Plomin, R. (2016) Predicting educational achievement from DNA, *Molecular Psychiatry*, 22, 2, 267–272.

Siddiqui, N., Gorard, S. and See, BH (2019) Can learning beyond the classroom impact on social responsibility and attainment? An evaluation of the Children's University youth social action programme, *Studies in Educational Evaluation*, 61, 74–82.

Stewart, K., Campbell, T. and Gambaro, L. (2019) The peer composition of pre-school settings in England and early recorded attainment among low-income children, *British Journal of Sociology of Education*, 40, 6, 717–741.

Strello, A., Strietholt, R. and Steinmann, I. (2022) Does tracking increase segregation? International evidence on the effects of between-school tracking on social segregation across schools, *Research in Social Stratification and Mobility*, 78, 100689.

Sugarman, B. (1970) *Sociology*, London: Heinemann Educational Books.

Taylor, C., Gorard, S. and Fitz, J. (2003) The modifiable areal unit problem: Segregation between school and levels of analysis, *International Journal of Social Research Methodology*, 16, 1, 41–60.

Treanor, M. (2020). *Income, poverty and deprivation among children – A statistical baseline analysis*, Department of Children and Youth Affairs, https://www.gov.ie/en/publication/a1580-income-poverty-and-deprivation-among-children-a-statistical-baseline-analysis-july-2020/

West, A. (2007) Poverty and educational achievement: why do children from low-income families tend to do less well at school?, *Benefits*, 15, 3, 283–297.

Xu, D. and Wu, X. (2022) Separate and unequal: *hukou*, school segregation, and educational inequality in urban China, *Chinese Sociological Review*, https://doi.org/10.1080/21620555.2021.2019007

Zeeuw, E. (2019) Socioeconomic status, genes and educational attainment, *Science of Learning*, https://npjscilearncommunity.nature.com/users/266633-eveline-de-zeeuw/posts/53123-socioeconomic-status-genes-and-children-s-educational-achievement?utm_source=newsletter_mailerandutm_medium=emailandutm_campaign=newsletter

KEY FINDINGS ON SCHOOL ATTENDANCE

3

REVIEW OF EVIDENCE ON TARGETED FUNDING TO IMPROVE ATTENDANCE AND PARTICIPATION

Introduction

The book has four chapters that contain findings from our inter-related reviews of the existing worldwide literature. This chapter looks at how cash transfers and other financial interventions can influence school enrolment, attendance and participation. Chapter 4 looks at the evidence on how attendance can be improved in other ways.

Chapter 6 looks at how financial interventions can improve student attainment at school, and Chapter 7 looks at other ways to improve attainment, including the deployment of teachers – how to encourage qualified staff to teach in poorer schools and areas. The results in Chapters 4 and 7 did not emerge from a bespoke structured review as such, but were found as part of the other reviews. Here we describe the overall approach we used for our reviews. The methods are similar across all reviews, of the kind reported in See et al. (2021, 2021).

Methods used in our structured reviews of evidence

Search strategy

In all reviews, we employed a broadly similar protocol, in line with current practice used in most structured or systematic reviews. The reviews differ only in terms of the syntax used. These are tailored to the research questions appropriate for each review.

In general, our reviews began with a broad search for studies that address the research questions. For example, one review, on interventions to increase school

DOI: 10.4324/9781003287353-5

enrolment, attendance, participation and attainment in low and middle income countries, used major search terms that included:

Developing/low or middle income nations

List of countries specified from Afghanistan★ to Zimbabwe★ OR "developing nation" OR "developing region" OR "developing countr★" OR "third world nation" OR "third world country" OR "third world region" OR "low income nation" OR "low income country" OR "low income region" OR "impoverished country" OR "impoverished region" OR "impoverished region" OR LMIC
AND

Evaluation

evaluat★ OR random★ OR controlled OR "control group" OR comparison★ OR propensity OR discontinuity OR match★ OR lotter★ OR "study design" OR rigorous OR trial OR experiment★ OR intervention★ OR "randomi★ control trial" OR "RCT" or "regression discontinuity" or "causal evidence" OR "quasi-experimen" OR "difference-in-difference" or "instrumental variable★" or strategy★ OR "approaches"
AND

Intervention

Impact★ OR effect★ OR effectiveness
AND

Enrolment outcomes

schooling OR enrol★ OR attend★ OR absent★ OR absence★ OR dropout★ OR "dropout" OR "drop-outs" OR "grade repetition" OR "repeat grade" OR "complete grade" OR "test score" OR "grade completion" OR "standardi★ test" OR matricul★ OR retention OR "staying on"
AND

Children

youth★ OR child★ OR student★ OR adolescent★ OR teen★ OR boy★ OR girl★ OR pupil★ OR youngster★ OR juveniles OR minors OR kids OR "primary" OR elementary OR "middle school" OR "junio★ school" OR "mobile child★" OR migrant★

For all reviews, a pilot review was first conducted to test out the sensitivity of the search terms on well-known sociological, educational and psychological databases, to ensure that the search terms picked up relevant pieces of literature and also studies already known to us. Following this, a very general and inclusive statement of search terms was generated for each database. These were adjusted to suit the idiosyncrasies of each. For different databases we had to modify the syntax but used similar key words.

The pilot reviews and previous reviews of literature suggested that there were few robust experimental evaluations of policy initiatives or approaches that aim to improve attendance, or the recruitment and retention of classroom teachers, for example. Therefore, we included any empirical studies with at least some type of comparative design, many of which will subsequently have low ratings for trustworthiness in terms of causal claims.

Databases

For all reviews, the search terms were applied to the main educational, psychological and sociological electronic databases. These included:

- Education Resources Information Clearinghouse (ERIC)
- JSTOR
- Social Sciences and Education Full Text
- Web of Science
- Science Direct
- Proquest Dissertations and Theses (http://library.dur.ac.uk/record=b2044198~S1)
- EBSCOhost (which covers the following databases: ERIC, PsychINFO, BEI, PsycARTICLES and IBSS
- plus Google and Google Scholar.

We also followed up on studies that were known to us from our previous work and from references in systematic reviews uncovered in our searches. For example, in our review of interventions that have an impact on learning outcomes of children in developing or low or middle-income countries, we found a number of really useful narrative reviews, particularly those conducted by the World Bank. These assessed the impact of a range of interventions and programmes on the outcomes of children in low and middle-income countries. The individual studies were then followed up, and many were added to our database.

All searches were limited to studies published in the English language. We intentionally did not set any date limits, to keep the search open. To avoid publication bias, the search included any material whether published or unpublished, that mentions both the substantive and causal terms. The identified reports were then exported to EndNote for screening.

Screening

In the first stage, studies were screened for duplicates and relevance, on the basis of their title and abstract. Inclusion and exclusion criteria were determined prior to screening. Only studies that related specifically to the research questions were retained.

Studies were included if they:

- were empirical research with an experimental, quasi-experimental or at least comparative design
- were relevant to the research questions
- had measurable outcomes (e.g. attainment, school attendance, school enrolment or teacher retention or recruitment)
- were related to mainstream education (i.e. not solely about special or alternative education).

Studies were excluded if they were:

- not primary research
- solely ethnographic, opinion pieces, guidance briefs, promotional reports or anecdotal accounts from schools or policy-makers about successful strategies
- not published or reported in English
- not actually a report of research at all
- simply descriptions of programmes or initiatives with no evaluation
- not about strategies or approaches to improve recruitment or retention of teachers in school or not about improvement in students' attainment and enrolment in school
- studies that had no clear evaluation of outcomes
- studies with no measurable outcomes

At this stage the retained reports were skim-read by one researcher. Any studies now thought not to meet the inclusion criteria were then reviewed by other members of the research team for consensus. Further, in order to establish inter-rater reliability, all members of the team independently reviewed 10 randomly selected reports to decide if they agreed on their inclusion or exclusion. Studies that were deemed relevant to the research questions and met our inclusion/exclusion criteria were retained for data extraction.

Data extraction

Information from the included reports was summarised, including details on research design, number of cases, method of allocation to groups, outcome measures, missing data, analyses and the results. At this stage further studies were excluded if it became clear that they were not relevant to the topic or not evaluations of interventions.

A PRISMA flowchart was created for each review detailing the number of reports identified and retained at each stage. As an example for the review of teacher supply, see Figure 3.1.

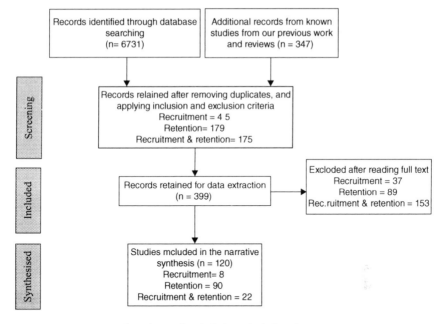

FIGURE 3.1   PRISMA flowchart of included/excluded studies

Quality assessment

Studies that were deemed to be both relevant and research-related were then assessed for the strength of their evidence based on their research design, scale and threats to validity using a quality assessment "sieve". This is a tool used to judge the trustworthiness or strength of each research report. If public investment is to be used for policies and practice in education, it is crucial that the most robust evidence is given the most weight. For this reason we synthesised the evidence by first assessing the trustworthiness of the findings in each report based on five criteria (Table 3.1). These criteria were having a research design appropriate for addressing a causal question (e.g. whether it is an RCT with random assignment of cases, or if there is a fair comparator group), scale of the study (based on the smallest cell size in any comparison), level of attrition and missing values, quality of outcome measurement (e.g. self-report or administrative data) and any other threats to validity. Each study is then assigned a score between 1🔒 (the minimum standard to be given any weight in our review, including some kind of comparison) and 4🔒, the most secure that could be expected in real life, meaning that the evidence is the most trustworthy (Gorard 2021). Studies that are not empirical or with no validity were rated 0 for our purposes, and excluded. These are not discussed further in the book.

We ignored the source of publication, reputation of the researchers/authors, and their reported outcomes and conclusions in our assessment. It is very common to find studies reporting a positive impact despite having no relevant data, and studies that claimed conclusions unwarranted by the data.

TABLE 3.1 Quality assessment "sieve"

Design	Scale	Dropout	Data quality	Threats	Rating
Strong design for research question	Large number of cases per comparison group	Minimal missing data, no impact on findings	Standardised, independent, accurate	No evidence of diffusion, demand, or other threat	4🔒
Good design for research question	Medium number of cases per comparison group	Some missing data, possible impact on findings	Standardised, independent, some errors	Little evidence of diffusion, demand or other threat	3🔒
Weak design for research question	Small number of cases per comparison group	Moderate missing data, likely impact on findings	Not standardised/ independent, contains errors	Evidence of diffusion, demand or other threat	2🔒
Very weak design for research question	Very small number of cases per group	High level of missing data, clear impact on findings	Weak measures, high level of error, or many outcomes	Strong indication of diffusion, demand or other threat	1🔒
No consideration of design	A trivial scale of study	Huge amount of missing data, or not reported	Very weak measures	No consideration of threats to validity	0

Synthesis

For the reviews on attendance and learning outcomes, we organised the studies by outcomes (e.g. school attendance, school enrolment, attainment or staying on in school) and then by interventions/programmes aimed at improving those outcomes (e.g. conditional cash incentives, unconditional cash incentives, school improvement initiatives or health/medical interventions).

For the review on teacher recruitment and retention, we first classified the research reports as being about recruitment, retention or both. These were then further sorted according to the types of incentives or initiatives.

Summaries of the results of all reviews appear in later chapters.

Why invest in school education?

We now present the results of the first of the structured reviews, here concerning the use of finance-based interventions to improve attendance at school. School attendance is considered a human right (Gaviria 2022). We consider here enrolment, absence and participation outcomes as well as measures of attendance.

And we include funding to create or expand schools, to eliminate the costs of attending school, and direct cash transfers to stakeholders such as schools, teachers, families and students. We excluded studies that are conducted in higher education institutions (universities) as our focus is on school age children, but we included studies of pre-school if they had school-relevant outcomes.

Education systems have adopted different policies for the age at which children start school, but usually the expected range of starting at a formal school has been between five to seven years of age (Sharp 2002). The evidence is inconclusive on the most appropriate starting age of school, and whether an early start leads to better academic attainment outcomes in later stages of education or not (Burger 2010). However, the evidence suggests some beneficial impacts for disadvantaged children if they start school earlier in life (Heckman 2006).

Introducing school to children's lives is intended to stimulate and accelerate the cognitive learning process in the early years of life (Black et al. 2017, Noble et al. 2015). Schools also act as a buffer zone against adversities and as a safe place when vulnerable children face challenges at home such as poverty, neglect, and family chaos impacting negatively on children's development and educational outcomes (Taggart 2010). Children out-of-school are at higher risk of abuse, poor health, violence, and participation in the labour force (UNICEF 2018).

There are several associated benefits of children's school attendance, such as assisting parental participation in the workforce (Morrissey 2017), women's participation in the labour market (Dahl & Lochner 2012). Tsai et al. (2009), prevention of child labour force participation (Berlinski & Galiani 2007), and delay in early child marriage and teenage pregnancy (Birchall 2018). Schools may also be useful in overcoming social and economic inequalities following periods of war, natural disaster, and economic adversity (Hermanussen et al. 2018). Universal school provision is linked to increased fairness, justice and opportunities for all, but especially for the children facing poverty at the household level (Raudenbush and Eschmann 2015).

However, this does not imply that schools are the only places where learning takes place. In countries where attendance at school is not enforced by state laws, many children do not attend school and learn to survive and adapt to their context (Amury and Komba 2010). There is also worldwide evidence suggesting attending schools is not making much difference. There is a persistent problem of some young people leaving schools after completing compulsory education without achieving minimum learning levels, even in OECD countries where school systems are well established and sufficiently resourced (Thomson 2019).

Previous reviews on this topic have suggested that financial incentives can encourage school attendance, and perhaps improve attainment outcomes (Slavin 2010). They have reported that conditional cash transfer programmes in developing (or low or middle-income) countries, especially the PROGRESA scheme in Mexico, have produced higher attendance, based on large-scale randomised trials. This has encouraged similar initiatives throughout the world, especially in poorer and less developed countries. In developed countries, that tend to have high attendance rates anyway, the evidence on school attendance is less clear.

Attendance can be encouraged by payments in kind, such as the health insurance given in Rwanda (Woode 2017), or vouchers to pay for private school attendance, especially for girls in Pakistan and Columbia (Morgan et al. 2013), or Chile (Sapelli and Vial 2002). See also Carnoy (2017), and DeAngelis and Hoarty (2018). Vouchers for attendance at state-funded schools can improve attendance whether given to the parents or the child, and the latter might also help improve student performance as well (De Walque and Valente 2018).

What does an up-to-date worldwide review suggest?

Common issues in the studies we rated

Before summarising the substantive findings, we mention here some of the common methodological and other issues we found in many studies that led them to be rated as 0 for trustworthiness of evidence, and so ignored in the summary below. Of course, some studies were ongoing or incomplete (e.g. Zulaika et al. 2019). A lot were very small-scale with no comparator. Many studies were poorly described, especially in terms of analyses. Perhaps the biggest omissions were lack of discussion of missing data, and not reporting "effect" sizes, or even providing the means and standard deviations or other information in order for the reader to compute effect sizes for themselves. There was a widespread and needless use of complex modelling, even in randomised control trials (RCTs) when there was reasonable balance between groups at the outset. And significance testing was routinely misused and misrepresented (Gorard 2021).

Summary of results

For each of our reviews we cannot claim to have found every relevant study. But we have found a lot, and it is unlikely that a few extra studies would substantially change the overall findings. In our summaries we mention the key features of each study that helped us to judge their trustworthiness, and so compare study quality with study outcomes.

Ignoring studies rated as zero for trustworthiness, there were at least 53 studies which evaluated the use of financial incentives to promote attendance and/or enrolment at school (Table 3.2). The vast majority were in developing countries, as expected, and they generally found that financial incentives are effective in increasing attendance and/or school enrolment. This is especially so for the strongest studies, which are clearly positive, and this is unusual in terms of other educational topics that we have reviewed.

The results in Table 3.2 include studies concerning attendance, enrolment and participation at school, and sometimes all of these (plus attainment, as covered Chapter 6). However, we classify them below in terms of the type of intervention involved. The intervention approaches with the most highly rated studies that show positive effects are considered the most promising. Approaches not mentioned or with no evidence of impact may be effective, but their absence in the summary

TABLE 3.2 Strength of evidence and impact for studies to improve school attendance/enrolment via finance

Strength of evidence	Positive	Unclear/mixed	Negative/neutral
4	2	1	–
3	11	2	–
2	16	7	2
1	11	1	–

here means that they have not been tested or that the existing evidence is unable to establish impact.

We wanted readers to understand a little about each study being reviewed, including any key factors that led to it being given a lower quality rating than might be expected. This means that the summaries below deal with each individual study, and for some sections in this chapter (and in the review chapters that follow) the text presents quite a long list. These sections are broken up as far as possible, with summaries and Tables like 3.2 but dealing only with the sub-set of pieces in that section. This permits readers both to see the quality of evidence on any topic, and to begin to work out which interventions look the most promising

Providing new schools

The first kind of intervention involves funding new schools. There are no 4 studies, representing the best we could hope to find on this topic.

3 studies

The Sindh Education Sector Reform Programme in Pakistan was intended to improve the enrolment and learning of primary school students, by providing new private schools (World Bank 2018). There is no universal access to government schools in remote areas. In a public–private programme, the government encouraged entrepreneurs to establish and operate free, co-educational primary schools in villages in remote areas by giving them a per student cash subsidy. The Sindh Education Foundation together with a World Bank team also provided free textbooks, teacher training, and regular visits from foundation staff to advise on how to improve teaching and learning. Schools had to meet minimum facility standards, exempt tuition fees for all students, and hire teachers with at least eight years of schooling themselves. Villages with poor school access were randomised to a subsidy of 350 rupees per student regardless of gender (82 villages), the same but with an additional 100 rupees for each female student (79 villages), or no subsidy (38). Enrolment in the treatment groups rose for boys and girls aged 6 to 17. And children continued in school longer. Children in treatment schools also did better on attainment tests, especially those who enrolled due to the programme. The additional subsidy for girls had no impact on enrolment or test scores. This study was rather poorly reported, and it is unclear whether the testing was independent of the developer.

In Afganistan, 13 villages were randomly assigned to receive community-based schooling a year before it was provided for the entire sample of 31 villages (Burde and Linden 2009). Outcomes were attendance and scores in maths and the local language. The presence of a community-based school increased enrolment by 42 percentage points and test scores by half a standard deviation, and the results were better for girls. Enrolment rates and test scores were lower by 15 percentage points for every mile a child had to walk to school, again especially for girls.

Levy et al. (2009) considered the BRIGHT Programme in Burkina Faso, which built 132 primary schools and improved school canteens, take-home rations, school kits and textbooks with the aim of increasing girls' enrolment rates. A regression discontinuity analysis was based on 293 villages that applied for BRIGHT, including 132 that were successful. A total of 21,730 children took tests in maths and French. The programme had a positive impact of 20 percentage points on girls' enrolment, and in maths and French attainment (effect size 0.4).

2🔒 studies

Barrera-Osorio et al. (2017) evaluated the impact of private schools created as a public–private partnership in rural Pakistan – to increase schooling in marginalised areas, reduce the gender gap in enrolment, and encourage learning. A per-student subsidy was paid to establish new private tuition-free primary schools. 100 schools were assigned to a flat subsidy per student. Both groups also had free school leadership and teacher training, free textbooks, other teaching and learning materials, stationery, and book bags. 100 schools were assigned to a higher subsidy for girls. Around 50 schools formed a control. The attrition level is not clear. The programme increased enrolment by 29% according to a verified headcount, and test scores by 0.63 standard deviations. The effect was similar across the two treatment groups and there was no obvious gender difference.

Kim et al. (1999) evaluated a programme of new schools designed to stimulate girls' schooling through the creation of private girls' schools in poor urban neighbourhoods of Quetta, Pakistan. Enrolment growth in these randomly selected neighbourhoods was compared to otherwise similar neighbourhoods that were randomly assigned to a control group. The analysis indicates that the programme increased girls' enrolment by around 33 percentage points. Boys' enrolment rose as well, partly because boys were allowed to attend the new schools and partly because parents would not send their girls to school without also educating their boys.

The Government of Uruguay built 414 classrooms in 1995, and 370 classrooms between 1999 and 2002. In addition, more pre-school teachers were recruited. The Encuesta Continua de Hogares collected retrospective information from

18,000 households each year on the number of pre-school years attended, for the years 2001–2005, The sample was restricted to children aged between 7 and 15 living in two-parent families (Berlinski et al. 2008). By age 8, children who attended pre-school had accumulated 0.17 more years of subsequent school education in comparison to children who did not attend preschool, while by age 15 they accumulated 1.03 extra years of education. Larger gains were found for disadvantaged children.

1🔒 studies

The Pakistan government provided funding for some communities to open a school for girls only, on condition that the community supplied a female teacher. A village committee was given the responsibility to motivate parents to send their daughters to school and monitor progress. The comparison schools were villages with a community support programme but without girls' schools (Kim et al. 1998). Girls' enrolment increased by an average of 22 percentage points. There was a possible spillover effect as boys' enrolment also increased by an average of 9 percentage points. The two groups were not balanced at the outset.

Berlinski and Galiani (2007) investigated the effect on pre-primary enrolment (for children aged 3 to 5) and maternal labour of a large infrastructure programme building new pre-school places in Argentina. From 1993 to 1999, the National Ministry of Education financed the construction of 3,531 rooms for pre-primary education across the country. Data from the Argentine household survey Encuesta Permanente de Hogares involved 29,817 mothers between the ages 19 and 49 with at least one child between ages 3 and 5. There was an increase in enrolment, and also in mothers' employment. There is no distinct comparison group.

Summary

In summary, there is considerable positive evidence here that providing more schools or pre-schools in poor areas will increase enrolment, attendance, and perhaps attainment. The issue is biggest in countries like Pakistan with less than 100% enrolment in school. In countries with near 100% school enrolment the private sector is usually a more minor element, and the state has a duty to provide schools for all citizens regardless of their area of residence.

Making schools free

In many countries school places exist but schooling is not free at the point of delivery, even if the fees are considered small. And in even more countries pre-schooling is not free. Some countries have abolished such fees, at least in part, or offered fee waivers to some families. So, the next section is about reducing or eliminating the cost of attending school or pre-school. This theme includes the first 4🔒 study.

4🔒 studies

Duflo et al. (2021) estimated the effects of free secondary education in Ghana using randomised assignment to secondary school scholarships for 682 young people, from a cohort of 2,064 youths who had places at high school but could not afford the fees. The students were followed up for 12 years until the age of 29, with relatively low attrition (6%). Perhaps unsurprisingly, scholarship recipients were 60% more likely than non-recipients to obtain secondary education. Women were less likely to become pregnant, and the scholarship recipients, especially women, were more likely to enrol in tertiary education.

3🔒 studies

An evaluation of public–private partnerships in Uganda allowed all students with an overall grade of 28 or higher on the Primary Leaving Examination to attend participating private secondary and vocational schools for free (Barrera-Osorio et al. 2016). 100 schools were randomised either to implement the programme in 2011, or a waiting list control. Enrolment in participating schools increased between 33% and 38% in grade 1 in the first year, and by 34% in grade 1 and 58% in grade 2 in the second year. Total enrolment increased by approximately 25% between 2007 and 2012. Students who were exposed to more than one year of treatment had slightly higher maths, English and biology scores (effect sizes range from 0.07 to 0.16).

2🔒 studies

Wong et al. (2013) looked at the impact on attendance of offering free pre-school and a cash transfer, in a poor rural area of China. A group of 141 four year old infants completed a school readiness test, and were then randomised to receive the help or not. The payment voucher to the parent(s) was conditional on at least 80% verified attendance by the child. Study attrition was 7%. Attendance was higher in the treatment group (74%) compared to the control (55%). Both groups improved school readiness, but this was actually higher in the control (reported effect size -0.07). The authors suggest that the poor quality of preschool education in rural China (in terms of both teaching and facilities) may be a contributing factor in the lack of effect on attainment. This would be in line with previous research, which has shown that in developing countries there is a potential trade-off between increasing access and improving quality (e.g., Sifuna 2007, Pritchett 2013). We could not verify the effect sizes as the authors did not report the standard deviations of the test scores.

Between 2001 and 2006 three reforms were implemented in China to counter the high dropout rate due to the cost of education. Although enrolment rates were high, completion rates for elementary and junior high school were rather low. Because the three reforms were introduced at different times, Chyi and Zhou (2014) used the variation in timing of the reforms in different counties to estimate their effects. They used a difference-in-difference approach to estimate the effects of tuition control, a tuition fee waiver and 2-waivers-one subsidy, on the school enrolment of poor children aged 6–16 in rural areas. Tuition control is a reform which controls the amount of fees charged at regulated levels. The 2-waivers-one subsidy policy provides tuition fee waiver, free textbooks and a living stipend for poor children. Only the 2-waivers-one subsidy policy is specifically targeted at poor families, which therefore affects the relevance of the study. The survey used for the study had high levels of attrition, and included children in some waves and not others. The number of cases varied, with each policy group and across years, from 162 to 1,071. Tuition control had a minimal effect on primary and junior high school enrolment. Tuition fee waivers alone had no overall impact. Tuition fee waivers, free textbooks, and living expense subsidies had a strong positive effect for rural girls, but not boys – largely due to improvement in the enrolment of girls from poor households.

School fees for all primary and secondary education in South Africa were abolished in a national policy. However, the implementation was staggered. Fees were first eliminated for schools located in high poverty neighbourhoods, permitting a kind of natural experiment (Garlick 2013). The impact of the policy was estimated using both difference-in-differences and regression discontinuity methods, where schools below the cutoffs (control) were compared with those above the cutoffs (the intended treatment group). Assuming that poverty scores are randomly assigned in the neighbourhood of the cutoffs, these two groups differ only in their treatment status and so any differences in enrolment between the two groups may be interpreted as a causal effect of the fee elimination intervention. Fee elimination had only a very small effect on enrolment – likely due to low returns to education for marginal students and the high labour market opportunity costs. School dropout rates fell marginally from 2.8% to 2.1%.

Giordono and Pugatch (2017) reported on the results of a scheme in Gambia which eliminated all public school fees for girls in grades 7 to 9, and provided costs for books, uniforms, shoes, bags, and supplementary mentoring. Students were selected based on their needs (disadvantaged families, orphaned, special needs, HIV/AIDS). Female enrolment in school increased by about 14%. However, female attainment actually fell (effect size -0.09). This may be because the new students were less well prepared or because the additional numbers created a school resource issue. Several studies have suggested that increased attendance is linked to lowered average attainment, at least in the short term.

Borkum (2012) looked at a national fee-elimination initiative in South Africa, and its short-term impact on enrolment. The programme raised enrolment by about 2 percentage points in treated secondary schools in comparison to untreated schools, but had little effect in primary schools. Schools may have exaggerated the number of enroled students to increase their payments.

1 🔒 studies

Barrera-Osorio et al. (2007) used a regression discontinuity design (eligibility based on poverty), to evaluate the impact of a fee reduction programme on enrolment, in

Colombia. It increased enrolment in both primary and secondary schools by a small amount. The number of participants is not stated clearly.

A school-level tuition waiver program in Haiti – "Programme de Subvention" provided public financing to non-public schools conditional on these schools not charging tuition, providing free textbooks for children and having class sizes no larger than 45. An RCT found an increase in enrolment, and reduction in grade repetition (Adelman et al. 2017). Although the increase in students at participating schools does not directly equate to a reduction in the number of children out of school, it does demonstrate strong demand from families for the programme. There was a very high level of missing data and unmatched data.

Summary

Table 3.3 summarises the studies on the first two themes of either adding new school places, or making schooling free, or both. The results are clearly positive overall, including for all of the higher quality studies.

In summary, fee waivers work in the sense that they lead to increased attendance, especially for poorer families and for girls. It seems that the waiver has to be complete – a fee at a controlled lower level is still off-putting. And there are other costs of going to school, such as books and uniforms, and opportunity costs for not doing paid work, that also need to be considered. Fee waivers are not so clearly effective for increasing enrolment, and the evidence suggests that increased attendance can then lead to lower attainment overall. This might be because of increased pressure on the schools, or the lower school-readiness of the students attracted by fee waivers. This issue is discussed further in Chapter 6.

PROGRESA conditional cash transfers

Some of the strongest overall evidence on financial incentives comes from the Programa de Educación, Salud, y Alimentación (PROGRESA) conditional cash transfer scheme in Mexico. This is a large-scale anti-poverty and human resource programme that began in 1997, and provided aid to about 10 million poor families. Its major goal was to stimulate investment in children's human capital. It provided transfer payments to families (average \$55 USD/month), contingent on children's

TABLE 3.3 Strength of evidence and impact for studies to improve school attendance/enrolment via expanding schools or making places free

Strength of evidence	Positive	Unclear/mixed	Negative/neutral
4 🔒	1	–	–
3 🔒	4	–	–
2 🔒	6	2	–
1 🔒	4	–	–

regular attendance at school. The transfer amount varies with the child's grade level and sex because older children are more likely to engage in work. The amount is intended to offset the opportunity costs of sending children to school. For example, families of children in Grades 3 to 9 received a cash transfer every two months if teachers and directors reported that those children attended 85% of classes, and parents attended monthly meetings. In addition to the educational subsidies, the programme also provided monetary aid and nutritional supplements for infants and small children that were not contingent on schooling. PROGRESA was replaced by the Oportunidades programme.

4🔒 studies

Buddelmeyer and Skoufias (2004) used a regression discontinuity design to look at the impact of the scheme across 506 localities (320 localities were assigned to the treatment group and 186 localities to the control). In each region, households were classified by their probability of being below the regional cut-off point or poverty line, whether they were in a locality where PROGRESA was in operation or not. Eligible households were those below the poverty line. The fact that the scheme was introduced in phases due to monetary constraints has rendered the study similar to an experiment. The programme increased boys' attendance by 5% or more, and girls' attendance by 7% or more.

3🔒 studies

Parker et al. (2006) studied Oportunidades using retrospective data to analyse the short-term and long-term impact on children's school outcomes and enrolment. The programme offered cash to poor families on condition that they send their children to school (85% attendance). The 2002–2004 Urban Evaluation Survey was used to create three groups of children from grade 9 to 12 – eligible households who live in intervention areas, households who miss the cut-off point for eligibility and who live in intervention areas, households who satisfy the eligibility criteria but do not live in intervention areas. Data were collected at baseline, and one and two years later. There was a benefit for school attendance among older children. A child who participated in the programme from age 6–17 would complete half an additional year of schooling. Long-term exposure to the programme also raised educational attainment by approximately half a year.

2🔒 studies

Behrman et al. (2000) evaluated the first two years of the PROGRESA programme (as above). Tests were administered at school and only the test scores for children who enrolled were available. Since the programme encouraged children to enrol who would otherwise have delayed or dropped out, the test scores for treated children could be affected. The treated children and the control were therefore not random anymore. The results suggest an impact on enrolment for older children but not those under 11. Transition to secondary school is higher for the treatment group compared to the control, while dropout is lower. Programme effects are greater for girls than for boys.

The second phase of PROGRESA was implemented as a trial, in which 506 rural villages were randomly assigned to either participate in the programme (2,162 households) or serve as controls (1,531). Attrition was over 10% (Todd and Wolpin 2003). Over the three-years covered, the households living in the control villages did not receive programme benefits. The treatment had no substantial effect on school attendance at ages 6–11 in the short run, when attendance is high anyway. However, it did have an effect on school attendance for older children at ages 12–15 in the short run. This report was mostly about creating a model. Clearly several of the studies of this programme overlap or use the same data.

1🔒 studies

An analysis by De Brauw and Hoddinott (2008) makes use of the fact that some recipients of the cash transfer did not have their attendance monitored, due to an administrative error. They were somewhat less likely to have high attendance, suggesting that the monitoring and conditionality are important components. Because the groups occurred naturally, they are not balanced.

In a study by Schultz (2000), the treatment group had higher school enrolment (by around 10 percentage points), but there was not much difference in actual school attendance. This study was poorly reported and measurements were unverified.

Summary

In summary, we found six studies of PROGRESA and school attendance, of somewhat varying quality, and not wholly distinct. Taken as a whole they suggest that the scheme worked well. Conditional cash transfers can increase attendance (and perhaps enrolment) at school. However, they must be conditional on attendance, and those conditions must be enforced. The cash transfers seem to be even more effective for girls than boys, in Mexico at least. Impact is greater for older students for whom school dropout is more likely. Long-term studies suggest that the gains remain even decades later (Caridad Araujo and Macours 2021).

More evidence on conditional cash transfers

There is a lot of further evidence on cash transfers, from around the world. These programmes are prevalent more in developing countries where chronic poverty is higher and cash transfer as safety-net programmes are perhaps the most practical solution to address socio-economic poverty (De Janvry et al. 2006). Children's outcomes associated with household poverty are of great concern therefore a large number of programme evaluation consider cash transfers directly or indirectly addressing children's access to education, attendance in school, and their attainment (González-Flores et al., 2012).

4🔒 studies

Edmonds and Shrestha (2014) examined the impact of two types of scholarship programme in Nepal, on school attendance and other outcomes for 660 children aged 10 to 16, and identified as vulnerable. The children were randomly allocated to one of the treatments or a control. One treatment was a scholarship for school-related expenses, and the second provided the same scholarship and an in-kind stipend conditional on school attendance. The aim was to promote schooling and deter child labour in the local carpet-weaving industry. There was little difference in attendance between the control and the scholarship group. The conditional stipend was more effective. It was more effective for girls, increasing attendance, and reducing the failure rate by 66%. The incentives substantively reduced child labour among girls (by 64%). Both interventions had a positive impact on test scores. However, there is no lasting impact on school enrolment after the support ended.

3🔒 studies

Chaudhury and Parajuli (2007) evaluated the impact of a female school stipend programme on enrolment in grades 6 to 8 of public schools in 15 of the lowest literacy districts in Punjab, Pakistan. Girls were given the stipend on condition that they enrolled in a public school and attended 80% of their classes. Three control groups were used – girls' schools in districts not receiving the programme, boys' schools in districts receiving the programme, and districts not receiving the programme. The main analysis was based on a difference-in-difference approach. There was a 9% increase in female enrolment, which was highest in grade 6.

Levy and Ohls (2010) looked at a cash transfer programme in Jamaica, which offered health and education grants to around 180,000 eligible poor children from age 6 to 17, conditional on 85% school attendance. A regression discontinuity analysis was used to compare the results of participants who were below the threshold (barely eligible) to those above the threshold (near eligible). The data was based on survey baseline and follow-up data collected by the Statistical Institute of Jamaica 18 months apart. The response rate was similar for both groups with 91% at baseline and 82% at follow-up. The programme had a positive impact on school attendance (0.5 days higher per month in the experimental group).

Galiani and McEwan (2013) reported on a conditional cash transfer in Honduras, known as the Family Allowances Programme. The study involved children enrolled in grades 1–4, in 40 poor municipalities, who were of low height for their age. Municipalities were randomised to four groups – control, cash transfer for health and education, cash transfer and direct investments in health and education, or just direct investments. The cash transfer was to children's families, and schools also received payments proportionate to their number of relevant students. The cash transfer increased enrolment by 8 percentage points compared to the control.

Ferreira et al. (2009) looked at the impact on middle school enrolment of the CESSP Scholarship Program, a cash transfer, in Cambodia. This was a regression discontinuity design, based on eligibility for support in terms of likelihood to drop out and exam scores. Based on 100 schools, 3,800 scholarships were offered, and given out three times per year without further conditions. Recipients were about 20 percentage points more likely to be enrolled in school, and 10 percentage points less likely to be in paid work, and this did not have a negative impact on the enrolment of their siblings. The effects were clear for both boys and girls.

Edmonds and Schady (2012) looked at an unconditional cash transfer scheme in Ecuador. Traditionally, children's education in poor families is often sacrificed for paid work to supplement family income. Mothers in poor families were individually randomised to receive a cash transfer that was equivalent to 7% of monthly expenditures, or not. The initial sample included 2,153 children aged 10 and above. Attrition was 6%. The cash transfer had a positive impact on reducing child labour, and the impact was largest among the poorest children, but there was no effect on those who were in paid employment at baseline (likely to be older children). School enrolment also improved. This was despite the payments being unconditional and probably less than the income foregone from employment.

In the Philippines, Chaudhury et al. (2013) looked at a conditional cash transfer based on 85% for attendance of children up to age 14. This was a waiting list design, with eligible households in treatment localities compared with eligible households in control localities. There were 1,418 treatment children. The programme increased the enrolment of young children (3–11) but this did not translate into changes in the overall number of years of schooling, nor enrolment of older children (slightly worse). At age 15, children in programme areas had a higher rate of dropout than those in the control areas, probably due to the cut-off age for the education grant. School attendance in treated areas was 4 percentage points higher among 6–11 year olds, 5 percentage points higher among 12–14 year olds, and 8 percentage points higher among 15–17 year olds compared to non-treated areas.

Chhabra et al. (2019) used a regression discontinuity design to evaluate the impact of a programme in Pakistan that offered cash benefits to households on condition that girls in grades 6 to 10 attended government schools regularly. The scheme started in 2004 with 16 low adult literacy districts in the treatment and 20 controls. The programme had a positive and stable effect on girls' secondary school enrolment – an increase of 30 to 50 girls per school. This gain was maintained up to 2015.

De Brauw and Gilligan (2011) assessed the Comunidades Solidarias Rurales in El Salvador – a poverty alleviation programme targeting households with children aged 6 to 15 who had not completed primary education. The cash transfer depended on 80% attendance at school. Children of all ages were more likely to enrol in schools.

2🔒 studies

Filmer and Schady (2009) analysed the effects of the CESSP Scholarship Program in Cambodia, which gave scholarships to poor children for the three years of lower secondary school. The scholarships were cash transfers to families of children selected for the scholarship, conditional on school enrolment, regular attendance and satisfactory grade progress. Pupils with the highest dropout risk in 100 high poverty schools were selected. Two-thirds of the scholarship recipients were girls because they were deemed more likely to drop out of school than boys. Regression discontinuity was used to compare students who were offered scholarships with those who just missed out. The scholarship group was 25 percentage points more likely to be enrolled in school, and more likely to attend school. And this was more common among lower ability children. The study was given a lower rating because of poor reporting.

Chitolina et al. (2016) evaluated the impact of the expansion of the Bolsa Família programme to families with youths aged 16 to 17 years in Brazil. This was a cash transfer, conditional on attendance. The dataset does not identify households receiving payments, but since the target is the poorest 20% of the households with young people age 16, these households are identified as beneficiaries using intention-to-treat. The control is made up of the 20% poorest households with 15 year olds. The programme appeared to increase school attendance for 16 year olds by 5 percentage points compared to 15-year-olds, especially in rural areas. The report is not clear about the number of cases, or the attrition.

Schady and Araujo (2006) evaluated a cash transfer scheme to increase school enrolment and reduce child labour, for low-income households in Ecuador – Bono de Desarrollo Humano. The transfer of $15 per month, approximately 7% of mean household expenditure in the study, was paid to the female of the house. This payment was not explicitly conditional on changes in behaviour, although many families reported believing that payment was conditional on school attendance. A sample of 1,391 households (3,072 children) was used, and 18 months later attrition was 6%. Because the budget was insufficient to cover all households, half were randomised to immediate treatment. The treatment increased school enrolment and reduced child work, compared to the waiting-list. Households believing that the payment was conditional had even higher enrolment and less likelihood of a child in work. The analysis and reporting are overly complex.

Data from the South African National Income Dynamics Survey was used to examine the link between the receipt of the South African Child Support Grant and school enrolment and attainment. No data was available for attendance. Introduced in 1998, the Grant was aimed at removing racial and gender inequality, targeting poor teenagers regardless of household status. This was extended in 2000 to children below age 7, and then to age 18 by 2012. The study took advantage of the phased roll out of the evaluation (Eyal et al. 2014). The grant was means tested, and take-up was low, because information about how to apply was not widely known. Grant recipients had higher enrolment rates than non-beneficiaries for older teens, suggesting that the grant did increase enrolment in further education. Those exposed to the grant for longer had higher enrolment rates. There was no impact on attainment. The two groups were not randomised.

Glewwe et al. (2003) evaluated the Programa de Asignacion Familiar, a government social welfare programme in Honduras. 20 municipalities were randomised to receive a cash transfer conditional on school attendance and frequent health clinic visits, 10 municipalities had improved schooling and health services, 20 had both of these, and 20 acted as a control. The total baseline sample was 5,784 households with 30,588 members. Attrition was 16%. The cash transfer was linked to a very small increase in attendance.

The Social Safety Net programme in Nicaragua was a cash transfer to female heads of household conditional on school attendance and regular visits to health clinics by the children. Prior research suggests that women are more likely than men to spend the cash transfers on their children's health, nutrition, and education. In an evaluation, 21 communities were randomised to treatment and 21 to control (Gitter and Barham 2008). Households with children aged 7–13 who had not completed fourth grade were eligible. The number of households appeared to vary considerably between analyses. There was some evidence of increased attendance but none that this was due to payments to females specifically. The study was poorly reported, with a complex analysis, and it was unclear how many cases were in each group.

Red de Protección Social was a government six-year conditional cash transfer project for poor households in rural Nicaragua, starting in 2000, and covering over 30,000 families. Cash transfers were paid to a designated female caregiver in the beneficiary household, conditional on school attendance of the child. 42 poor areas were randomised to receive the treatment from 2000 to 2003 (1,330 households) or 2003 to 2005 (1,379). The attrition rate was about 12%. By 2002, the first group had an 18% increase in the enrolment rate, and a 62% reduction in the number of schools days missed in the past month (Barham et al. 2013).

The Punjab Female School Stipend Program, a female-targeted conditional cash transfer program in Pakistan, was implemented in response to gender gaps in education. An early evaluation of the programme showed that the enrolment of eligible girls in middle school increased in the short term by nearly 9 percentage points (Alam et al. 2011). Regression discontinuity and difference-in-difference analyses suggested a positive impact five years later. Beneficiary adolescent girls were more likely to complete middle school and have less paid work. There is evidence that participating girls delayed their marriage and had fewer births by the time they were 19. Girls exposed to the programme later, and eligible for the benefits given in high school, increased their rates of matriculating into and completing high school.

Evans et al. (2014) analysed the impact of the Tanzania Social Action Fund, a community-based programme where payments were conditional on school aged children (7–15) having 80% attendance at school. A total of 1,764 poor households in 80 villages were randomised to treatment or not. Almost all households had no electricity, and over 90% had homes with mud floors. The treatment effect was estimated by comparing the difference in the change between treatment and control groups using an intention-to treat-analysis. School attendance, based on reports from the communities, suggested positive results, but school reports showed little improvement, largely because school attendance was already high at the outset. Children aged 15–18 in treatment villages were more likely to complete school (15% point difference), especially girls.

The New Cooperative Medical System in rural China was offered to 49% of the 5.9 million population in eight low-income rural counties in 2006. The average take-up rate was 87% in 2007, 93% in 2008 and 93% in 2009. It covered medical expenses and the cost of books, meals and educational activities for school children. An evaluation used data collected at the household level from the 2006 China Agricultural Census (Chen et al. 2010), involving 1.4 million school-age children across 3,977 villages. The treatment areas had a slightly more educated population and better houses at the outset. A cross-sectional propensity score matching method was used to estimate the effect of the treatment, with the assumption that treated and untreated individuals were similar in unobservable characteristics if they were matched on observable characteristics. By 2006, school enrolment was 89% in treatment counties and 84% in non-NCMS counties. However, a difference-in-difference propensity score analysis suggested that the programme had zero effect on the average population.

Angrist and Lavy (2009) looked at an incentive scheme in Israel offering cash to low-achieving high school students for progressing from tenth to eleventh grade, from eleventh to twelfth grade, and for passing the high school matriculation exam. Forty of the lowest scoring schools were randomised to treatment or not (20:20). One school closed and three were non-compliant. Outcomes were based on administrative data. There was an increase in progression for girls but not boys, and no impact on post-secondary enrolment. The reporting is weak, the analysis overly complex, and the mean scores of the outcomes are not reported.

Rodriguez-Planas (2012) evaluated the US Quantum Opportunity Programme – a five-year after-school programme combining mentoring, educational services and financial incentives throughout high school. This was offered to disadvantaged high school students to improve high-school graduation and post-secondary school enrolment. It appeared to be effective in the short term, increasing the likelihood of high-school completion and college enrolment by 18% and 23% respectively, especially for female students. But the impact was short-lived, and the programme may have reduced intrinsic motivation. Reporting of the study is poor – including of missing data and effect size calculations.

In Kenya, the chance of sponsorships for free school uniforms was provided to a randomised group of 550 students in 12 schools for three years, while 602 students formed the control. Attrition after eight years was about 5% (Evans and Ngatia 2018). Those receiving a uniform had 37% fewer absences. There were no differences after eight years. Those not in school at the outset did not receive a uniform, which creates a bias.

Ravallion and Wodon (2000) evaluated the impact of an educational subsidy programme (Food for Education) in Bangladesh that provided monthly food rations to families that sent their children to primary school for 95% of classes. They used an instrumental variable approach with geographic placement as an instrument. The subsidy did reduce the incidence of child labour but did not increase school enrolment.

Dean and Jayachandran (2019) examined a scheme which offered scholarships to children in India aged 3.5 to 4.5 to encourage attendance in a private kindergarten. The premise is that attending kindergarten improves children's cognitive development. Scholarships were randomly allocated to half of 808 eligible children (not attending pre-school) in 71 villages, if parents agreed to enrol their children in the private kindergarten. 22 children were missing scores at the end. The scholarship had no effect on primary school enrolment, or on social emotional development. However, the treatment group scored higher on cognitive tests (effect size 0.8).

1🔒 studies

Cahyadi et al. (2018) looked at a cash transfer, Program Keluarga Harapan, in Indonesia, launched in 2007. It offered payments to poor households with children or pregnant women, on condition that they fulfilled some health-related (immunisation and check-ups) and educational obligations. 360 sub-districts (about 14,000 households) were randomly chosen for data collection (180 sub-districts in the treatment group and 180 sub-districts in the control group). This study focused on the survey data collected six years afterwards. There was a considerable health impact after six years. The programme also led to an 8 to 9 percentage point increase in enrolment of children aged 13 to 15, and a decrease in child labour, and smaller gains for children aged 7 to 12. Attrition was very high in the control districts (only data on 39 of the 180, compared to 179 in the treatment group).

The Programa Nacional de Becas Estudiantiles was a conditional cash transfer programme in Argentina, targeting students entering grades 8 and 9, but at risk of dropping out (Heinrich 2007). The study followed a cohort of students enrolled in 24 schools over a period of five years. Data for beneficiaries were compared to eligible students who received no scholarship. The treatment and comparison groups were unmatched, and attrition was high. Attendance (and performance) increased in the treatment group, while grade repetition reduced.

The Food for Education programme in Bangladesh provided wheat or rice for parents to help send their children to school and ensure regular attendance, and then shifted to cash incentives. Pupils had to attend 85% of classes each month and maintain an average of 50%. The programme started in 1993, and covered 65,000 schools and supported 5.5 million pupils. Bhandari (2013) used a difference in difference analysis with a counterfactual group of students who were too young to start school at the time the programme started. The survey used data from 600 households in 60 villages. The programme reduced dropout rate before completion of primary school by 10 percentage points for girls and 7 percentage points for boys. The treatment children were more likely to enrol in school by 20 percentage points, and to continue to later years of school. The two groups were not equivalent at the outset.

Microfinance provides financial services for low income families with no other access to banking. Bhuiya (2016) evaluated the impact of three such schemes in rural Bangladesh by comparing naturally occurring groups of users and non-users. Data were collected from 439 households in twenty villages. Poverty was higher among microfinance members than non-members. School enrolment was higher in the microfinance group, but there was no difference in school attendance, and attainment was actually lower.

Cueto and Chinen (2008) conducted a quasi-experiment to examine the effect of a breakfast programme on children's attendance and drop-out rates in Peru. The programme was for Grade 4 classes in three of the poorest departments in Peru. Eleven treatment schools (300 students) were selected from one province, and nine schools (290 students) in the other two provinces were used as a waiting-list comparison. The treatment led to no substantial improvement in tested memory, and to a small disadvantage in arithmetic and reading. The programme had a positive effect on attendance and drop-out rate. The groups were not balanced at the outset.

Acosta (2006) showed, in a cross-sectional survey of 11,953 households belonging to 11 villages in El Salvador in the year 1998, that payments to households of 11–17 year old students led to a 7.1% increase in school retention, and a reduction in child labour, especially for girls. However, the recipient families in these areas were already better educated than non-recipient families and had better facilities in their homes.

Bui et al. (2020) looked at a conditional cash transfer programme in Vietnam. Tuition fee reduction and the provision of an education subsidy formed the two treatments while the outcome was enrolment. The research used a survey of over 4,000 households in 2006 and 2008, and in 2016 and 2018. Both treatments were deemed effective for enrolment, especially for girls. The two groups are not really comparable.

Attanasio et al. (2005) evaluated a conditional cash transfer programme in Colombia – "Familias en Acción". Mothers from poor backgrounds received cash on condition that they promoted certain activities with their children, including school attendance. The comparator group was not balanced. Older children aged 12 to 17 from families receiving the incentive improved attainment, more so in rural areas (10.1 percentage points) than urban (5.2 percentage points). Younger children aged 8 to 11 already had a high attendance rate of 90%, and the programme had no discernible effect on attendance for them.

Summary

Table 3.4 summarises the studies on the theme of conditional cash transfers.

In summary, there is a considerable body of evidence worldwide that cash transfers work in terms of improved attendance at school. Although the contexts are often different, and the quality of research is very variable, there is a relatively clear overall finding. Money works for attendance, and probably for enrolment. It is most effective for older students who are more likely to take paid work otherwise. However, creating free school places (above) has been shown to be more consistently effective.

TABLE 3.4 Strength of evidence and impact for studies to improve school attendance/enrolment via cash transfers

Strength of evidence	Positive	Unclear/mixed	Negative/neutral
4🔒	1	1	–
3🔒	7	2	–
2🔒	10	5	2
1🔒	7	1	–

How should cash transfers be paid?

So the next question is how is the money best paid, and to whom? There are no 4🔒 studies relevant to this, and only one 3🔒.

3🔒 studies

Positive effects on children's cognitive outcomes were reported from a conditional cash transfer programme targeted at adolescent girls in Malawi. The programme was evaluated in a three-armed cluster randomised control trial where enumeration areas were randomly assigned to conditional (based on at least 80% attendance) or unconditional payments or a control (Baird et al. 2011). The final sample was 2,284 girls in 161 treatment areas, who were at school at the outset (which weakens the study). The conditional group generally scored better than the other two on all measures. Their self-reported enrolment was higher, and remained so after the funding ceased. Attendance was also higher (by 8 percentage points). The difference was greater in Term 1 for two years. The authors suggest that this might be because Term 1 coincides with the lean season when food is scarce and malaria cases are high. Perhaps the condition for regular school attendance is effective when the cash is most needed. This group also scored higher in English, maths and cognitive ability. However, conditional cash transfer may have a negative impact on non-schooling outcomes. Teenage pregnancy and marriage rates were substantially higher than in the unconditional arm. The authors suggest that it is possible that for girls with a high probability of dropout and marriage at baseline, the attendance requirement may be too onerous (and perhaps the cash offer too small) to make regular school attendance more attractive than marriage.

2🔒 studies

Barrera-Osorio et al. (2008) looked at three conditional payments in poor areas of Colombia to improve attendance at secondary schools. In one group the child received the incentive paid into the bank on condition that they attended at least 80% of school days per month. In the second, two thirds of the incentive is for attendance and the rest is paid when children re-enrol for the next school year.

A third group had incentives paid on condition of graduation and tertiary enrolment rather than attendance. Students offered cash incentives were more likely to attend school, more likely to remain enrolled, more likely to matriculate to the next grade, more likely to graduate, and more likely to matriculate to a tertiary institution. Postponing payment to a larger lump-sum at the time of a re-enrolment decision increased enrolment at secondary and tertiary levels, without reducing daily attendance. Incentivising for graduation and matriculation is more effective than just for attendance, increasing attendance and enrolment at secondary and tertiary levels. However, there is a side effect in that siblings (sisters) of treated students attended school less than students who received no incentives. Attrition was low (2%). The impact analysis is poorly described.

The Education Maintenance Allowance (EMA) was a UK government cash transfer paid directly to young people aged 16–18, in the first two years of post-compulsory full-time education. Holford (2015) used data from the Longitudinal Study of Young People in England, to find that a payment of £30 per week reduced teenagers' labour supply by three hours per week, and increased the probability of education by 13 percentage points from a base of 43%. Providing the money to the parents was inefficient, because the money was partly used for other things, and did not reduce young people's working time (and so make time available for education and training) as much as would be expected. The study concluded that it is preferable to make this cash transfer directly to the young person.

Akresh et al. (2013) conducted a two-year randomised trial in rural Burkino-Faso to assess the impact of four cash transfer delivery mechanisms – a conditional cash transfer given to fathers or mothers, or unconditional cash transfer given to fathers or mothers. The condition was that children aged 7–15 enrol in school and attend classes regularly (90%). Children who were less likely to enrol in primary or secondary school, such as girls and younger children, in 75 villages were randomly assigned. Eligible households received the type of cash transfer assigned to their village. Stipends were paid quarterly, and the amount varied with the age of the child (older children were given more). Difference-in-difference models were used to control for variation across villages. Take-up in the conditional group declined because of the enforced conditions. By the second year there was a positive impact on school enrolment for the conditional group only, which was more marked for girls, younger children, and lower ability groups – all of which are traditionally less likely to enrol. The same pattern was found for attendance rates. No difference was found in maths and French tests, which might suggest that children who would otherwise not have enrolled in school perform just as well as their peers on average. Household attrition was low, even after two years (3.6%). There was no clear reporting of effect sizes.

Benhassine et al. (2015) randomly assigned 320 primary school sectors in Morocco to one of four variants or a control – conditional (on attendance) cash transfer made to the father, or mother, or a labelled cash transfer (not conditional on attendance) to father, or mother. School participation was recorded through surprise school visits by the research team (44,000 children) and household survey

(4,000), including households whose children were not in school. Because the programme was run from the school, households with no contact with the school system were excluded, which is an important limitation. Results indicate no differences in school attendance between conditional and unconditional cash transfers. There was no difference whether cash was given to fathers or mothers. The unconditional transfer was actually better for re-enrolment of those who had dropped out, and slightly better for attainment. The study was quite poorly reported.

Summary

In summary, the evidence shows that payments should be conditional, on balance, but the evidence is not strong and the picture is quite mixed. It does not seem to matter if the payment is to father or mother. And for older students, it might be better to give them the cash directly, and delay at least part of it until they reach a target such as re-enrolment or matriculation. Otherwise, the evidence is that cash payments are less effective for maintaining subsequent enrolment than for current attendance.

Conclusion

In poorer countries, and those with less than full school attendance, financial incentives can improve the situation. But there must be enough school places for this to work. Distance from home to school matters, especially for girls. It is generally the responsibility of governments to provide sufficient school places, even in the remotest areas. This costs money, and it may not be sustainable to provide free places for all and continue to pay students for attendance. The money in many of the studies above came from charities or organisations like the World Bank. Are there other and perhaps cheaper ways of encouraging schooling? We address this question in the next chapter.

References

Acosta, P. (2006) *Labor supply, school attendance, and remittances from international Migration: the case of El Salvador*, World Bank Policy Research Working Paper 3903.

Adelman, M., Holland, P. and Heidelk, T. (2017) Increasing access by waiving tuition: Evidence from Haiti, *Comparative Education Review*, 61, 4, 804–831.

Akresh, R., De Walque, D. and Kazianga, H. (2013) Cash transfers and child schooling: Evidence from a randomized evaluation of the role of conditionality, *World Bank Policy Research Working Paper*, (6340).

Alam, A., Baez, J. and Del Carpio, X. (2011) *Does cash for schools influence young women's behavior in the longer term? Evidence from Pakistan*, Policy Research Paper No. 5669, Washington DC, World Bank.

Amury, Z. and Komba, A. (2010) *Coping strategies used by street children in the event of illness*, REPOA, https://media.africaportal.org/documents/Coping_Strategies_by_Street_Children.pdf

Angrist, J. and Lavy, V. (2009) The effects of high stakes high school achievement awards: Evidence from a randomized trial, *American Economic Review*, 99, 4, 1384–1414.

Attanasio, O., Battistin, E., Fitzsimons, E. and Vera-Hernandez, M. (2005*) How effective are conditional cash transfers? Evidence from Colombia*, Institute for Fiscal Studies, Briefing Note No. 54.

Baird, S., McIntosh, C. and Özler, B. (2011) Cash or condition? Evidence from a cash transfer experiment, *The Quarterly Journal of Economics*, 126, 4, 1709–1753.

Barham, T., Macours, K. and Maluccio, J. (2013) *More schooling and more learning? Effects of a three-year conditional cash transfer program in Nicaragua after 10 Years*, Inter-American Development Bank.

Barrera-Osorio, F., Bertrand, M., Linden, L. and Perez-Calle, F. (2008) *Conditional cash transfers in education design features, peer and sibling effects*, National Bureau of Economic Research, Working Paper 13890.

Barrera-Osorio, F., Blakeslee, D., Hoover, M., Linden, L., Raju, D. and Ryan, S. (2017) *Delivering education to the underserved through a public-private partnership program in Pakistan*, New York: The World Bank.

Barrera-Osorio, F., De Galbert, P., Habyarimana, J. and Sabarwal, S. (2016) *Impact of Public-private Partnerships on private school performance: Evidence from a randomized controlled trial in Uganda*, Policy Research Working Paper 7905.

Barrera-Osorio, F., Linden, L. L. and Urquiola, M. (2007) *The effects of user fee reductions on enrollment: Evidence from a quasi-experiment*, Columbia University.

Behrman, J., Sengupta, P. and Todd, P. (2000) *The impact of PROGRESA on achievement test scores in the first year*, Impact of PROGRESA on achievement test scores in the first year, IFPRI: International Food Policy Research Institute.

Benhassine, N., Devoto, F., Duflo, E., Dupas, P. and Pouliquen, V. (2015) Turning a shove into a nudge? A "labeled cash transfer" for education, *American Economic Journal: Economic Policy*, 7, 3, 86–125.

Berlinski, S. and Galiani, S. (2007) The effect of a large expansion of pre-primary school facilities on preschool attendance and maternal employment, *Labour Economics*, 14, 3, 665–680.

Berlinski, S., Galiani, S. and Manacorda, M. (2008) Giving children a better start: Preschool attendance and school-age profiles, *Journal of Public Economics*, 92, 5–6, 1416–1440.

Bhandari, D. (2013) *Two essays in educational spending in developing countries*, (Ph.D.), Oklahoma State University, EBSCOhost ecn database.

Bhuiya, M. (2016) *Impact of microfinance on health, education and income of rural households: Evidence from Bangladesh*, Bhuiya_2016_whole.pdf (usq.edu.au).

Birchall, J. (2018) Early marriage, pregnancy and girl child school dropout, Institute of Development Studies, Early Marriage, Pregnancy and Girl Child School Dropout (ids. ac.uk).

Black, M., Walker, S., Fernald, L., Andersen, C., DiGirolamo, A., Lu, C., ... and Lancet Early Childhood Development Series Steering Committee (2017) Early childhood development coming of age: Science through the life course, *The Lancet*, 389, 10064, 77–90.

Borkum, E. (2012) Can eliminating school fees in poor districts boost enrolment? Evidence from South Africa, *Economic Development and Cultural Change*, 60, 2, 359–398.

Buddelmeyer, H. and Skoufias, E. (2004) *An evaluation of the performance of regression discontinuity design on PROGRESA*, World Bank Policy Research Working Paper, 3386.

Bui, T., Nguyen, C., Nguyen, K., Nguyen, H. and Pham, P. (2020) The effect of tuition fee reduction and education subsidy on school enrollment: Evidence from Vietnam, *Children and Youth Services Review*, 108, N.PAG-N.PAG, https://doi.org/10.1016/j. childyouth.2019.104536

Burde, D. and Linden, L. (2009) The effect of proximity on school enrollment: Evidence from a randomized controlled trial in Afghanistan, Unpublished working paper, http://sticerd.lse.ac.uk/seminarpapers/dg11052009.pdf

Burger, K. (2010). How does early childhood care and education affect cognitive development? An international review of the effects of early interventions for children from different social backgrounds, *Early Childhood Research Quarterly*, 25, 2, 140–165.

Cahyadi, N., Hanna, R., Olken, B., Prima, R., Satriawan, E. and Syamsulhakim, E. (2018) Cumulative impacts of conditional cash transfer programs: Experimental evidence from Indonesia, *National Bureau of Economic Research, Working Paper No. 24670*.

Caridad Araujo, M. and Macours, K. (2021) *Education, Income and Mobility*, halshs-03364972, https://halshs.archives-ouvertes.fr/halshs-03364972

Carnoy, M. (2017) School vouchers are not a proven strategy for improving student achievement, *Economic Policy Institute*.

Chaudhury, N., Friedman, J. and Onishi, J. (2013) Philippines conditional cash transfer program impact evaluation, *Manila: World Bank Report*, (75533-PH).

Chaudhury, N. and Parajuli, D. (2007) Conditional cash transfers and female schooling: the impact of the female school stipend program on public school enrollments in Punjab, Pakistan, *World Bank Policy Research Working Paper 4102*.

Chen, Y., Jin, G. and National Bureau of Economic Research (2010) *Does health insurance coverage lead to better health and educational outcomes? Evidence from Rural China*, NBER Working Paper No. 16417.

Chhabra, E., Najeeb, F. and Raju, D. (2019) *Effects over the life of a program: Evidence from an education conditional cash transfer program for girls*, World Bank Group: Policy Research Working Paper 9094.

Chitolina, L., Foguel, M. and Menezes-Filho, N. (2016) The impact of the expansion of the Bolsa Família Program on the time allocation of youths and their parents, *Revista Brasileira de Economia*, 70, 2, 183–202,

Chyi, H. and Zhou, B. (2014) The effects of tuition reforms on school enrollment in rural China, *Economics of Education Review*, 38, 104–123.

Cueto, S. and Chinen, M. (2008) Educational impact of a school breakfast programme in rural Peru, *International Journal of Educational Development*, 28, 2, 132–148.

Dahl, G. and Lochner, L. (2012) The impact of family income on child achievement: Evidence from the earned income tax credit, *American Economic Review*, 102, 5, 1927–56.

De Brauw, A. and Gilligan, D. (2011) *Using the regression discontinuity design with implicit partitions: The impacts of comunidades solidarias rurales on schooling in El Salvador*, (No. 1116) International Food Policy Research Institute (IFPRI).

De Brauw, A. and Hoddinott, J. (2008) Must conditional cash transfer programs be conditioned to be effective? The impact of conditioning transfers on school enrollment in Mexico, Must conditional cash transfer programs be conditioned to be effective? The impact of conditioning transfers on school enrollment in Mexico (repec.org).

De Janvry, A., Finan, F., Sadoulet, E. and Vakis, R. (2006). Can conditional cash transfer programs serve as safety nets in keeping children at school and from working when exposed to shocks? *Journal of development economics*, 79(2), 349–373.

De Walque, D. and Valente, C. (2018) *Incentivizing school attendance in the presence of parent-child information frictions*, World Bank Policy Research Working Paper 8476.

Dean, J. and Jayachandran, S. (2019) *Attending kindergarten improves cognitive but not socioemotional\development in India*, Working Paper.

DeAngelis, C. and Hoarty, B. (2018) Who participates? An analysis of school participation decisions in two voucher programs in the United States, Policy Analysis No. 848, *Cato Institute*.

Duflo, E., Dupas, P. and Kremer, M. (2021) *The impact of free secondary education: Experimental evidence from Ghana* (No. w28937), National Bureau of Economic Research.

Edmonds, E. and Schady, N. (2012) Poverty alleviation and child labor, *American Economic Journal: Economic Policy*, 4, 4, 100–124.

Edmonds, E. and Shrestha, M. (2014) You get what you pay for: Schooling incentives and child labor, *Journal of Development Economics*, 111, 196–211.

Evans, D., Hausladen, S., Kosec, K. and Reese, N. (2014) *Community-based conditional cash transfers in Tanzania: Results from a randomized trial*, World Bank Publications.

Evans, D. and Ngatia, I. (2018) *School costs, short-run participation, and long-run outcomes: Evidence from Kenya*, World Bank: Policy Research Working Paper 8421.

Eyal, K., Woolard, I. and Burns, J. (2014) Cash transfers and teen education: evidence from South Africa, Cash Transfers and Teen Education: Evidence from South Africa | Semantic Scholar.

Ferreira, F., Filmer, D. and Schady, N. (2009) *Own and sibling effects of conditional cash transfer programs: theory and evidence from Cambodia*, Own and sibling effects of conditional cash transfer programs: theory and evidence from Cambodia (worldbank.org).

Filmer, D. and Schady, N. (2009) School enrollment, selection and test scores, *World Bank Policy Research Working Paper* 4998.

Galiani, S. and McEwan, P. (2013) The heterogeneous impact of conditional cash transfers, *Journal of Public Economics*, 103, 85–96.

Garlick, R. (2013) How price sensitive is primary and secondary school enrollment? Evidence from nationwide tuition fee reforms in South Africa, *Unpublished working paper*, http://pubdocs.worldbank.org/en/3241466186067633/garlickschoolfees.pdf

Gaviria, J. (2022) Education: a compulsory right? *British Journal of Educational Studies*, https://doi.org/10.1080/00071005.2021.2024136

Giordono, L. and Pugatch, T. (2017) Non-tuition costs, school access and student performance: Evidence from the Gambia, *Journal of African Economies*, 26, 2, 140.

Gitter, S. and Barham, B. (2008) Women's power, conditional cash transfers, and schooling in Nicaragua, *The World Bank Economic Review*, 22, 2, 271–290.

Glewwe, P., Olinto, P. and de Souza, P. Z. (2003) Evaluating the impact of conditional cash transfers on schooling: An experimental analysis of Honduras' PRAF program. Unpublished manuscript, University of Minnesota.

González-Flores, M., Heracleous, M. and Winters,. P. (2012). Leaving the safety net: an analysis of dropouts in an urban conditional cash transfer program. *World Development*, 40(12), 2505–2521.

Gorard, S. (2021) *How to make sense of statistics: Everything you need to know about using numbers in social science*, London: SAGE.

Heckman, J. (2006) Skill formation and the economics of investing in disadvantaged children, *Science*, 312, 1900–1902.

Heinrich, C. (2007) Demand and supply-side determinants of conditional cash transfer program effectiveness, *World Development*, 35, 1, 121–143.

Hermanussen, M., Bilogub, M., Lindl, A., Harper, D., Mansukoski, L. and Scheffler, C. (2018) Weight and height growth of malnourished school-age children during re-feeding: Three historic studies published shortly after World War I, *European Journal of Clinical Nutrition*, 72, 12, 1603–1619.

Holford, A. (2015) *The labour supply effect of Education Maintenance Allowance and its implications for parental altruism*, IZA Discussion Paper No. 8822, https://ssrn.com/abstract=2564955

Kim, J., Alderman, H. and Orazem, P. (1998) *Can cultural barriers be overcome in girls' schooling? The Community Support Program in rural Balochistan*, World Bank Working Paper Series on Impact Evaluation of Education Reforms, 10.

Kim, J., Alderman, H. and Orazem, P. (1999) Can private school subsidies increase enrollment for the poor? *The World Bank Economic Review*, 13, 3, 443–465.

Levy, D. and Ohls, J. (2010) Evaluation of Jamaica's PATH conditional cash transfer programme, *Journal of Development Effectiveness*, 2, 4, 421–441.

Levy, D., Sloan, M., Linden, L. and Kazianga, H. (2009) *Impact evaluation of Burkina Faso's
BRIGHT Program*, Final Report.

Morgan, C., Petrosino, A. and Fronius, T. (2013) *A systematic review of the evidence of the impact
of school voucher programmes in developing countries*, London: EPPI Centre.

Morrissey, T. (2017) Child care and parent labor force participation: a review of the research
literature, *Review of Economics of the Household*, 15, 1, 1–24.

Noble, K., Houston, S., Brito, N., Bartsch, H., Kan, E., Kuperman, J., … and Sowell, E.
(2015) Family income, parental education and brain structure in children and adolescents,
Nature Neuroscience, 18, 5, 773–778.

Parker, S., Todd, P. and Wolpin, K. (2006) *Within-family program effect estimators: The impact of
Oportunidades on schooling in Mexico*, Universidad de Pennsylvania, mimeografiado.

Pritchett L. (2013) *The rebirth of education: Schooling ain't learning*, Washington, DC: Center
for Global Development.

Raudenbush, S. and Eschmann, R. (2015) Does schooling increase or reduce social inequality? *Annual Review of Sociology*, 41, 443–470.

Ravallion, M. and Wodon, Q. (2000) Does child labour displace schooling? Evidence on
behavioural responses to an enrollment subsidy, *The Economic Journal*, 110, 462, 158–175.

Rodriguez-Planas, N. (2012) Longer-term impacts of mentoring, educational services, and
learning incentives: Evidence from a randomized trial in the United States, *American
Economic Journal: Applied Economics*, 4, 4, 121–39.

Sapelli, C. and Vial, B. (2002) The performance of private and public schools in the Chilean
voucher system, *Cuadernos de Economía*, 39, 118, 423–454.

Schady, N. and Araujo, M. (2006) *Cash transfers, conditions, school enrollment, and child work:
Evidence from a randomised experiment in Ecuador*, The World Bank.

Schultz, P. (2000) *Impact of PROGRESA on school attendance rates in the sampled population*,
Impact of PROGRESA on School Attendance Rates in the Sampled Population (psu.
edu).

See, B.H., Gorard, S., Lu, B., Dong, L. and Siddiqui, N. (2021) Is technology always helpful?
A critical review of the use of education technology in supporting formative assessment
in schools, *Research Papers in Education*, https://doi.org/10.1080/02671522.2021.1907778

See, B.H., Gorard, S., Siddiqui, N., El Soufi, N., Lu, B. and Dong, L. (2021) A systematic
review of technology-mediated parental engagement on student outcomes, *Educational
Research and Evaluation*, Full article: A systematic review of the impact of technology-mediated parental engagement on student outcomes (tandfonline.com).

Sharp, C. (2002) School starting age: European policy and recent research, NFER, https://
defenddigitalme.com/wp-content/uploads/2020/05/44414.pdf

Sifuna D. (2007) The challenge of increasing access and improving quality: An analysis
of universal primary education interventions in Kenya and Tanzania since the 1970s,
International Review of Education, 53, 5–6: 687–99.

Slavin, R. (2010) Can financial incentives enhance educational outcomes? Evidence from
international experiments, *Educational Research Review*, 5, 68–80.

Taggart, B. (2010) Vulnerable children: Identifying children 'at risk', in *Early Childhood
Matters* (pp. 182–207), London: Routledge.

Thomson, D. (2019) *Some thoughts on 'the children leaving school with nothing'* Family Fisher Trust, https://ffteducationdatalab.org.uk/2019/09/some-thoughts-on-the-children-leaving-school-with-nothing/

Todd, P. and Wolpin, K. (2003) Using a social experiment to validate a dynamic behavioural model of child schooling and fertility: Assessing the impact of a school subsidy programme in Mexico, *American Economic Review*, 96, 5, 1384–1417.

Tsai, W., Liu, J., Chou, S. and Thornton, R. (2009) Does educational expansion encourage female workforce participation? A study of the 1968 reform in Taiwan, *Economics of Education Review*, 28, 6, 750–758.

UNICEF (2018) Out-of-School Children in the Balochistan, Khyber Pakhtunkhwa, Punjab and Sindh Provinces of Pakistan, https://www.itacec.org/document/sector_plans/UNICEF_UIS_pakistan_oosc_report_2013_en.pdf

Wong, H., Luo, R., Zhang, L. and Rozelle, S. (2013) The impact of vouchers on pre-school attendance and elementary school readiness: A randomized controlled trial in rural China, *Economics of Education Review*, 35, 53–65.

Woode, M. (2017) Parental health shocks and schooling: The impact of mutual health insurance in Rwanda, *Social Science and Medicine*, 173, 35–47.

World Bank (2018) *Pakistan: Can private schools catering to the poor increase access and improve learning? From evidence to policy*, http://search.ebscohost.com/login.aspx?direct=trueanddb=ericandAN=ED589943andsite=ehost-live

Zulaika, G., Kwaro, D., Nyothach, E., Wang, D., Zielinski-Gutierrez, E., Mason, L., ... Phillips-Howard, P. A. (2019) Menstrual cups and cash transfer to reduce sexual and reproductive harm and school dropout in adolescent schoolgirls: Study protocol of a cluster-randomised controlled trial in western Kenya, *BMC Public Health*, 19, 1, 1317–1317.

4

IMPROVING SCHOOL ATTENDANCE IN OTHER WAYS

Introduction

Persistent poverty and adverse circumstances interact with children' chances of access to education, attendance at school, and attainment outcomes. Poverty may present in the form of poor health, shortage of nutrition, and lack of access to child-care. To a large extent such factors are malleable, and it sounds reasonable to invest financial resources in addressing these factors.

This chapter continues from the previous one, looking at similar studies about attendance/enrolment at school, and rating them in the same way. However, the previous chapter focused on financial incentives while this chapter is about other interventions, including food and incentives in kind.

Summary of results

We found a further 21 studies of at least 1🔒 quality, as summarised in Table 4.1. Again the majority have reportedly positive results. However, among the strongest studies the pattern is perhaps not as clear as it was for financial incentives. Each

TABLE 4.1 Strength of evidence and impact for further studies on improving attainment

Strength of evidence	Positive	Unclear/mixed	Negative/neutral
4🔒	–	–	–
3🔒	5	–	1
2🔒	4	1	3
1🔒	4	2	–

DOI: 10.4324/9781003287353-6

study is summarised below in terms of whether it involved providing food, a health intervention, pre-school experience, or something else.

Evidence on the use of food and school attendance

There are no 4🔒 studies on this theme.

3🔒 studies

Tan et al. (1999) evaluated the Dropout Intervention Programme in the Philippines, on dropout behaviour and student learning. Five groups were compared – one where all pupils in beneficiary schools received a free school meal, another where all teachers received pedagogical materials and attended a training course on their use with differing abilities of students, and the other two were the same but with parent meetings at school and parental involvement. There was also a control. There were 10 schools with high initial dropout in each group. Student dropout declined in general, but most clearly in the groups with teaching materials. Feeding alone made little difference. There was little impact on attainment, but more so for languages than maths.

Is it better to feed children in school or provide take home rations, both conditional on 90% school attendance? In Burkina Faso, 46 village schools in areas of severe food shortage were randomly assigned to three groups (school meals, take home rations of 10 kg of cereal flour, or a control). Girls were between 5 and 15 years old. The groups were balanced at the outset in terms of enrolment, child health and nutritional status, household and socio-economic characteristics. All school age children had a pre- and post-test in maths and cognitive skills (Kazianga et al. 2008). The programme increased girls' attendance rate by 6% points after one year, but there was no clear benefit for their attainment. Girls also shifted from farm labour to more domestic tasks that were probably more compatible with the school schedule.

2🔒 studies

In the Bangladesh Food for Education programme, households received food resources (wheat or rice) on condition that their children enrolled in primary school and attended at least 85%. To evaluate the results, a standard achievement test was given to 3,369 students enrolled in both treatment and other schools (Meng and Ryan 2003). The programme significantly raised calorie and protein consumption in beneficiary households but did not improve the nutritional status of preschool-age children. Enrolment in treatment schools increased but average attainment did not. This could be because of the increased numbers, the strain on the schools, and the background of the new recruits.

1🔒 studies

The School Feeding Programme in Ethiopia provided a daily hot lunch of wheat, corn, or beans. Its purpose, other than feeding, was to encourage school attendance. A small trial compared three schools implementing the programme with three others in the same district, matched as far as possible, and involved 390 students aged 10–14 (Zenebe et al. 2018). However, there were differences between the two groups in wealth, household food insecurity, parental education and occupation, and child age at the outset. Diet was improved in the treatment schools, and absences were less.

Jacoby et al. (1996) looked at the impact of a school breakfast programme for 30 days on the diet, attendance, and cognition of students in grades 4 and 5 in an Andean region of Peru. 10 schools were randomised to treatment or a waiting list control. The treatment consisted of breakfast (energy, iron and protein). The programme raised dietary intakes and improved attendance rates. There was slightly more improvement in attainment in coding and vocabulary for the treatment group but not in maths.

Summary

In summary, the evidence is weak on whether providing food in school or outside improves attendance or enrolment. Most studies say yes. There is no real evidence at all that food programmes improve attainment.

Evidence on health interventions and school attendance

We found no 4🔒 studies on health and attendance.

3🔒 studies

Montgomery et al. (2016) used a cluster quasi-randomised control trial to determine the effect of puberty education and/or free sanitary pads on the attendance and psychological wellbeing of girls in Uganda. Eight schools (1,124 girls in grades 3–5) were allocated to puberty education, reusable sanitary pads, puberty education and pads, or a control. Over two years there was very high dropout, especially in the intervention groups. Intention-to-treat analysis was used. School attendance declined in all groups but remained greatest in the control condition.

2🔒 studies

Oster and Thornton (2009) recruited four schools in Nepal, and 60 girls (grade 7 and 8) from each school were invited, with their mothers, to participate in the study. Participation depended on attendance at the first meeting where girls received pens and stickers and mothers received money. Students were then randomly allocated to receive a menstrual cup during their monthly period or to the control group. A baseline survey was administered, and students were followed for a period of 15 months. Post-intervention data was available for 89% of the girls who took the baseline test. The intervention had only a negligible impact on girls' attendance during their period (or at other times), or on their test scores, or self-reported measures of self-esteem or gynecological health.

Save the Children implemented a school-based malaria treatment programme in Malawi primary schools. Teachers participated in training on when and how to utilise malaria treatment kits, including persuading children to come to school when sick, and get treated. Free tablets were provided. Simwaka et al. (2009) assessed the impact of the intervention over five years, based on 63 treatment and 30 comparison schools. There was high student attrition from the study (30%). The treatment schools had fewer deaths, fewer student days sick (effect size 0.23), and slightly less general absenteeism (effect size 0.03).

1 🔒 studies

The 1985 Turkish National Immunisation Campaign sought to immunise Turkish children under five against infectious diseases. Within three months 27 million vaccines had been administered nationwide. Alsan (2017) examined the spill-over effect of the campaign on the years of schooling of older siblings who were not targeted by the campaign. Using administrative data, the study compared individuals born between 1971 and 1980, to those born between 1961 and 1970. Based on 7,698 cases a one standard deviation increase in vaccine prevalence is associated with a 2% increase in completing at least compulsory education for elder sisters of vaccine-eligible children, but there is no spill-over impact on years of education beyond the compulsory stage, or for brothers. No mention of missing data, likely confounds.

Summary

Table 4.2 summarises the results for the themes of nutrition and health interventions.

In summary, we found few studies of health interventions and attendance, and there will surely be more not covered by our search criteria. Here, there is some promise, especially for girls.

TABLE 4.2 Strength of evidence and impact on studies of nutrition and health

Strength of evidence	Positive	Unclear/mixed	Negative/neutral
4 🔒	–	–	–
3 🔒	3	–	–
2 🔒	2	–	1
1 🔒	2	1	–

Evidence on pre-schools and school attendance

Can attending pre-school improve subsequent school attendance? There were no 4 🔒 studies on this.

3🔒 *studies*

Martinez et al. (2017) considered a community-based pre-school programme in Mozambique. Thirty communities were randomised to the programme and 46 remained as the control. Tests of vocabulary and development were used at the baseline and after treatment. Children who attended pre-school scored higher on cognitive development, communication, fine motor skills, and socio-emotional skills on average. They were more likely to enrol in primary school, and at the standard age, especially those from the most vulnerable households.

2🔒 *studies*

A sample of 103 families in North Carolina, with children deemed at developmental or educational risk because of poverty, were randomised to a programme lasting from infancy to kindergarten (57 children) or to a control condition (54 children). Children as young as 6 weeks of age were given educational activities and games in a year-round child-care facility (Campbell et al. 2012). At age 5, children were admitted to kindergarten. Children in the experimental group were more likely to achieve more years of education (effect size 0.62) and to attend university than their counterparts by the age of 21. They were also more likely to work full time by the age of 30.

Baker-Henningham et al. (2012) assessed a pre-school-based intervention called the Incredible Years Teacher Training Programme in Jamaica. This involved training teachers and principals, the use of collaborative and experiential learning, individual goal setting and self-monitoring, building teachers' self-efficacy, a focus on teachers' cognitions, behaviour and emotions, and emphasis on teachers' ability to generalise the skills learned. In a cluster randomised design, 24 community schools were assigned to receive the treatment or to a control. Three children from each class with the highest levels of teacher-reported conduct problems were selected for evaluation. This included 225 aged 3–6 years children in total, and 15 pupils dropped out during the process. Children's school attendance is taken from school records. Children in the treatment group showed an increase in school attendance (effect size 0.30).

1🔒 *studies*

A small study of one early childhood centre in Zambia used a natural comparator of 40 children not attending to compare to 40 attendees (Zuilkowski et al. 2012). It reported greater school preparedness in the treatment group.

Summary

In summary, this small body of evidence suggests that pre-school experience is linked to improved enrolment and attendance at school, but not necessarily to greater school readiness.

Other approaches

3 studies

Banerjee et al. (2010) looked at three schemes to improve attendance and participation in India. One involved a small-group discussion to share information about the structure and organisation of local services, including the role of the local Village Education Committee (VEC). Villagers such as heads, teachers, parents, and VEC members were invited to attend the meetings. VEC members also received a pamphlet on their roles. The second intervention added training sessions in which interested villagers were taught to evaluate their children using a simple test. The third treatment supplemented the previous two by introducing the villagers to a teaching technique (Read India). Volunteer villagers were trained for four days and started giving free after-class reading courses to children. Each village in the third treatment received seven visits from NGO staff who offered extra support. 65 villages were randomly selected for each treatment group, and 85 for the control, totalling 17,533 children aged 7 to 14. Attrition was 4%. Neither of the first two treatments made any difference to children's reading. There was a small increase in the practice of reading for the third treatment, and this was more marked among the children who actually attended the reading classes. There was no clear impact for maths. The proportion of pupils missing school actually went up for all treatments. The tests were not independent of the programme developers.

As described in Chapter 6, Skoufias and Shapiro (2006) looked at the Quality Schools Programme in Mexico, intended to expand autonomy and improve learning in pre, primary, and secondary schools. Staff and parents planned the steps for improving the school quality, principals got training, and a five-year grant to carry this out. The researchers constructed a panel of 1,767 schools in the treatment group and 65,457 in the comparator, based on matching. Dropout after three years was slightly lower for the treatment schools (effect size -0.04).

2 studies

Leos-Urbel and Sanchez (2015) looked at the impact of Playworks – a US programme that provided children in low-income elementary schools with a safe play area, inclusive play and coaching in recess time. The treatment group was 17 schools and 12 schools provided the comparator, with a focus on grades 1 to 5. There was a small 0.2% increase in attendance.

Social-emotional learning programmes aim to foster student emotional intelligence (a non-cognitive skill), helping students to deal with their anxiety and relationships at school. Wang et al. (2016) conducted a cluster-randomised trial of such a programme with grade 7 and 8 students in public junior high schools in China. Seventy-five paired schools were randomised to treatment (3,694 students) and control (3,801). For the intervention, the principal would choose a music, art, or physical exercise teacher with previous experience as a homeroom teacher to get five-day training on how to execute the 32 scripted 45-minute sessions per week. Social-emotional skills were taught mainly through activities and games. The data are drawn from a baseline, midline, and endline survey. In the middle survey, the treatment group had less dropout (effect size -0.07) and learning anxiety. However, by the final survey there was no impact on dropout or attainment. Attrition was around 20%.

Lee et al. (2020) looked at a US family truancy intervention programme for primary schools. In Minnesota, parents of truant primary school students would usually be directly referred to child protection services or juvenile court. In the alternative court-diversion programme, parents were educated about the importance of school attendance and had an attendance contract that included social service referrals. After five unexcused absences, responsible staff members contacted parents about their child's absenteeism, met with parents and implemented attendance-promotion activities. If ignored, this could lead to filing a petition for educational neglect with the juvenile court. Based on administrative data, 1,197 students were in the treatment group, and 2,615 matched students were in the control. The programme effect based on difference in difference was close to zero in terms of student attendance. Attrition was over 20%.

1🔒 studies

Asim and Dee (2016) studied the impact of mobile-phone calls made by trained agents to school-council members (parents, community members, and head-teachers) on pupil enrolment and attendance. The calls provided guidance and orientation to members about their roles and responsibilities every month, for 17 months. Most schools were primary, and segregated by sex, in 26 school districts of which five received the programme. Difference in difference analysis suggested that the treatment increased student enrolment by 7.5% points and teacher attendance by 1 point. There was no benefit in terms of student attendance (effect size -0.4).

Graeff-Martins et al. (2006) evaluated the impact of a package intended to prevent student dropout from schools in Brazil. The study compared two matched schools with high dropout, one of which had two workshops with teachers, five informative letters to parents, three school meetings with parents, a school telephone helpline, and a one-day cognitive intervention. There was an effect size of 0.64. Poorly reported, especially about missing data.

TABLE 4.3 Strength of evidence and impact of other approaches

Strength of evidence	Positive	Unclear/mixed	Negative/neutral
4 🔒	–	–	–
3 🔒	2	–	1
2 🔒	2	1	2
1 🔒	2	1	–

Summary

Table 4.3 summarises the results for this miscellaneous group of interventions.

In summary, this mix of other approaches to improving attendance are mostly either not very promising, or have not been robustly evaluated, or both. Involving local communities may actually worsen local attendance. Involving parents more makes no apparent difference, and increasing autonomy of schools, adding play areas, or addressing socio-emotional intelligence, have only marginal benefits for attendance.

Conclusion

Encouraging pre-schools, like creating new school places, seems to be related to improved later attendance at school. But a new large-scale study in the US by Durkin (et al. 2022) found that low-income children randomised to a pre-kindergarten programme had lower test scores as late as grade 6, along with worse discipline and school attendance. So, the interventions evaluated in this chapter, whatever their other merits, do not seem to be as effective as financial incentives in terms of attendance (although of course issues like health matter in their own right). In Chapter 5, we begin to examine more about how and why attendance at school might matter, in the context of our own fieldwork in Indian and Pakistan.

References

Alsan, M. (2017) *The gendered spillover effect of young children's health on Human Capital: Evidence from Turkey*, National Bureau of Economic Research, Inc, NBER Working Papers: 23702.

Asim, M. and Dee, T. (2016) Mobile phones, civic engagement, and school performance in Pakistan, *National Bureau of Economic Research*, Mobile Phones, Civic Engagement, and School Performance in Pakistan | Center for Education Policy Analysis (stanford.edu).

Baker-Henningham, H., Scott, S., Jones, K. and Walker, S. (2012) Reducing child conduct problems and promoting social skills in a middle-income country: Cluster randomised controlled trial, *The British Journal of Psychiatry*, 20–1, 2, 101–108.

Banerjee, A., Banerji, R., Duflo, E., Glennerster, R. and Khemani, S. (2010) Pitfalls of participatory programs: Evidence from a randomized evaluation in education in India, *American Economic Journal: Economic Policy*, 2, 1, 1–30.

Campbell, F., Pungello, E., Burchinal, M., Kainz, K., Pan, Y., Wasik, B., Barbarin, O., Sparling, J. and Ramey, C. (2012) Adult outcomes as a function of an early childhood educational program: an Abecedarian Project follow-up, *Developmental Psychology*, 48, 4, 1033.

Graeff-Martins, A., Oswald, S., Obst Comassetto, J., Kieling, C., Rocha Gonçalves, R. and Rohde, L. (2006) A package of interventions to reduce school dropout in public schools in a developing country, *European Child and Adolescent Psychiatry*, 15, 8, 442–449.

Jacoby, E., Cueto, S. and Pollitt, E. (1996) Benefits of a school breakfast programme among Andean children in Huaraz, Peru, *Food and Nutrition Bulletin*, 17, 1, 1–11.

Kazianga, H., De Walque, D., Alderman, H. and Faso, C. (2008) *Educational and health impact of two school feeding schemes. Evidence from a randomized trial in rural Burkina Faso*, The World Bank: Policy Research Working Paper 4976.

Lee, W., McNeely, C., Rosenbaum, J., Alemu, B. and Renner, L. (2020) Can court diversion improve school attendance among elementary students? Evidence from five school districts, *Journal of Research on Educational Effectiveness*, 13, 4, 625–651.

Leos-Urbel, J. and Sanchez, M. (2015) *The relationship between playworks participation and student attendance in two school districts*, John W. Gardner Center for Youth and Their Communities.

Martinez, S., Naudeau, S. and Pereira, V. (2017) *Preschool and child development under extreme poverty: Evidence from a randomized experiment in rural Mozambique*, World Bank: Policy Research Working Paper 8290.

Meng, X. and Ryan, J. (2003) *Evaluating the food for education program in Bangladesh*, International Food Policy Research Institute: FMRSP Working Paper No. 35.

Montgomery, P., Hennegan, J., Dolan, C., Wu, M., Steinfield, L. and Scott, L. (2016) Menstruation and the cycle of poverty: A cluster quasi-randomised control trial of sanitary pad and puberty education provision in Uganda, *Plos One*, 11, 12.

Oster, E. and Thornton, R. (2009) *Menstruation and education in Nepal*, National Bureau of Economic Research: NBER Working Paper No. 14853.

Simwaka, B., Simwaka, K. and Bello, G. (2009) Retrospective analysis of a school-based malaria treatment programme demonstrates a positive impact on health and education outcomes in Mangochi district, Malawi, *Journal of Development Effectiveness*, 1, 4, 492–506.

Skoufias, E. and Shapiro, J. (2006) *Evaluating the impact of Mexico's quality schools programme: the pitfalls of using nonexperimental data*, The World Bank.

Tan, J., Lane, J. and Lassibille, G. (1999) Student outcomes in Philippine elementary schools: An evaluation of four experiments, *The World Bank Economic Review*, 13, 3, 493–508.

Wang, H., Chu, J., Loyalka, P., Xin, T., Shi, Y., Qu, Q. and Yang, C. (2016) Can social–emotional learning reduce school dropout in developing countries? *Journal of Policy Analysis and Management*, 35, 4, 818–847.

Zenebe, M., Gebremedhin, S., Henry, C. and Regassa, N. (2018) School feeding programme has resulted in improved dietary diversity, nutritional status and class attendance of school children. *Italian Journal of Pediatrics*, 44, 1, 16–16.

Zuilkowski, S., Fink, G., Moucheraud, C. and Matafwali, B. (2012) Early childhood education, child development and school readiness: Evidence from Zambia, *South African Journal of Childhood Education*, 2, 2, 20.

5

THE IMPORTANCE OF ATTENDANCE AT SCHOOL IN INDIA AND PAKISTAN

Introduction

This chapter reports on our study of the experiences and impact of young children attending school/pre-school or not in two countries that do not have anything like full enrolment in school, especially in more rural areas. According to estimates from UNESCO (2017), 6 million children in India and 5 million in Pakistan in the age group of 5-9 years have never been enrolled in school. And school dropout for those enrolled gradually increases after primary-school age.

The chapter summarises the results of our study of school attendance in India and Pakistan. We present relatively simple findings from this recently competed project, to add to our reports of the pilot study (Siddiqui et al. 2020a), and the interim report after the first wave (Siddiqui et al. 2020b), all building on our earlier work in Pakistan (Siddiqui 2017, Siddiqui and Gorard 2017, Siddiqui 2019). Here we focus on who goes to school and who does not, their attainment and wider development, and the views of participants in the study.

Methods used in our study of school attendance in India and Pakistan

This section outlines the methods we used.

The study looks at the differences in development between young children who attend school and those who do not, and how they have developed after one year. In both India and Pakistan, school enrolment is substantially less than 100% and this provides the opportunity for a natural research comparison. This is helpful because it is not feasible to envisage an experiment or similar in which children of school age were randomised to attend school or not. The research questions are:

DOI: 10.4324/9781003287353-7

- What is the apparent impact of schooling on children's learning and social development?
- What level of progress in cognitive development is made by children who attend one year of formal pre-primary schooling (Kindergarten, Nursery, Reception, Grade 1) compared to those who do not?

Due to school closures in the period of the Covid-19 pandemic 2020-21, all children included in the study sample had the same status of not attending school, for a period of around five months (lockdown and summer/ winter breaks). This made the fieldwork harder, and the analysis more complex than it would otherwise have been.

The study design

The study was based on a natural quasi-experimental design where children included in the sample were of comparable age and in terms of household socio-economic characteristics, in both of the categories of attending school and not attending school. This unique and naturally occurring phenomenon of not attending school exists in some poorer countries, giving a reasonable number of cases for assessing the link between attending school and children's learning. This study is also longitudinal, using household surveys, school surveys and a baseline assessment, with the same sample of young children reassessed after a year of attending or not attending school.

Participants

The sample was based on 12 districts in Punjab, Pakistan and six in Gujarat, India. From each district, two villages were selected, and from each village 10 volunteer households were invited to participate. The achieved sample from the first data sweep in June 2020 was 1,129 children from 783 households. Of the total, 322 households and 616 children were from Pakistan (51% rural), and 451 households and 513 children from India (49% rural). Further characteristics of the sample appear below. In the second data sweep in June 2021 we could not track 106 of these children as the enumerators lost contact with 53 households. This attrition constitutes 9% of the initially recruited sample, and our analysis looked at the characteristics of the missing cases to understand whether attrition leads to any threats to the findings of the study. The results presented are for the 1,023 children and their families who took part in both waves.

Data collection

Children aged 4 to 8 (according to parental reports of their children's age) were assessed and parents were interviewed regarding household socio-economic conditions, reasons for use of school, children's general health and interest in attending school, and experience of access to their children's school during lockdown.

School closures created a natural disruption to the study. Covid-19 led to school closures, travel restrictions and social distancing measures, announced in both countries in March 2020. We developed new protocols for children's assessment using mobile phone technologies and conducted a new round of pilot tests. The pilots were successful in using mobile and internet technology. We found that access to internet connections did not really pose any major challenge to our modified remote assessment plans. The internet coverage was very good in Gujarat, India and Punjab, Pakistan. However, access to mobile devices was sometimes a barrier because very poor families sometimes do not possess a smart phone. We provided the enumerators with extra mobiles with internet connection so that they could temporarily share a hotspot with the households who did not possess a mobile phone or internet (and we provided masks and gloves).

We recruited and trained 90 enumerators from the local communities who had access to households. Most of the enumerators had prior experience of collecting research data from children. We conducted two online workshops on collecting data using the mobile technology (instead of face to face). And all enumerators conducted four practice sessions. The study involved a repeated survey, measurements, and interviews with parents. The data sweeps took place in May to June 2020 and May to June 2021.

Instruments

The child assessment instrument used was based on the International Development and Early Learning Assessment (IDELA), developed by Save the Children. IDELA has been translated into several languages, and adopted in 32 countries to assess children's learning and development. There is good evidence that IDELA had been successfully implemented with children, and that the items in the four major learning domains clearly demonstrate children's early years of development and their learning profile. We piloted IDELA and selected the most appropriate features of the assessments that could be implemented remotely or in open air, using mobile phone and internet technologies. Because of the lockdown, we had to curtail the assessment by eliminating exercises which required the child to perform physical activities such as completing jigsaw puzzles, sorting shapes, writing their names, drawing, and hopping.

The test was individually administered with each child, and the enumerator scored each item, and recorded how long the test took. Test materials were pre-prepared and packed in a small test-kit, which included the following items:

- Original copy of the test
- Score sheets for 10 tests
- Two cards for size comparison
- One card for shape identification
- One card for number identification
- Two cards for addition and subtraction

- A picture card of a child with crying face
- A card with printed story text so that the assessor could read it to the child (only for the assessor)
- A card with numbers printed to test short-term memory (only for the assessor)

The test we used covered the following three domains of learning and development in early years (Table 5.1). Full details of all our instruments appear in Siddiqui et al. (2020a, 2020b)

For listening comprehension, a story was read from a card in Guajarati or Urdu. The assessor added emotions to make the story interesting for children. There was no change in wording. The questions were read as they were written for the face-to-face test. The test also scored children's persistence and engagement in this activity.

As another example, for basic comparison of size and length, the child was first shown a card with pictures of three sticks, and the assessor asked them to point at the longest stick and then at the shortest (Figure 5.1). Similarly, with the second card with three circles, the assessor them asked to point at the biggest circle and then at the smallest circle.

Shape identification involved identifying shapes printed on a card (Figure 5.2). The assessor asked each child to identify a circle, rectangle, triangle, and square,

TABLE 5.1 IDELA domains and subdomains

Emergent literacy and language	Emergent numeracy	Social-emotional development
Expressive vocabulary	Comparison by size and length	Peer relations
Letter identification	Number identification	Emotional awareness
Initial sound discrimination	Classification/Sorting	Empathy
Listening comprehension	Shape identification	Self-awareness
	Simple operations	
	One-to-one correspondence	
	Addition and subtraction	

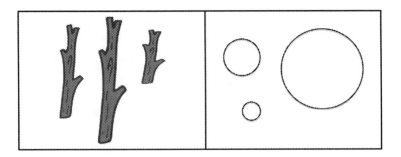

FIGURE 5.1 Comparison by size and length

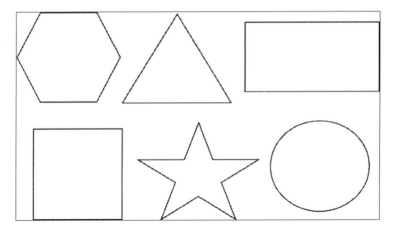

FIGURE 5.2 Shape identification

by pointing. An additional question was to ask the child to look at their surroundings and suggest something that is shaped like a circle.

As a final illustration of the larger test, in simple operations, we used a set of 50 small balls kept in a box. Children were asked to pick balls from the box according to the number stated by the assessor and put them aside. We used the same numbers (3, 8, and 15) on each occasion. The test scored children's concentration and motivation in this activity.

Parents were also interviewed regarding their household socio-economic conditions, reasons for school choice, children's general health and interest in attending school, and experience of access to their children's education during lockdown.

The modified IDELA test involving observations, literacy, numeracy, and social and emotional components, was conducted by trained enumerators, sometimes with researcher observation and participation, and it went well. Perhaps because of Covid-19 lockdown, households preferred open air but face-to-face interactions. Those enumerators who worked in both urban and rural areas said that children in urban areas were less hesitant to talk with strangers – and this may be influenced by the nature of housing (privacy) and the number of other people present. Children generally enjoyed the activities, especially listening to stories and answering questions. They liked having physical items like cards to look at. All of this can be seen in our video recordings of the process. In many cases both the child and parent expressed disappointment that the assessment was over so soon, although a few began to lose interest by the end. A few asked "will you come again tomorrow?" Some were less interested in talking about their friends, names of animals, and things like food items. Children in rural areas were seen as better at naming locally found animals and food items. Children generally had difficulties understanding the sad feeling portrayed by a picture on a card, but were usually good at explaining how to make a crying baby laugh. Children as young as three can successfully complete our modified IDELA test.

Descriptive results

Here we consider some aspects of the sample, and how certain characteristics of individuals are related to school attendance. The achieved sample consisted of 1,023 cases who took part in the first survey and assessment in 2020 and in the second round in 2021. Of these, 72.8% were recorded as attending school in 2020, and 85.2% in 2021. However, this was not a simple increase in attendance over one year. A further 180 children were reported as attending school in 2021, but 53 of those who had attended in 2020 no longer did (Table 5.2).

Overall, 49.1% of the samples were boys, and 50.9% girls – a reasonable balance. Of these, 73.5% of the boys went to school in 2020, and 72.2% of girls did (Table 5.3). Again, this is reasonably balanced. In 2021, boys' attendance had increased, with age presumably, to 84.7%, and girls' attendance had overtaken them at 85.8% (Table 5.4).

As expected from the nature of the household sampling, the children ranged in age from 3 to 8 at the outset, with most being aged 5 (Table 5.5).

Children's age is clearly linked to whether they are reported as attending school (Table 5.6). Those attending school tend to be up to a year older on average. This difference will be taken into account in the multivariate analyses that follow.

Of the 14 assets such as mains electricity or a computer that children's homes could have had, some homes had as few as two, and some all 14. The overall mean was 8.6 (Table 5.7). Given incomplete data on parental education and occupation,

TABLE 5.2 School attendance in each year of the study

	School 2021	Not school 2021	Total
School 2020	692	53	745
Not school 2020	180	98	278
Total	972	151	1,023

TABLE 5.3 School attendance in 2020, by sex

	Boys	Girls	Total
School 2020	369	376	745
Not school 2020	133	145	278
Total	502	521	1,023

TABLE 5.4 School attendance in 2021, by sex

	Boys	Girls	Total
School 2021	425	447	872
Not school 2021	77	74	151
Total	502	521	1,023

TABLE 5.5 Frequency of age in years, sample

Age	Frequency	Percentage
3	17	1.7
4	281	27.5
5	288	28.2
6	237	23.2
7	107	10.5
8	93	9.1

TABLE 5.6 Mean age of school attenders in 2020 and 2021

	2020	2021
Attending school	5.6	6.6
Not attending school	4.8	5.6

TABLE 5.7 Mean number of household assets in 2020 and 2021, by attendance at school

	2020	2021
Attending school	9.0	8.7
Not attending school	7.6	8.3

this is a feasible measure of socio-economic status. Those attending school had more assets on average, but the difference was minimal by 2021. But assets (as well as age) will be taken into account in our multivariate analyses.

Children who were reported as attending school in 2020 were ahead of those not attending school on all five of our measured outcomes. The same is true for 2021. And both groups of children, whether attending school or not, improved their average outcome scores over time from 2020 to 2021. It is important to recall this fact. Children learn and develop both inside school and outside. Our question is – can we assess to what extent school makes a difference over and above the development achieved simply through getting older, and above what is learnt at home and from family and friends? For this purpose we will present the results for those attending school or not in 2021.

The scores in Table 5.8 are somewhat subjective, based on the enumerators' judgements and observations about the behaviour, motivation and attention of the child during the test. They show that children attending school in 2021 were judged to be more alert and so on, in the 2020 test and in 2021. And both those attending school and those not attending improved their scores over time. However, the children attending school had higher scores in 2020 (with a standardised difference or "effect" size of 0.09 in 2020). This grew to 0.48 in 2021. The children

TABLE 5.8 Observation scores by school attendance or not

	Observation score 2020	Standard deviation	"Effect" size	Observation score 2021	Standard deviation	"Effect" size
Attending school 2021	74.28	21.46		75.69	24.19	
Not attending school 2021	72.28	22.57		64.85	21.74	
Total	74.44	21.64	**+0.09**	74.09	22.43	**+0.48**

at school were ahead at the outset had pulled further ahead over one year (despite Covid-19 disruptions).

A similar result appears for literacy scores (Table 5.9). In 2020, children attending school in 2021 were already ahead of their peers who did not attend, and the gap widened slightly over one year (from 0.7 to 0.75).

The gap is bigger in terms of numeracy and it grows more over time from an "effect" size of 0.79 in 2020 to 1.04 in 2021 (Table 5.10).

The pattern continues for social and emotional development (as assessed by the IDELA test) as well. Children attending school in 2021 are more developed in this respect than non-attenders, and have made more progress since 2020 (Table 5.11).

Finally in this section, we look at the overall IDELA test score (combining literacy, numeracy and social and emotional development, but not the observation scores). As expected from the foregoing the pattern is the same (Table 5.12). The 2021 school

TABLE 5.9 Literacy scores by school attendance or not

	Literacy score 2020	Standard deviation	"Effect" size	Literacy score 2021	Standard deviation	"Effect" size
Attending school 2021	50.69	28.88		63.33	25.69	
Not attending school 2021	30.31	22.38		41.98	27.72	
Total	47.68	28.94	**+0.70**	60.17	28.45	**+0.75**

TABLE 5.10 Numeracy scores by school attendance or not

	Numeracy score 2020	Standard deviation	"Effect" size	Numeracy score 2021	Standard deviation	"Effect" size
Attending school 2021	72.27	25.79		81.96	21.83	
Not attending school 2021	51.62	21.92		56.95	25.73	
Total	69.22	26.29	**+0.79**	78.27	24.13	**+1.04**

TABLE 5.11 Social emotional scores by school attendance or not

	Social emotional score 2020	Standard deviation	"Effect" size	Social emotional score 2021	Standard deviation	"Effect" size
Attending school 2021	53.50	20.12		62.15	19.22	
Not attending school 2021	46.00	19.60		48.61	20.78	
Total	52.40	20.21	**+0.37**	60.15	20.03	**+0.68**

TABLE 5.12 Total IDELA scores by school attendance or not

	Total IDELA score 2020	Standard deviation	"Effect" size	Total IDELA score 2021	Standard deviation	"Effect" size
Attending school 2021	58.82	21.79		69.15	20.13	
Not attending school 2021	42.64	18.16		49.18	21.52	
Total	56.43	22.05	**0.73**	66.20	21.53	**0.93**

attenders are ahead on test scores at the start in 2020 ("effect" size 0.73), and have pulled further ahead after one year (0.93).

However, before we can conclude that school is responsible for either the initial gap or the differential progress over time, we need to take the previously noted differences between the two groups into account. In particular, we need to allow for the fact that those attending school are somewhat older, on average.

Modelling the results

To do this we have created simple regression models for each of the four separate outcomes and the IDELA test total. Each model is used to predict or explain the 2021 result for each child using their known characteristics, the 2020 result, and whether the child was reported as attending school in 2020 and again in 2021. In the first step we added the sex, age in years and sum of household assets for each child, using forward entry. In the second step for each model we added the prior score for that element of the test. And finally we added whether the child went to school in 2020, and in 2021.

The most important part of the model for observation scores is shown in Table 5.13 – how much of the variation in the outcome measure is linked to each predictor when entered in the order shown. Putting school attendance last allows its relationship to be considered net of the impact of the other factors. As expected from the descriptive findings, the strongest predictor of the observation scores is the

TABLE 5.13 Model for Observation score, 2021

Step	R	Increase in R
Age in years	0.27	–
Sum of assets	0.32	0.05
Observation score 2020	0.41	0.09
Child went to school 2020	0.41	0
Child went to school 2021	0.43	0.02

Sex of the child is not relevant

age of the child (R = 0.27, explaining over 7% of the variation in the outcome). SES, as estimated by the sum of household assets, plays a smaller role in the prediction. The sex of the child is not relevant to any of the models, and is ignored in the table. This is not apparently a gendered issue. Unsurprisingly, the 2020 score in the equivalent test adds to the prediction (R = 0.09). Net of these factors, school attendance (reported in 2021) is positively linked to the outcome score but only by a very small amount. Most of the differences in outcomes shown above are created by differences between the kinds of children who attend school or not, and are not chiefly associated with school attendance itself. Presumably this is partly because those attending school in 2020 had higher average prior scores. This pattern, with slight variations, appears for all five models

The model creates a coefficient for every variable in it, regardless of the amount of variation it explains/predicts. This is why the first table is the more important in each model (it gives the best idea of the "effect" size, which is the square of the R value). Nevertheless, we report the coefficients for completeness (Table 5.14). Older children with more assets and higher prior scores tend to have higher outcomes. The standardised coefficient for attending school at the outset is near zero, and for attending after one year the coefficient is 0.12 –suggesting a small benefit from school attendance for this outcome.

The picture is similar for literacy (Tables 5.15 and 5.16). Once age has been accounted for, there is a role for SES and prior literacy score. After this there is a very small benefit from attending school at the end of the year. This shows several important things. As already explained in Chapter 3, children can learn in any context, in

TABLE 5.14 Coefficients for model of Observation score, 2021

Variable	Unstandardised coefficient	Standardised coefficient
Age in years	3.47	0.20
Sum of assets	1.04	0.11
Observation score 2020	0.30	0.29
Child went to school 2020	−1.82	−.004
Child went to school 2021	7.44	0.12

TABLE 5.15 Model for Literacy score, 2021

Step	R	Increase in R
Age in years	0.35	–
Sum of assets	0.46	0.11
Literacy score 2020	0.58	0.12
Child went to school 2020	0.58	0
Child went to school 2021	0.59	0.01

TABLE 5.16 Coefficients for model of Literacy score, 2021

Variable	Unstandardised coefficient	Standardised coefficient
Age in years	3.42	0.15
Sum of assets	1.90	0.16
Literacy score 2020	0.41	0.42
Child went to school 2020	−1.37	−0.02
Child went to school 2021	9.87	0.12

school or outside. In fact, much of the progress that children make happens with age and experience, and is not related to school attendance at all (Luyten et al. 2020). The explicit teaching and directed learning that take place at school are meant to enhance this natural early progress, but may not always do so to the extent that educators fondly imagine.

As perhaps predictable from the "effect" sizes in the last section, the potential role of school is slightly greater for numeracy than literacy ($R = 0.03$). This may be because the role of SES is slightly less in this model (Table 5.17 and 5.18). The coefficient for school attendance in 2021 is also correspondingly higher (0.21).

Two methodological points are worth making. The non-school attenders started at a lower level in both literacy and numeracy – a position that it might be easier to show progress from. The tests were relatively simple, and this might mean that the more advanced learning that could be taking place in school might not be registered by the test. It may be, of course, that other factors are at play, including other but unknown differences in the types of children attending and not attending school.

The only real difference in the model for social and emotional development is that there is a tiny benefit for those attending school in 2020 as well as 2021 (Tables 5.19 and 5.20). Schools are places where children learn to socialise. It is worth emphasising at this stage, and as referred to in Chapter 2, schools are about a lot more than attainment. They are where children might learn to interact with others, including adults. Otherwise the model and coefficients are similar to those for literacy.

The final model is for the IDELA test combined total (Tables 5.21 and 5.22). In many ways, this is the headline result. Age matters, SES matters (to some extent non-attendance at school is a result of poverty), and as in all such educational

TABLE 5.17 Model for Numeracy score, 2021

Step	R	Increase in R
Age in years	0.44	–
Sum of assets	0.50	0.06
Numeracy score 2020	0.61	0.11
Child went to school 2020	0.61	0
Child went to school 2021	0.64	0.03

TABLE 5.18 Coefficients for model of Numeracy score, 2021

Variable	Unstandardised coefficient	Standardised coefficient
Age in years	3.80	0.20
Sum of assets	0.89	0.09
Numeracy score 2020	0.39	0.42
Child went to school 2020	−2.22	−0.04
Child went to school 2021	14.34	0.21

TABLE 5.19 Model for Social emotional score, 2021

Step	R	Increase in R
Sum of Assets	0.24	–
Age in years	0.34	0.10
Social emotional score 2020	0.54	0.20
Child went to school 2020	0.55	0.01
Child went to school 2021	0.56	0.01

TABLE 5.20 Coefficients for model of Social emotional score, 2021

Variable	Unstandardised coefficient	Standardised coefficient
Sum of Assets	0.87	0.11
Age in years	1.58	0.10
Social emotional score 2020	0.43	0.43
Child went to school 2020	2.11	0.05
Child went to school 2021	7.70	0.14

TABLE 5.21 Model for Total IDELA score, 2021

Step	R	Increase in R
Age in years	0.38	–
Sum of Assets	0.49	0.11
Total IDELA score 2020	0.65	0.16
Child went to school 2020	0.65	0.00
Child went to school 2021	0.67	0.02

TABLE 5.22 Coefficients for model of Total IDELA score, 2021

Variable	Unstandardised coefficient	Standardised coefficient
Age in years	2.31	0.14
Sum of Assets	1.01	0.11
Total IDELA score 2020	0.50	0.51
Child went to school 2020	−1.99	−0.04
Child went to school 2021	10.42	0.17

predictions prior attainment matters. Over and above those factors there is a small advantage in progress for the school attenders ($R = 0.02$, coefficient of 0.17).

Estimating the difference made by school attendance

Those who attend school are different to those who do not, as shown by the models above. The key question for us is what difference does attending school make. So here the focus is on the progress made by the children who did not attend school at the outset. To understand these data better, we consider how the four patterns of school attendance (both years, first year only, second year only and never) are related to the test scores in each year. Unsurprisingly the children who attended school in both years have the highest scores in all five outcomes (Table 5.23). The lowest outcomes are for the children who went to school in the second year but not the first. This may be an age issue, but also ties in with our review findings so far, that interventions to improve attendance can lead to lower average attainment in the first instance. This may also explain why the premium for school attendance is rather low in terms of improved attainment, especially in 2020 (see above).

A year later the situation has been transformed (Table 5.24). Although the children attending school for two years clearly still have the highest scores in all five outcomes, those who attended for only the second year have the second highest scores. This is perhaps the clearest way of visualising the benefit of schooling. These same children have gone from easily the lowest scoring to the second highest in one year, and are actually catching up with the children who attended school from

TABLE 5.23 Outcomes 2020 by patterns of school attendance

	Attended both years	Attended first year	Attended second year	Did not attend
Observation score	78.27	73.79	61.55	71,47
Literacy score	57.05	33.40	26.22	28.63
Numeracy score	79.81	63.81	43.26	45.03
Social emotional score	56.27	50.55	42.85	43.54
IDELA total score	64.38	49.25	37.44	39.07

TABLE 5.24 Outcomes 2021 by patterns of school attendance

	Attended both years	Attended first year	Attended second year	Did not attend
Observation score	77.31	64.13	69.46	65.25
Literacy score	66.89	43.49	49.64	41.16
Numeracy score	85.28	61.54	69.20	54.46
Social emotional score	64.39	51.67	53.53	46.95
IDELA total score	72.19	52.23	57.46	47.52

the outset. Those who have never attended school now generally have the lowest scores. This is why school matters.

Looking at the attainment gap

In this section, we have computed a simple attainment gap comparing the attainment in literacy and numeracy of children whose homes have 8 or fewer of the 14 households "assets", compared to their wealthier peers whose households have 9 or more. And we looked at how these differ between children attending school (in 2021) and those not attending. We are unable to look at a more extreme gap, such as those with 3 or fewer assets compared to those with 11 or more because that would leave so few cases not attending school. Of the 1,023 cases overall, 151 did not attend school in 2021, of which 76 had 8 or fewer assets, and 75 had 9 or more. Of the total, 872 attended school in 2021, of which 441 had 8 or fewer assets, and 431 had 9 or more. The results are therefore based on a relatively small cell size (75), and must be treated with caution.

The gap in literacy scores is of a similar size for children in and out of school. As already portrayed, the absolute scores are worse for those not at school, on average, however many assets they have. However, the poverty attainment gap is larger for children in school (Table 5.25).

In the same way, the gap in numeracy scores is of a similar size for children in and out of school, and again the absolute scores are worse for those not at school, on average, however many assets they have. For numeracy however, the poverty attainment gap is noticeably smaller for children in school (Table 5.26).

TABLE 5.25 The poverty attainment gap for literacy

	Attended school 2021	Not attending school
Richer, 9+ assets	69.51	47.03
Poorer, 8- assets	57.28	37.00
Overall standard deviation	27.72	25.69
Effect size	0.44	0.39

TABLE 5.26 The poverty attainment gap for numeracy

	Attended school 2021	*Not attending school*
Richer, 9+ assets	85.14	61.66
Poorer, 8- assets	78.86	52.30
Overall standard deviation	21.83	25.73
Effect size	0.29	0.36

TABLE 5.27 The poverty attainment gap for overall IDELA scores

	Attended school 2021	*Not attending school*
Richer, 9+ assets	73.80	53.34
Poorer, 8- assets	64.60	45.06
Overall standard deviation	20.13	21.52
Effect size	0.40	0.46

The poverty attainment gap for the total IDELA scores is again similar for those attending school and the rest, with the scores clearly worse for those not attending school (Table 5.27). Overall, the attainment gap is lower for children attending school.

What do the participants say?

In this section we listen to the views of the families who took part in the study. A common observation by the enumerators was that children who had a delay in language development, sometimes struggled to communicate and engage in activities. There could be several reasons for this delay. Children from families with a high level of poverty sometimes had limited opportunities for verbal engagement with parents. Many migrant workers' native language or dialect is different from what people usually speak in urban areas, including the language of instruction in schools. Some children who were not attending school in the daytime when both parents were working, spent long hours without the presence of an adult in the house every day. We asked parents how their children spend their time if they do not attend school. Most common activities reported by their parents were – they play in the street with other children or stayed at home locked inside, and spend time watching TV, or looking after, or being looked after by, other siblings. This was observed in rural areas and where immigrant workers moved from rural to urban settings and lived in temporary accommodation or rented servant quarters. Most immigrant women worked as domestic helpers while men worked as security guards, drivers or domestic helpers. There were few opportunities for verbal interaction between such parents and children. When we asked a mother as a domestic helper working in 10 different homes, how she spends time with her children, she said:

> When I come back home after a long day of working in homes, I am too tired to talk with anyone. I can't talk and it is just so difficult. I can just make

> dinner and make sure they have eaten enough, and they have some food for breakfast in the morning as I leave home very early. On weekends I have so much cleaning and work at home.

Another said:

> There is so much to do at home. I spend all my day in cleaning, cooking and doing laundry. Children just play on their own.

We observed that many children not in schools struggled with the language of emotions and feelings. This was not because they had no empathy or sense of feeling for pain, happiness and sadness but due to lack of vocabulary to name their emotions and feelings. Most children could identify what happiness is and what makes them happy, but identifying or recognising sadness and pain was difficult for many children not attending school. However, those who attended school attributed sadness to experiences at school such as "when teacher shouts at me", "my friend hit me", or "when no one plays with me". We asked one such child what makes them sad and he said:

> My mother does not live with us here. She has left us and now gone to another city and this makes me sad. I want her to come back home.

The home environment of children from above average income groups had more learning resources and materials and more attention from parents to help with learning activities. Mothers' (usually) engagement in this process was in the form of reading stories, helping with homework, attending parent teacher meetings, and studying together. Many families also had grandparents living in the household. Grandparents were helpful for working women as they provided support for childcare when mothers were working outside. Children had a stronger social network with live-in or nearby grandparents, and more opportunities for language development.

Support for schooling

Unsurprisingly perhaps, many families and children expressed support for schooling. Sending a child to school or not is a choice. However, a large number of children are now attending schools in both countries which shows that more parents are choosing school for their children. More women are joining the labour workforce in both countries which is also the reason that more children are attending school, as a kind of child-care if nothing else.

Schools provide more than learning experiences and tuition. Children can enjoy the social interactions. One girl aged 6 said:

> I had lots of friends. I used to go to school. I had many cousins to play with. When we came in the city it is better, but I don't go to school anymore and I miss all my friends and cousins who I used to play with. Here we have a TV

only and I just spend all day watching dramas. There is no one to talk. School is so much fun. I have friends and we play. At home it is nice but boring.

Several families discussed the importance of formal education during the Covid-19 lockdown. A father said:

> For very young children schools could not do much because it was difficult to use online methods for this age group. Schools are open since last five months and I have seen that children are catching up now. It is just that parents have to be consistent in sending children to school. I think that is the most important thing at the moment.

A mother said:

> I tried to keep my youngest daughter and son engaged in learning but it is very hard. I don't know the syllabus. I don't know what school wanted us to teach. They sent us things to teach but it is very hard to keep up the same way as done by school teachers. Now proper school has started.

Disruption in attending school can disconnect children and families from accessing school and lead to a permanent drop out. Most common disruptions were school closure due to lockdown, moving from a rural to urban region, disruption in income flow, transitions in school phase, trauma or death in the family, and children's long term sickness.

One parent said:

> Lockdown was a big change in our lives. Our younger daughter was 3 years old and we wanted to start school but then schools were closed for new enrolments. My older children continued whatever form of schooling was available at that time but the younger one has not seen school and she is five now. We have applied to the nearest school and we are waiting for the invitation letter now. She will start from March session. Lockdown has delayed her school admission but I think it is for all children in the world. Children catch up very quickly. I think if all children had experienced the same then it will not just effect my child only.

A mother expressed support for schools, even in some adversity:

> In pandemic and lockdown the children really suffered. We had our family problems as well. My husband lost his job and we moved from Karachi to Islamabad. Schools were closed and were not taking new admissions. Education was disrupted. We are now very close to getting children enrolled in new school here in Islamabad but these last few months have been very difficult. I hope that children will catch up as they will start school in the March session.

Another father said:

> We got a private tutor for our children. The youngest one just continued Quran but not school learning. The older children in primary and secondary were taught by tutor during the lockdown. It is not the same as school because school has a proper structured learning. Tutoring is better for revision exercise but not for new learning. My youngest is in nursery but children in this age were not learning as they could have learned in school. Tutors don't know how to teach children as young as my daughter.

Most of these families are from urban areas, and many are of average income or above.

No support for schooling

Even in urban settings, the lowest income group who are mostly daily wage earners, immigrants from rural areas without any qualifications, and those who have no stable source of income, often choose not to send children to schools. Low income can be a barrier to attending cheap private schools, and another is the distance to elementary government schools. The safety of children was a concern when free school provision was not available near home. Children's education is not a priority when income resources are very limited and there is no government provision to support children's enrolment in school. Parents expressed the following views:

> I can't leave my younger child alone at home. She is a toddler. Her elder sister look after her. I can't afford to send them to school unless both go to school. I know my elder daughter is missing school but there is no other way. None in our family have ever gone to school. There is a school but we just don't bother. Children are happy like this.
>
> I have a 12 year old daughter who works now. When my husband lost job in the pandemic we had no means to support our family. He worked in the city and we were in the village where there was no work for him. We were in real difficult times after a few months and then someone asked if we could send our elder daughter to work as house cleaner and helper for a family in the city. We had no choice. I went with my daughter at first to see the family and I was very satisfied to know that they were kind people. She was not going to school anyway so living in that big city house with educated people would give her some skills. She lives in that house and we get her monthly salary in the village. This is our only means of survival. She is happy there because she is looked after well by that family. Her education finished then but at least she is happy and safe there. That's more important for me than her school education.
>
> School is for people who understand its value. No one in our family have gone to school and children just help their parents in farming, construction,

fields and house work. Our children grow up learning these skills. We see school education is relevant for jobs in the city. Our children will never do those jobs. We don't get anything from that education from school. Our children learn from doing things with elders and then they take up those tasks themselves.

Some families, especially in rural areas, justify their decision not to use schools because they feel that what children learn in school will be of no value. These families seem to assume that their children's future will be the same as their own.

I want my son to become a carpenter and this is how he is going to support himself and our family. School cannot help him learn any such thing. A lot of labour migrants go to middle-east on skilled jobs. No one asks if they completed school or not. We have progressed financially by working on construction sites. I want my son to join that workforce as it brings good amount of money. They ask what we know in construction of houses and buildings. These skills are learned as we saw our parents doing and this is how our children will learn. School education is for people who will work in offices.

I am a refugee from Afghanistan. My family came to Pakistan and the only thing that helped me to survive in the construction sites was skill as plumber. As a child I worked with my father's friend and slowly I learned this work. This is not what school had taught me. I wasted my time in school whatever years I spent. I want my son to learn skills as early as possible so that he becomes financially independent. School wastes our time. I know that school opens opportunities for children but we are not in that race.

One of the daughters is very good in school and the teachers encouraged us to help her in coming to school every day. She is continuing school and we will do our best that she completes education. The older daughter was not good in getting good results. Teachers were not happy so I thought it is better to take her out from school and she could spend time in learning some other skills. Spending school fee on her was a waste of our limited income resources. She was not happy in school and never liked teachers. She now helps me at home and in the evening she spends a few hours at my friend's place in learning skills for stitching clothes. She can cook now and she could stitch as well.

One of the reasons some children drop out from school was that they had learning difficulties. Their school experiences were not happy, and teachers might have struggled to keep them up with peers in their class. Children struggling in school may not enjoy going to school, and gradually parents stopped sending them to school. Some parents said that schools were hostile places:

School teacher was so unfriendly with my child. My child wasn't happy. She used to cry all day in the school. I thought that next year would probably a better year as she would be older and more clever to stay in school without crying. Then Covid-19 came that year and she further delayed as schools were closed for admissions.

Another child's father was asked why his child does not attend school and he said:

There were lots of family problems. His mother does not live with us anymore. It is difficult for me to manage my job and his education. He was always unhappy at school. He is slow in learning and the teacher always complained about him. We changed school as well, but he never liked going to school because it was difficult for him. He is at home now and we have arranged a private tutor for him. At least he is happy now and doesn't cry every morning. We live in a joint family and there are always people around him to look after but responsibility for his school is something no one cares about. I am not able to do it myself so I can't expect others to do so. It is just so difficult to manage.

Others said that they could not afford the (relatively) small fees:

I sent them to local private school. It was good but then we had to change work place to another city and after that our financial circumstances became worse. School was an extra expenditure. More than the fee school has additional demands to fulfil. Pick and drop to school is difficult when we are both working. I take my child with me when I work in houses.

A mother of four children said:

I am dependent on my brother's income. My husband is in jail for a minor crime. And I have a few months old baby to look after. I can't even work under such condition. I have no other means to support my children. Two of them used to go to school before but now I can't pay the fees, so they don't go to school anymore. These are very hard times.

Another said:

We decided to come to city so that we could earn some money and make a pukka house in our village. If I spend on school fees, I can't save money.

Most of these families were from rural areas. There was a difference in the reported quality of early years' schools and nurseries so that even children attending them were not all receiving high quality care and education as expected. High cost schools had more resources and qualified teachers to support children's learning. However, many low-cost nurseries were not sufficiently equipped with learning resources and qualified teaching staff. The number of children attending low-cost nurseries was quite high but it seemed that the private low-cost sector needed a lot of support and infra-structure. The same was observed in government elementary schools in sub-urban regions where the staff-student ratio was very low and resources were sparse.

Children were sent to school with whatever resources parents could provide such as school uniform, a school bag and in some cases a packed lunch. Parents with average income level generally chose low-cost nursery schools instead of government elementary school provision mainly because the government elementary schools are not nearby. There was also a perception that government elementary schools were not sufficiently resourced with qualified teachers, and sending children to these schools will not support their learning. On the contrary children's early years may be damaged if they attend such schools. This perception was more prevalent among the high income group where parents were both more educated and had the means to choose high cost private schools and they could also afford the additional cost of school.

Safety

Many reasons were given by families for why they use or do not use schools. One recurring theme was child safety, which was a particular issue for families where both parents were working away from home, and for girls in more rural areas.

> I leave children at home because they are safe inside rather than on the street. I don't like the idea that they walk to school by themselves. I feel streets are unsafe for children. We can't do pick and drop service to school because we are both working. We can't afford school fees and transport services. It is a walking distance from my house to school but streets are not safe for children.
>
> In our village the environment is not good. Girls are not safe and that is one of the reasons that parents prefer early marriage of girls.
>
> I prefer that my daughter has left this village and gone to live in city as a family helper. She is living safely with an educated household. She is living a safe and comfortable life. She sends her salary to us here in the village. When she was in village she was not happy. Her school closed during Covid-19 and her father lost his job. The year of pandemic she just stayed in house and there was nothing to do and we needed some income resource for survival. I have another daughter who is year 1 and I will wait few more years and will send her to a city family for work where at least they have a safe environment and some income to live. In the villages only rich landowners have good life. A majority is of poor people and their lives are always at risk. Going to school is a risk for girls.

A mother was asked why she does not send her daughter to school and said:

> The school is not near, and I worry if she walks to school then it is not safe for her. It is at least safe that she is at home.

Of course, staying at home unattended is not necessarily safe for young children either. One mother reported:

> We have moved to the city from a remote village. We can earn better wages here. I work as cleaner in a number of houses. When I leave home early in the morning I lock my children in the house, give them food and tea so that they are fed. My husband works as a security guard and sometimes he comes in the mid of the day to check if children are fine. All day long they watch TV. It is dangerous to leave them like this all day and I remember once my elder one tried to warm milk and he burnt his leg as he could not hold the pan properly. We took him to the emergency services and it took months to heal the wound.

Conclusion

The realities of (rural) poverty are clear in the opportunities that children in India and especially Pakistan have to go to school or not. This is partly how a poverty attainment gap arises. Families need free school places near to their home for ease and safety. It is worrying that parents feel that young girls are not safe. Over and above the restrictions caused by fees, distance, the need to work, and child-care, many of the stories above suggest that parents have a subjective opportunity structure reminiscent of those in our prior work in the ex-coalfield valleys of South Wales and elsewhere (Gorard and Rees 2002). Context and experience have inevitably created a kind of learner identity for themselves that either does or does not encompass schooling as a key factor in their children's lives. To some extent, and only to some extent, the specific reasons given for using or not using schools may merely be attributed by participants rather than being the real primary causes. For the poorest families the need to work and so provide food and shelter for their children is the priority. All else is considerably higher up the hierarchy of needs.

Parents from low income groups may not see that school is as relevant or purposeful if school education does not provide a return on the cost of time children spend in school. Children who work with parents reportedly learn skills which schools do not provide, and what school provides (literacy/numeracy) is not going to return anything of value to parents in the short term. This is perhaps partly why cash transfers work (Chapter 3).

This chapter confirms that children make progress by learning in or out of school, but they make even more progress in school than by not attending. Sometimes the premium for school attendance seems rather low, in comparison to the progress that takes place anyway, but a careful analysis of our findings suggests that the school "effect" of attendance is there and it is relatively substantial. Our reviews have already suggested that attendance does not necessarily lead to much greater attainment, and the average results of school after improved attendance are sometimes worse because of the nature of the extra children enrolled – who may have been less ready for school.

So one message is that school does matter in these less than full enrolment school systems (and of course there are wider social and workforce benefits as well). And the attainment gap suggests that school attendance by poorer children is more important for learning numeracy than literacy. Perhaps another message is that mere attendance at school is necessary but not sufficient for improved progress. What actually happens at school also matters greatly. This applies to more developed school systems as much as to countries with incomplete enrolment such as India and Pakistan. Mere attendance at school does not make as much difference as educators and policy-makers might want to imagine (Gorard 2016). There must also be a focus on what happens in school, and what happens there must be evidence-led. These issues are the chief focus for the remainder of the book.

References

Gorard, S. (2016) Does missing one week of school lead to lower grades? *Significance*, 13, 5, p. 13.

Gorard, S. and Rees, G. (2002) *Creating a learning society?* Bristol: Policy Press.

Luyten, H., Merrell, C. and Tymms, P. (2020) Absolute effects of schooling as a reference for the interpretation of educational intervention effects, *Studies in Educational Evaluation*, 67, 100939.

Siddiqui, N., Bulsari, S., Gorard, S., See, BH, Dixon, P., Pandya, K., Saeed, S. and Saeed, S. (2020a) *Pilot study report 2020 Assessing Early Years Schooling*, Access and Student Outcomes (AESAS): Establishing routes for sustainable education in Pakistan and India.

Siddiqui, N., Bulsari, S., Gorard, S., Saeed, S., Saeed, S., See, BH, Dixon, P. and Pandya, K, (2020b) *Interim project report on ECE project in India and Pakistan*.

Siddiqui, N. (2017) Socio-economic segregation of disadvantaged children between schools in Pakistan: comparing the state and private sector, *Educational Studies*, 43, 4, 391–409.

Siddiqui, N. and Gorard, S. (2017) Comparing government and private schools in Pakistan: The way forward for universal education, *International Journal of Educational Research*, 82, 159–169.

Siddiqui, N. (2019) What do we know about children's access to school and their learning outcomes in Pakistan? *Journal of International Development*, 31, 8, 752–763.

KEY FINDINGS ON SCHOOL ATTAINMENT

6

USING TARGETED FUNDING TO IMPROVE ATTAINMENT

Introduction

This chapter presents the results of the second strand of our structured reviews, here concerning the use of finance-based interventions to improve attainment at school. The policy of using targeted additional funding to try and improve student attainment is a widespread phenomenon internationally. It has been used by governments and other agencies for decades (Children's World Report 2020), where poverty is assumed to be a barrier to the attainment of academic objectives for some students. There have been many variations, with money given to the school system to deploy, or to areas with high levels of disadvantage, to families either for them to deploy or as an incentive (so that parents encourage school attendance, for example), to teachers, or to the disadvantaged students themselves (Toutkoushian and Michael 2007). This makes it important not just to assess the impact of cash transfers but also how best to implement them.

While the function and objectives of cash transfers are generally the same, the implementation and delivery has differed between studies. In some studies the magnitude of the incentives was varied, which allows for investigation into whether the size of the incentives made a difference, while in others comparisons were made between incentives awarded to students, parents or schools/teachers or a combination of these. A large quasi-experiment, with standardised outcome measures, has suggested that providing extra resources for schools led to greater gains than incentives for teachers did, for example (Lavy 2002). Some studies compared delayed or immediate rewards. In some countries rewards were in the form of money paid into the child's bank account, in others they were paid to the mothers or families.

DOI: 10.4324/9781003287353-9

In some cases, these awards were in the form of vouchers which the child could exchange for items in a shop. Some studies looked at the impact of financial awards for efforts into inputs (e.g. homework completion, number of books read), and in others, students were rewarded for outputs (e.g. performance on tests/exams and grade completion or enrolment in post-secondary education).

Some researchers have studied the impact of conditional and unconditional incentives, and tried to test the impact of cash transfers conditioned on input and output. These experiments were to test whether financial incentives help motivate students to do better if the lack of motivation or lack of information on the benefits of schooling was the reason for their low performance. If students' low performance was the lack of structural resources or knowledge then financial incentives would have no impact. And if financial incentives undermine intrinsic motivation then giving students money could lead to negative outcomes.

Cash incentives can also be seen as an investment in human capital, targeted at groups that would otherwise not be in school, would drop out of school early or fail to progress in education. The assumption is that offering financial incentives to students or families provides the motivation for children to attend school and continue in their education. Offering cash or financial aid should increase students' effort to study and thus improve their performance at school (Smith and Walker 1993, Gibbons 1997, Lazear 2000). Money appears to be more of an incentive in poorer countries than in the US (Hanushek et al. 2019). Behavioural psychologists might claim that if financial reward is given for the performance of an unpleasant activity, such as studying, or completing homework, it will reduce aversion to that activity, thus leading to a long-term positive effect. Cognitive psychologists, however, argue that financial rewards may reduce intrinsic motivation (performing the task for its own sake), and any positive effects will be short-lived when that reward is removed (Deci et al. 1999, Kohn 1999, Kruglanski et al. 1971, Lepper and Greene 1973). Economists, on the other hand, argue that there are other motivating factors besides money and effort, such as the understanding of the consequences or returns from small compensations (Bénabou and Tirole 2003, Frey and Oberholzer-Gee 1997, Titmuss 1970).

In the US, school vouchers to pay for places at private schools have been justified in terms of improved student outcomes. But the evidence on this is mixed, being perhaps as much negative as positive (Lubienski and Malin 2020). There are other interventions involving incentive programmes in primary and secondary education such as in the Baltimore City Public School District (Ash 2008) and in Texas (Jackson 2007). It is rarer that funding is used in more developed or richer countries to improve attainment for the most disadvantaged students particularly. It is even rarer that funding is used to try to reduce the attainment gap between economically disadvantaged students and their peers, and almost unheard of that the funding is intended to change the nature of school intakes by making disadvantaged students more attractive when schools are allocating places. These issues, as they appear in England, are addressed in later chapters. This chapter focuses on some of the poorer countries around the world.

Evidence on incentives and attainment

Here we present a summary of the findings that relate financial incentives to attainment at school. Ignoring studies rated as zero for trustworthiness, there were at least 30 studies which evaluated the use of financial incentives to promote attainment outcomes at school (Table 6.1). These mostly reported positive results, including some of the strongest studies. As with increasing attendance (Chapter 3) and reducing socio-economic segregation between schools (Chapter 13), financial incentives appear to work for improving attainment.

As in Chapter 3, the findings are considered in more detail in terms of whether they are based on providing new school places, reducing or eliminating the cost of schooling, or conditional cash transfers. The final section looks at the evidence on how cash transfers are best implemented to improve attainment.

Providing new school places

One way of investing in education is to provide new school places. Is this effective? Unfortunately, there are no high quality studies on this in our review.

2🔒 studies

As discussed in Chapter 3, the World Bank (2018) evaluated subsidies for new free schools in remote areas of Pakistan. Children in treatment schools did better on attainment tests, especially those who enrolled due to the programme. An additional subsidy for girls had no impact on their test scores. The study was rather poorly reported, and it was unclear whether the testing was independent of the developer.

Duflo et al. (2009) looked at the impact of smaller classes in grade 1 in Kenya. Out of 140 schools, 70 were randomly selected for extra funding to hire an extra teacher and open a second classroom. Children were randomised to classes. In independent assessments of language and maths, treatment classes scored higher (effect size 0.16). There was 23% attrition of student scores after one year.

As discussed in Chapter 3, Burde and Linden (2009) assessed a community-based schooling initiative in Afghanistan. The presence of a community-based school increased test scores by half a standard deviation, and was particularly important for girls.

TABLE 6.1 Strength of evidence and impact for studies linking financial incentives to attainment

Strength of evidence	Positive	Unclear/mixed	Negative/neutral
4🔒	1	–	–
3🔒	4	1	2
2🔒	10	1	2
1🔒	6	3	–

1 🔒 studies

As described earlier, Barrera-Osorio et al. (2017) evaluated a programme in Pakistan to increase schooling in marginalised areas, to reduce the gender gap in enrolment, and foster learning. The programme offered private school operators a per-student subsidy to establish new private tuition-free primary schools. 100 schools (82 villages) were assigned to the treatment group (no gender differentiation) and another 100 schools (79 villages) to the gender-differentiated treatment group, in which the subsidy was higher for each female student. Other benefits included free school leaders and teacher training, free textbooks, other teaching and learning materials, stationery, and book bags, which are the same for both treatment groups. The study reported positive effects on test scores (and enrolment). But the evidence is relatively weak, as there were no details about the kind of tests used, and no reports of attrition or missing data.

Taiwo and Tyolo (2002) selected 60 grade 1 students across 12 diverse primary school classes in Botswana who had pre-school experience and 60 who had not. At the start of schooling children were assessed on five English-related, five mathematics-related, and five science-related items. Those with pre-school outperformed the others in all areas (effect size 2.01). Since the groups were naturally allocated, they cannot be assumed to have been balanced at the outset.

Aboud (2006) compared children attending pre-school in some villages in Bangladesh to those not in pre-school in neighbouring villages, in a cross-sectional design. Cognitive, school readiness and social play scores of pre-school children were higher than those of the comparison children with large "effect" sizes (up to 1.0 for school readiness). The groups were not comparable at the outset.

Chen et al. (2022) looked at the One-Village-One-Preschool initiative to guarantee early childhood education to all children in high-poverty villages in China. Following 23,775 children from preschool to fourth-grade in a high poverty area, the study found that children with two years of pre-school entered first grade with similar attainment to children from a more prosperous urban area (having been behind at the outset). However, those who had only one year of pre-school actually fell slightly further behind. That extra year seems to matter.

Summary

In summary, there is some weak evidence here that creating new school places leads to improved overall attainment. In Chapter 3 we showed that enrolment and attendance can be improved through investment, and it might be assumed that attainment will follow. However, the students who might previously have not attended school may have lower initial attainment (as in Chapter 5). The true test would be not what the average attainment of those at schools is, but what the average attainment of all children is and whether it is improved by having more of these children at school? Presumably it is.

Making schools free

Another approach is to make schools more accessible by reducing or eliminating schools fees, where applicable. Here the studies are rather stronger.

4🔒 *studies*

As described in Chapter 3, Duflo et al. (2021) estimated the effects of free secondary education in Ghana using randomised assignment to secondary school scholarships. The students were followed for 12 years until the age of 29, with relatively low attrition (6%). Scholarship students scored higher on maths and reading comprehension, five years after the study (effect size 0.16).

2🔒 *studies*

Kremer et al. (2009) evaluated a merit scholarship programme in which girls in grades 5 and 6 who scored well in academic exams in Kenya received a scholarship for the next two years. This covered fees, school supplies, and public recognition in a big school assembly. A total of 11,728 students competed for the scholarships in 64 schools. 12 schools withdrew but their scores were included in an intention to treat analysis. The results were mixed. Only 65% of baseline students provided subsequent test scores. In one district girls in the treatment group were ahead (effect size 0.12). In the other district attrition was too high to decide on impact.

As described later, Das et al. (2013) conducted a natural experiment in Zambia where schools became free in 2001, and a fixed cash grant of $600 per school was introduced, meaning it was the same for large and small (rural) schools. Small schools therefore received more funding per pupil. However, 24% of schools still received (unanticipated) discretionary funding in 2002. Based on 172 schools, the study showed a positive correlation between discretionary/unanticipated funding and test scores for English and maths (effect size 0.1).

1🔒 *studies*

Angrist et al. (2002) looked at Programa de Ampliacion de Cobertura de la Educacion Secundaria in Colombia. The programme offered school vouchers to more than 125,000 children from low-income families, covering more than half the cost of their private secondary school. Vouchers were awarded by lottery and students could receive more vouchers as long as they maintained good academic performance. Out of the 473 invited for testing in literacy, maths, and multiple choice, 283 children were tested resulting in a response rate of about 60%. Lottery winners scored higher than losers (effect size 0.2). Scores were not clearly reported. A follow-up study suggested that there was a long-term impact on learning outcomes and high school graduation, especially for females. However, the evidence is weak as only 35% of the original voucher recipients could be matched successfully (Angrist et al. 2006).

Summary

Overall, the body of evidence on school places and attainment is positive (Table 6.2).

There is some evidence that providing free places at school improves average attainment. But several of these studies are based on selective criteria, and one suggests little or no impact. However, the strongest single study suggests that making schooling free is not only beneficial for wider enrolment and attendance, but also improves results.

Cash incentives or grants

As with attendance, we also looked at the evidence of direct cash transfers, and who they are best paid to. There are no 4🔒 studies on this, but a reasonable number of 3🔒 studies.

3🔒 studies

Fryer (2011) evaluated the impact of financial incentives on student achievement from four different field experiments in 200 low-performing urban schools across three US cities. Money was paid to students to help motivate them to do better, and see if lack of motivation or lack of information on the benefits of schooling was the reason for their low performance. Within each city, schools were randomly assigned to treatment or not. In New York City, payments were given to fourth- and seventh-grade students conditional on their performance on 10 standardized tests. In Chicago, incentives were paid to ninth graders every five weeks for grades in five courses. The Dallas program gave second graders $2 per book read, with an additional requirement of passing a short quiz on the book. In Dallas the treatment was combined with Accelerated Reader (a program to encourage reading). There was no impact on maths and reading in any city. In a fourth city, Washington, incentives were given to sixth, seventh, and eighth grade students based on a composite index intended to capture their school attendance, behaviour, and measures of inputs in educational production. The results suggested positive impacts on behaviour. Fryer concluded that incentives are best tied to inputs rather than outcomes as students do not necessarily know what behaviours lead to improved test performance.

TABLE 6.2 Strength of evidence and impact for studies linking free school places to attainment

Strength of evidence	Positive	Unclear/mixed	Negative/neutral
4🔒	1	–	–
3🔒	–	–	–
2🔒	5	–	–
1🔒	4	1	–

Stampini et al. (2018) used a regression discontinuity design to examine the effect of the Programme of Advancement through Health and Education on the Grade 6 achievement test for urban children aged 11–12 in Jamaica. Receipt of the cash was conditional on at least 85% attendance. The amount varied with gender and grades, with boys receiving more. Data from 341 secondary schools, including a sample of 15,509 urban children for which data could be merged, was used for the analysis. Eligibility was means tested. Outcomes of children above the eligibility cut-off (intent-to-treat group) were compared with those below the cut-off (control). The results showed an improvement in the attainment of boys, but there was no effect on girls. The authors proposed that this was because girls had higher pre-treatment GSAT scores, so there was less room for improvement.

Burgess et al. (2021) conducted an RCT involving 10,000 students in England, and found little or no impact of incentives for KS4 students. There was a negative overall outcome for maths and science, and a slightly positive one for English.

Baird et al. (2011), described in Chapter 3, found improvements in attainment for girls in Malawi who received a cash payment conditional on 80% attendance at school.

Schools in Senegal were invited to submit a proposal to apply for a grant for local changes to improve learning outcomes. 633 high quality proposals were received and randomly assigned to receive funding in three separate years (211 in each). This allowed the first cohort to be the experimental group and the other two cohorts formed a natural control (Carneiro et al. 2015). A random sample of children in grades 2 and 4 were selected. The policy had positive effects on maths, French, and oral reading for the younger grades with girls showing bigger overall effect sizes (0.25) than boys (0.08). This persisted for at least two years, but there was no long term effect, presumably because of the wait-list design. Attrition was 17%.

Glewwe et al. (2003) evaluated a two year teacher-reward programme in Kenya, based on the performance of students in grades 4 to 9. The prize value was up to 43% of a teacher's typical monthly salary. 50 schools were randomly selected from 100 low-attaining schools. Students in both groups had similar grades at the outset. Students in the treatment schools were more likely to take later examinations, less likely to drop out, and had some increase in scores (mainly in year 2). Students who did not take the exams were given low grades so that weak students were not discouraged from taking the exam. The gains were not maintained.

Fernald et al. (2008) analysed the cumulative impact of a conditional cash transfer programme for low income households in Mexico, known as Oportunidades (formerly Progresa, as described in Chapter 3) – a conditional cash incentive for families in exchange for regular school attendance, health clinic visits and nutrition support. This was a wait-list cluster RCT wherein 6,695 households with children aged 24–68 months were randomly selected to receive the treatment first and another 4,029 households to receive it later. Randomisation was done at community level. Cash transfers had positive effects on children's health and cognitive development, and the amount and duration of payments matters. A doubling of the cash transfer was associated with improvement in long-term and short-term memory, visual integration and language development.

2🔒 studies

Barrow and Rouse (2013) evaluated two performance based scholarship programmes – one for students in their last year of high school (California) and one for post-secondary students (New York City). The post-secondary students were recruited at campus and randomly assigned to receive a performance-based scholarship up to $1,300, or not. The incentive was intended to reward attendance and performance at the end of the semester, and the amount varied with achievement. In California, high school students from low income families who attended a "Cash for College" workshop were randomly assigned to either a performance-based scholarship (2,474 cases) paid directly to them, or the money went to their institution (4,188). The scholarships led to more time spent on educational activity, but this did not continue once the brief scholarships were completed. The amount of money seemed to make no difference. It is possible that there is a limit to how much students can change, or that the increased money reduced intrinsic motivation. The situation was confused by students having other state grants available.

Bettinger (2012) evaluated a pay-for-performance programme for primary students in grades 3 to 6 in Ohio. Children received payments for successful completion of standardised tests – in maths, reading, writing, science, and social studies. Eligible students received $15 vouchers for each test in which they scored "proficient", and $20 for a higher score. Grades were randomised to treatment or not in each school. The study reported improvement in maths (effect size 0.13). The incentive was not effective in moving students from non-proficient to proficient, only in moving some students from proficient to higher levels. There were no effects for other subjects. There is no clear pre-post comparison of treatment and control groups.

Barrera-Osorio et al. (2021) looked at teachers receiving in-kind incentives for the academic improvement of disadvantaged children in Guinea, compared to recognition of services, and business as usual. Based on 420 schools, the treatment led to improvement in the first year and fading effects in the second.

Dean and Jayachandran (2019), as discussed in Chapter 3, examined a scholarship scheme in India to encourage attendance in a private kindergarten. The treatment group scored higher on cognitive tests (effect size 0.8).

Akresh et al. (2013) conducted a two-year randomised trial in rural Burkino-Faso, as described in Chapter 3. Neither conditional nor unconditional cash transfers for attendance made a difference to attainment scores.

Filmer and Schady (2009), as described more fully in Chapter 4, analysed the effects of the CESSP Scholarship Program in Cambodia, which gives scholarships to poor children for the three years of lower secondary school. It improved enrolment but did not improve maths and vocabulary test scores 18 months later.

Skoufias and Shapiro (2006) examined the impact of a school improvement programme in Mexico where schools were offered a five-year grant to carry-out improvement plans with parents involved, and training offered to principals.

The Quality Schools Programme was aimed at expanding autonomy and improving learning in disadvantaged urban schools. The authors constructed a panel of schools and used difference-in-difference regression analysis and propensity score matching to create a control group. There were 9,244 schools in the treatment group and 65,457 in the control. The programme was found to reduce the student failure rate by 0.24 percentage points, grade repetition by 0.31 and the dropout rate by 0.21 in comparison to the control group.

Heinrich (2007) examined the impact of the Programa Nacional de Becas Estudiantiles, a conditional cash transfer programme in Argentina using a retrospective cohort design comparing scholarship recipients with those who were eligible but did not receive scholarship due to a quota. The programme targeted students between the ages of 13 and 19 years, at risk of dropping out. Scholarship recipients appeared to perform better than non-recipients, and greater impact was seen among those in the programme for more than one year. The programme also increased students' attendance, and reduced grade repetition. Attrition was high, and the two groups were not randomly assigned.

1 🔒 studies

Behrman et al. (2000) presented the results of the impact of the PROGRESA enrolment programme on students' test scores in Mexico. There was no benefit for the treatment group in terms of student test scores. However, the two groups were not balanced, and data was missing.

In a study by Riccio (2010), low-income families were offered cash rewards to encourage parents to engage in activities related to children's education (among a range of other things such as health and employment). There were more than 50 outcome measures, making the claims for the success in any one outcome very weak. There appeared to be a small benefit for maths scores for one year, and some improvements in attendance.

Andrew et al. (2018) looked at a non-conditional cash transfer programme in Colombia, and 96 towns were randomly allocated to control, psychosocial stimulation, nutrient supplementation, or a combined intervention. 1,419 children aged 12–24 months from households that benefitted from a cash transfer programme formed part of a cluster randomised trial that lasted 18 months. Attrition was 11%. The stimulation intervention showed a short-term impact on cognition (0.26) and language development (0.22). None of the other interventions had any effect. In fact, there was a small negative effect of combining the supplements and stimulation treatments (e.g. language -0.13). This cast some doubts on the other results. It is difficult to tell from this study whether the cash transfer alone had any impact.

Fullard (2019) reported that a 10% increase in teacher salary is equivalent to a one pupil reduction in class size or a one hour increase in weekly instructional time. The effect size is small.

List et al. (2018) suggested that cash incentives for school performance might actually have a negative effect by damaging intrinsic motivation. Using 9 low attaining US elementary and middle schools, tutor groups were allocated, in a strange manner, to control, or a treatment of incentive payments to student, parent and/or teacher. On a low-stakes test the incentives produced better results, but on a high-stakes test there was a small negative impact. The cases were not properly randomised.

Summary

The body of evidence linking cash transfers to improved attainment is quite mixed (Table 6.3).

The overall evidence is nowhere near as positive as the evidence for improving attendance in Chapter 3. Several studies here of varying quality found no clear benefit, or worse. It is easier to pay people to attend school than to do well at school. It is also easier to pay students for other inputs like behaviour or completing homework than to reward them for outcomes. Students know what it means to attend, but they may not understand what they have to do to improve attainment. Money may therefore not be enough, especially for the weakest students. The impact also seems to be stronger with low-stakes tests. The cash is usually given to families or older students and this is where the strongest evidence lies. There is less on giving cash to schools or teachers. The impact seems to be sensitive to length and amount of payment, and there is evidence that once the payments cease there is no long-term impact on attainment at all. This leads to the next research question. How are cash transfers best organised?

How should cash transfers be paid?

There are many variations on how cash transfers are paid, when and to whom. We found no 4🔒 evidence on this.

3🔒 studies

Behrman et al. (2015) reported on the Aligning Learning Incentives programme in Mexico that offered monetary incentives conditional on secondary student performance in maths in grades 10 to 12. This was a cluster randomised trial in which 88 Mexican high schools with over 40,000 students were randomised to three

TABLE 6.3 Strength of evidence and impact for studies linking cash transfers to attainment

Strength of evidence	Positive	Unclear/mixed	Negative/neutral
4🔒	–	–	–
3🔒	4	1	2
2🔒	5	1	2
1🔒	2	2	–

treatment groups and a control. In one group students were paid for their maths performance, in another teachers were paid for student performance, and in the third students, teachers and other school staff were paid for their performance and that of their peers. The results are reasonably clear. The improvement for schools in which teachers were paid for results was about the same as for the control. The group with students paid scored higher than the control. But the group with the combined incentive of school, student and teacher produced by far the strongest effect. These differences lasted for at least three years. There was some diffusion as some schools also received a separate attendance subsidy.

Are incentives given to parents or students more effective in improving children's reading? Berry (2015) used eight government primary schools (grades 1– 3) in India. Incentives of a toy (or toy voucher) or cash equivalent were randomly assigned to either the parent or child. Children were pre-tested, given a reading competency goal, and retested after two months. If the child attended free after-school classes and achieved the goal the incentive was paid. Both attendance and attainment improved more if parents were paid when the child had higher initial test scores. But attendance and attainment improved more if the child was paid when the child had low initial test scores.

Mbiti et al. (2019) conducted an RCT with 350 schools in Tanzania, with three treatment groups – schools with unconditional incentive grants, teacher incentives based on student performance, and both of these. The school grants led to no impact on test scores. The teacher incentives led to a small increase. The best results came from providing both kinds of payment. Adding teacher incentives to standard school grants could increase the cost-effectiveness of education.

The school block grant experiment in India ran for two years across 200 state primary schools, selected by lottery to receive a small grant (around $2 per pupil) over and above what they would have received in their regular school allocation (Das et al. 2013). The condition was that the funds had to be spent on items used directly by students and not infrastructure, for example. In the first year the grant was a surprise, but was anticipated by the second year. Students in the 100 treatment schools performed better than those in the 100 control schools in the first year – effect size of 0.08 in language and 0.09 in maths. There was no difference in the second year. Unanticipated inputs may generally have a larger impact on test scores than anticipated inputs.

Muralidharan and Sundararaman (2006) randomly selected 500 schools in India to receive one of two kinds of incentive (3% of teachers' annual pay). Some teachers got an incentive based on their own student's performance, and some on the average school performance. Further, 100 schools acted as controls (but not randomly allocated). Student attrition was 14.2%. Students in treatment schools performed better than the control (effect sizes 0.19 in maths and 0.12 in language). They also did better in subjects like science for which there was no incentive. This might be a spillover effect, or the schools might not have been comparable anyway. Students in individual incentive schools did very slightly better than students in group incentive schools. Attrition 14%.

2🔒 studies

Levitt et al. (2010) evaluated the effects on educational achievement of a performance-based incentive that gave monthly payments to grade 9 students or their parents in two low-performing high schools in a Chicago suburb. The incentives were based on school attendance, behaviour, grades, and test scores. Despite the small scale, students were randomised to four treatment groups and a control. The treatments were incentives given to either students or parents, and whether the incentive was a fixed rate or a lottery. The expected value was $50 per month. There were immediate gains in achievement, especially for those at the threshold of meeting basic standards at the outset. Perhaps incentives are more effective in improving the attainment of those who have the potential to achieve, but have not done so yet for some reason. There is no difference between incentives awarded to parents or students, or fixed or by lottery. However, after three years all gains disappeared.

List et al. (2018) used two experiments to assess the impact on students' high stakes test scores of providing cash incentives to students, parents, and/or tutors, in nine elementary and middle schools in Chicago. Tutor groups were allocated to six arms – the "randomisation" was repeated 500 times to achieve best balance between groups, so the groups are not actually random at all. Other than the control, incentives were given to students, parents, tutors, parents and students, or all three. Given there were only 380 students, this is too many groups. In one experiment the rewards came after test success and in the other the rewards came later. The results were mixed. There were apparent improvements in the incentivised low-stakes test but not in the non-incentivised high stakes test.

Li et al. (2010) compared a cash incentive for achieving grades, incentivized peer tutoring, and parental communication, for primary school students in China. This was a school-level RCT. In 12 schools, 47 classes received cash incentives, and 18 did not. In 11 schools, 44 classes were given peer-tutoring, and 18 not. The cash incentive alone was least effective, incentivised peer-tutoring better, and combined with parental communication the best (effect size 0.2 for standardised test scores). The study is poorly reported.

Nong et al. (2021) used a regression discontinuity design to study a poverty alleviation programme in rural China, and its impact on the school attainment of 13 year olds. The programme included farming subsidies, business subsidies, housing improvements, and education and health benefits. The two groups at the cut-off score on initial need were fairly similar. There was no impact on boys' scores, but an improvement for girls.

Summary

In summary, the evidence here is slightly confusing. There are indications that combining cash transfers with other measures, such as tutoring, might be more effective. There is a primacy effect, with new cash transfers being more effective than established, taken for granted, ones. For young children, it makes more sense to give the cash to their parents, but as they get a bit older this appears to make less difference and when the child is a young adult it is preferable to pay them directly. Payments to families/students are somewhat more promising than incentive payments to teachers, which in turn may be more promising than payments to schools. As with attendance, the use of conditions is important. For teachers, these conditions are better as individual, not based on average school outcomes.

Conclusion

The results in this chapter suggest that government policies involving the use of cash incentives have promising results, particularly in low-and middle-income countries. Of these, the stronger studies rated 3🔒 and above mostly suggest that the use of monetary incentives have positive effects on children's learning outcomes. However, the three 3🔒 studies that looked longer term found no long-term impact. There is no delayed effect and the impact generally disappears when the incentives are withdrawn.

There is less robust evidence on which, if any, of the approaches described above is most effective. Large experimental studies suggest that simply paying students to improve does not improve their intrinsic motivation, and sometimes does not lead to improved attainment, largely because students say that they do not know how to improve. Several evaluations suggest that giving the funding to students to improve their performance directly or through enhanced extrinsic motivation does not work in most subject areas. Students also need to know <u>how</u> to improve their attainment. Therefore, paying them for the building blocks of improvement, such as for classroom behaviour or school attendance where students are more likely to know what to do, is more promising. In a large experimental study where students were paid for academic achievement in five core subjects, there was only a benefit in maths, not for reading or other subjects. So far, the evidence on paying students directly is not as strong as for attendance, but it might be a better approach than providing the money to teachers.

One reason why policy-makers prefer using monetary incentives rather than directly intervening in the process of education is that we do not have knowledge about what is the most effective way to improve education outcomes given the complex and heterogeneous characteristics of students, teachers and the school environment. Offering monetary incentives allows schools and teachers to use the incentives for programmes or resources that they judge will most benefit students in their own contexts. We consider the importance of this in later chapters.

References

Aboud, F. (2006) Evaluation of an early childhood preschool program in rural Bangladesh, *Early Childhood Research Quarterly*, 21, 1, 46–60.

Akresh, R., De Walque, D. and Kazianga, H. (2013) Cash transfers and child schooling: evidence from a randomized evaluation of the role of conditionality, *World Bank Policy Research Working Paper* 6340.

Andrew, A., Attanasio, O., Fitzsimons, E., Grantham-McGregor, S., Meghir, C. and Rubio-Codina, M. (2018) Impacts 2 years after a scalable early childhood development intervention to increase psychosocial stimulation in the home: A follow-up of a cluster randomised controlled trial in Colombia, *PLOS Medicine*, 14, 4, e1002556.

Angrist, J., Bettinger, E., Bloom, E., King, E. and Kremer, M. (2002) Vouchers for private schooling in Colombia: Evidence from a randomized natural experiment, *American Economic Review*, 92, 5, 1535–1558.

Ash, K. (2008) Promises of money meant to heighten student motivation, *Education Week*, February 13.

Baird, S., McIntosh, C. and Özler, B. (2011) Cash or condition? Evidence from a cash transfer experiment, *The Quarterly Journal of Economics*, 126, 4, 1709–1753.

Barrera-Osorio, F., Blakeslee, D., Hoover, M., Linden, L., Raju, D. and Ryan, S. (2017) *Delivering education to the underserved through a public-private partnership program in Pakistan*, The World Bank.

Barrera-Osorio, F., Cilliers, J., Cloutier, M. and Filmer, D. (2021) *Heterogenous teacher effects of two incentive schemes*, https://openknowledge.worldbank.org/bitstream/handle/10986/35565/Heterogenous-Teacher-Effects-of-Two-Incentive-Schemes-Evidence-from-a-Low-Income-Country.pdf?sequence=1

Barrow, L. and Rouse, C. (2013) *Financial Incentives and Educational Investment: The Impact of Performance-Based Scholarships on Student Time Use*, Working Paper 2013-07.

Behrman, J., Parker, S., Todd, P. and Wolpin, K. (2015) Aligning learning incentives of students and teachers: Results from a social experiment in Mexican high schools, *Journal of Political Economy*, 123, 2, 325–364.

Behrman, J., Sengupta, P. and Todd, P. (2000) *The impact of PROGRESA on achievement test scores in the first year*, Impact of PROGRESA on achievement test scores in the first year | IFPRI: International Food Policy Research Institute.

Bénabou, R. and Tirole, J. (2003) Intrinsic and extrinsic motivation, *Review of Economic Studies*, 70, 489–520.

Berry, J. (2015) Child control in education decisions: An evaluation of targeted incentives to learn in India, *Journal of Human Resources*, 50, 4, 1051–1080.

Bettinger, E. (2012) Paying to learn: The effect of financial incentives on elementary school test scores, *Review of Economics and Statistics*, 94, 3, 686–698.

Burde, D. and Linden, L. (2009) The effect of proximity on school enrollment: Evidence from a randomized controlled trial in Afghanistan, Unpublished working paper, http://sticerd.lse.ac.uk/seminarpapers/dg11052009.pdf

Burgess, S., Metcalfe, R. and Sadoff, S. (2021) Understanding the response to financial and non-financial incentives in education, *Economics of Education Review*, 85, https://doi.org/10.1016/j.econedurev.2021.102195

Carneiro, P., Koussihouede, O., Lahire, N., Meghire, C. and Mommaerts, C. (2015) *Decentralizing education resources: School grants in Senegal*, Centre for microdata methods and practice, download (psu.edu).

Chen, S., Zhao, C., Chen, C., Wu, Z., Snow, C. and Lu, M. (2022) Does one more year matter? Dosage effect of the one-village-one-preschool intervention in rural China, *Journal of Research on Educational Effectiveness*, https://doi.org/10.1080/19345747.2021.2006383

Children's World Report (2020) *A unique worldwide view of children's perspectives*, https://isciweb.org/wp-content/uploads/2020/07/Summary-Comparative-Report-2020.pdf

Das, J., Dercon, S., Habyarimana, J., Krishnan, P., Muralidharan, K. and Sundararaman, V. (2013) School inputs, household substitution, and test scores, *American Economic Journal: Applied Economics*, 5, 2, 29–57.

Dean, J. and Jayachandran, S. (2019) *Attending kindergarten improves cognitive but not socioemotional\development in India*, Working Paper.

Deci, E., Koestner, R. and Ryan, R. (1999) A meta-analytic review of experiments examining the effects of extrinsic rewards on intrinsic motivation, *Psychological Bulletin*, 125, 6, 627–668.

Duflo, E., Dupas, P. and Kremer, M. (2009) *Additional resources versus organizational changes in education: Experimental evidence from Kenya*, Unpublished manuscript, Abdul Latif Jameel Poverty Action Lab (JPAL), Cambridge, Mass.: Massachusetts Institute of Technology.

Duflo, E., Dupas, P. and Kremer, M. (2021) *The impact of free secondary education: Experimental evidence from Ghana* (No. w28937), National Bureau of Economic Research.

Fernald, L., Gertler, P. and Neufeld, L. (2008) Role of cash in conditional cash transfer programmes for child health, growth, and development: an analysis of Mexico's Oportunidades, *The Lancet*, 371, 9615, 828–837.

Filmer, D. and Schady, N. (2009) School enrollment, selection and test scores, *World Bank Policy Research Working Paper* 4998.

Frey, B. and Oberholzer-Gee, F. (1997) The costs of price incentives, *American Economic Review*, 87, 4, 746–755.

Fryer, R. (2011) Financial incentives and student achievement: Evidence from randomized trials, *The Quarterly Journal of Economics*, 126, 4, 1755–1798.

Fullard, J. (2019) Relative wages and pupil performance, Evidence from Timss, Work in Progress: Institute for Social and Economic Research, 2021-07.pdf (essex.ac.uk).

Gibbons, R. (1997) Incentives and careers in organizations, in D. Kreps and K. Wallis (eds.) *Advances in economic theory and econometrics*, Vol. II, Cambridge, U.K.: Cambridge University Press.

Glewwe, P., Ilias, N. and Kremer, M. (2003) Teacher incentives, Cambridge, MA: National Bureau of Economic Research, *NBER Working Paper Series*, Number 9671.

Hanushek, E., Peterson, P., Talpey, L. and Woessmann, L. (2019) The Achievement Gap fails to close: Half century of testing shows persistent divide between haves and have-nots, *Education Next*, 19, 3, 8–17.

Heinrich, C. (2007) Demand and supply-side determinants of conditional cash transfer program effectiveness, *World Development*, 35, 1, 121–143.

Jackson, C. (2007) A little now for a lot later: A look at a Texas Advanced Placement Incentive program, http://works.bepress.com/c_kirabo_jackson/1

Kohn, A. (1999) *Punished by rewards: The trouble with gold stars, incentive plans, A's, praise, and other bribes*, Bridgewater, NJ: Replica Books.

Kremer, M., Miguel, E. and Thornton, R. (2009) Incentives to learn, *The Review of Economics and Statistics*, 91, 3, 437–456.

Kruglanski, A., Friedman, I. and Zeevi, G. (1971) The effect of extrinsic incentives on some qualitative aspects of task performance, *Journal of Personality and Social Psychology*, 39, 608–617.

Lavy, V. (2002) Evaluating the effect of teachers' group performance incentives on pupil achievement, *Journal of Political Economy*, 110, 6, 1286–1317.

Lazear, E. (2000) Performance, pay and productivity, *American Economic Review*, 90, 5, 1346–1361.

Lepper, M. and Greene, D. (1973) Undermining children's interest with extrinsic rewards, *Journal of Personality and Social Psychology*, 28, 129–137.

Levitt, S., List, J. and Sadoff, S. (2010) *The effect of performance-based incentives on educational achievement*, Working paper, Univ. Chicago.

Li, T., Han, L., Rozelle, S. and Zhang, L. (2010) Cash incentives, peer tutoring, and parental involvement: A study of three educational inputs in a randomized field experiment in

China, *Unpublished manuscript, Peking University, Beijing, China.* http://mitsloan.mit.edu/neudc/papers/paper223.pdf

List, J., Livingston, J. and Neckermann, S. (2018) Do financial incentives crowd out intrinsic motivation to perform on standardized tests? *Economics of Education Review*, 66, 125–136.

Lubienski, C. and Malin, J. (2020) Moving the goalposts: the evolution of voucher advocacy in framing research findings, *Journal of Education Policy*, https://doi.org/10.1080/026809 39.2020.1730977

Mbiti, I., Muralidharan, K., Romero, M., Schipper, Y., Manda, C. and Rajani, R. (2019) Inputs, incentives, and complementarities in education: Experimental evidence from Tanzania, *The Quarterly Journal of Economics*, 134, 3, 1627–1673.

Muralidharan, K. and Sundararaman, V. (2006) *Teacher incentives in developing countries*, Teacher Incentives in Developing Countries: Experimental Evidence from India (vanderbilt.edu).

Nong, H., Zhang, Q., Zhu, H. and Zhu, R. (2021) Targeted poverty alleviation and children's academic performance in China, *Review of Income and Wealth*, https://onlinelibrary.wiley.com/doi/full/10.1111/roiw.12517

Riccio, J., Dechausay, N., Greenberg, D., Miller, C., Rucks, Z. and Verma, N. (2010) *Toward reduced poverty across generations: Early findings from New York City's conditional cash transfer program*, New York, NY: MDRC.

Skoufias, E. and Shapiro, J. (2006) *Evaluating the impact of Mexico's quality schools programme: The pitfalls of using nonexperimental data*, The World Bank.

Smith, V. and Walker, J. (1993) Monetary rewards and decision cost in experimental economics, *Economic Inquiry*, 31, 2, 245–61.

Stampini, M., Martinez-Cordova, S., Insfran, S. and Harris, D. (2018) Do conditional cash transfers lead to better secondary schools? Evidence from Jamaica's PATH, *World Development*, 101, 104–118.

Taiwo, A. and Tyolo, J. (2002) The effect of pre-school education on academic performance in primary school: A case study of grade one pupils in Botswana, *International Journal of Educational Development*, 22, 2, 169–180.

Titmuss, R. (1970) *The gift relationship*, London: Allen and Unwin.

Toutkoushian, R. and Michael, R. (2007) An alternative approach to measuring horizontal and vertical equity in school funding, *Journal of Education Finance*, 32, 4, 395–421.

World Bank (2018) *Pakistan: Can private schools catering to the poor increase access and improve learning? From evidence to policy*, http://search.ebscohost.com/login.aspx?direct=trueanddb= ericandAN=ED589943andsite=ehost-live

7

STUDIES OF IMPROVING ATTAINMENT IN OTHER WAYS

Introduction

As suggested by the work on pre-school attendance, enrolment and providing more school places, in previous chapters, extra schooling also tends to improve attainment. For example, an extra year of schooling produces higher scores in maths, by 30% in Brazil, according to a regression discontinuity analysis of PISA scores by Marchionni and Vazquez (2018). Also cash transfers generally work. One promising approach, evaluated in a randomised control trial in China, is to tie the additional school funding to peer-tutoring (Tao et al. (2010). What other ways are there?

An outline of the evidence on school/home interventions

Following consideration of financial incentives and attainment in Chapter 6, this new chapter looks at improving attainment in other ways. Table 7.1 shows a summary of the results of 14 further studies.

Again, these are largely positive in outcome, although the higher quality studies are more mixed. There are not any really strong studies on attainment here. The first group of studies covers health and nutrition.

Health and nutrition

One consideration is the health and nutrition of students. We found no 4🔒 evidence linking these factors to attainment.

3🔒 *studies*

In rural Jamaica, 814 children in grades 2 to 5 in 16 schools were randomised either to receive a free breakfast every day for a year, or else a quarter of an orange

DOI: 10.4324/9781003287353-10

TABLE 7.1 Strength of evidence and impact for further studies on improving attainment

Strength of evidence	Positive	Unclear/mixed	Negative/neutral
4 🔒	–	–	–
3 🔒	4	–	2
2 🔒	5	–	1
1 🔒	1	1	–

(Powell et al. 1998). Both groups made poor progress in reading, spelling and arithmetic. But the breakfast group made more progress (as did those children judged as adequately nourished at the outset). Scores are missing for 45 children.

Simeon et al. (1995) recruited 407 mainstream primary school pupils in Jamaica who had high levels of T. trichiura infection, and 206 were randomly assigned to receive a treatment of 800 mg of albendazole, and the others received a placebo. Fifteen children were not included in the post-test analyses because they changed schools during the academic year. Post-test measurements were taken about 26 weeks after the first round of treatment. The medical treatment was effective but the impact on school attainment was marginal or non-existent (effect sizes of 0.04 for arithmetic, and 0.02 for both spelling and reading).

McKay et al. (1978) conducted a cluster randomised trial of health, nutrition and education activities for pre-school children in Colombia. Five groups with varying levels of treatment were created using 333 children with signs of poor nutrition. Short cognitive tests were administered at five measurement points. 53 children were lost due to emigration factors and death. Children with the treatment had higher cognitive test scores, especially when they started the programme younger. The effect was maintained a year after the programme ended.

1 🔒 studies

Watanabe et al. (2005) looked at the lasting effects of an early childhood development and nutrition intervention on the cognitive performance of school-age children in rural communes in Vietnam. This included improving existing centre-based pre-schooling through material support and teacher training on child-centred teaching methods, training sessions for fathers and mothers separately on child care and development, a small local library for parents, and it promoted play corners in the homes of participating children. One commune with 172 students had been exposed only to the nutrition intervention, and another with 140 students had both. The attrition rate was 27%. The group with both interventions had slightly higher test scores at later primary school.

Walker et al. (2005) evaluated the impact of a community aid programme, including food supplement and weekly home visits, on "growth-stunted" children in Jamaica. This cohort study consisted of three post-tests carried out when participants turned 7, 11 and 17 years old. 129 children were recruited from Kingston,

Jamaica. There is data for 103 of these. Children receiving just the food supplement showed no improvement in IQ scores, maths, or language compared to a control. Children with extra psychosocial stimulation had improved scores (effect sizes averaging 0.5).

Summary

In summary, health and nutrition interventions are found to have only a small impact on progress and attainment in poorer countries. As shown in previous chapters, providing schools, and getting students to attend schools, are the first steps in dealing with a poverty attainment gap. But being healthy enough to prosper at school is also important. Some of the evidence here is of reasonable quality.

Other approaches – information and resources

We found a variety of other approaches, including giving families information, and giving schools specific resources. Again none of the studies was rated 4🔒.

3🔒 studies

A study by Nguyen (2008) looked at the impact of randomly assigning 604 schools to be statistics schools where teachers reported to parents and children the average earnings and the implied gain at each level of education, or schools with a role model, or schools with both. The interventions consisted of parent-teacher meetings. A further 69 schools had no intervention. Final data was collected from grade 4 students (aged 9 to 15) after five months. Attrition was 12%. The statistics group had slightly better attendance, and better average test scores (effect size 0.2). The role model schools only showed improvement if the role model was a successful student from a poor background.

Loyalka et al. (2013) looked at the impact of career counselling, or providing information about school returns, on student dropout and achievement at school in rural China. 131 junior high schools and 12,786 students were randomised to one of the two treatments or a control. Students in the counselling group received four 45-minute lessons in career planning. Students in the information group were given one lesson about statistical graphs on wage differences with regards to educational attainment. A maths test was used pre and post. Neither intervention had an impact on maths, or on dropout or plans to go to high school. The interventions were of very short duration.

Dillon et al. (2017) compared the impact of a game-based pre-school curriculum in maths, for pre-schools in India. There were three arms for four months – 70 schools had maths games designed to improve children's skills in numbers and geometry, 70 schools used games focusing on social cognitive abilities without mathematical content, and 72 schools used a standard curriculum. The groups were similar at baseline. The age range of the 1,540 children was 2 to 12. The maths game group improved more than both other groups in geometric sensitivity and especially the non-symbolic maths test. The longer term impact was not so clear.

2🔒 studies

Duflo and Hanna (2005) conducted a trial involving a camera with a tamper-proof date and time function to study teacher absenteeism and children's primary level achievement in India. 120 education centres were randomised to two groups. Absence is common due to the geographical nature of the area, which makes it difficult for teachers to reach schools. In the treatment group teachers' salaries were based on attendance as recorded by pictures. In the control group salaries were fixed but teachers were warned of dismissal for absences. Teacher absence declined (halved compared to the baseline), and student instruction time increased in the treatment group, compared to the control. After a year, treatment students who had been illiterate at the outset scored higher in oral and written tests (effect size 0.17), and were more likely to enrol in regular schools. Attrition was 11%.

In rural Kenya, the use of flip charts for schools where textbooks were sparse was found to improve test scores for children in grades 3 to 8 with an effect size of 0.2 (or perhaps less in an alternative computation). Two years later, there was no difference between the groups (Glewwe et al. 2004). The number of cases is unclear, and there is some attrition.

Banerjee et al. (2007a) looked at remedial education, the Balsakhi Program, for students lagging behind in urban India. It required a young woman from the community to work on literacy and numeracy with grade 3 and grade 4 children who did not have these basic skills, out of regular classrooms for 2 hours per day during normal school hours. In Vadodara, 98 out of 122 government primary schools participated. In year 1, half of them were given the treatment in grade 3 and the other half were given the treatment in grade 4. In year 2, the grades were reversed, and 24 more primary schools participated and were randomly assigned to the two groups. In Mumbai, 77 schools were stratified by test scores and language, which were randomly assigned to receive the treatment in grade 3 or grade 2. In the second year, the order of treatment was again reversed. The treatment improved average test scores by 0.14 standard deviations in the first year, 0.28 in the second year, and this dropped 0.1 once the programme was over. There was no impact on school attendance/drop-out. The tests and testing were not independent of the developer. Attrition is variable between groups.

Banerjee et al. (2007b) evaluated a computer-assisted maths learning program for 5,945 grade 4 children in 67 schools. Children were offered 2 hours of shared computer per week to solve maths problems by playing games. Schools were randomised in a waiting list design. The treatment had an impact on maths of 0.35 standard deviations in the first year and 0.47 in the second year. The effect dropped to 0.1 standard deviations one year after finishing the programme. There was no impact on school attendance/drop-out. The tests and testing were not independent of the developer. Attrition is 7%.

As discussed in Chapter 3, Levy et al. (2009) considered the BRIGHT Programme in Burkina Faso, and found an improvement in maths and French (effect size 0.4).

In 1995, the Ministry of Education selected 100 (of the most "needy") primary schools in Kenya to participate in the School Assistance Program, and divided them into four groups. Group 1 received free textbooks in 1996. Group 2 received educational materials including textbooks in 1997, Group 3 in 1998, and Group 4 in 2000. In year 1, the 25 schools can be compared to the 75 schools that did not receive the treatment. In year 2, the 25 schools can be compared to the 50 schools that did not receive the treatment and so on. The impact was very little (effect size 0.02). Only students with high initial scores appeared to gain, perhaps because the textbooks were in English and they could read them better (Glewwe et al. 2009). A lot of students dropped out of school anyway.

Summary

In summary, there is some promise here on the basis of providing information for families of the value of education, providing schools with pedagogical resources, encouraging teacher attendance in remote areas, and additional tutoring. As in most reviews on the use of technology in schools, the evidence on EdTech is mixed (See et al. 2021a, 2021b). It depends on the application and context. Technology *per se* is not the solution.

An outline of evidence on recruiting teachers to poorer areas and schools

We have previously also conducted a review of how (good) teachers can be attracted to and retained in poorer areas and schools (with high levels of student disadvantage), including in more developed countries like the UK. Our work looked at financial incentives and other approaches. This is another possible route to improving the attainment of poorer students. Classroom teachers around the world are usually and mostly paid to a fixed schedule and by a pre-set amount, often linked to their experience and qualifications. Financial incentives might be able to improve the apparent performance of teachers (Dee and Wyckoff (2015). However, there is also a growing interest in whether performance-based incentives can improve teacher retention and performance. We only present an outline of the synthesis here, rather than a summary of each study. The full reports can be found in (See and Gorard 2019; See et al. 2020a, 2020b).

Most promising approaches for attracting teachers

The only approach that seems to have evidence of working at all is the offer of monetary inducements, but there are caveats. First, it works only in attracting those who are already interested in teaching. Second, such incentives have to be large enough to compensate for the relatively challenging working conditions, and competitive enough to offset the opportunity costs of not being in better paid jobs. Monetary incentives can also attract teachers to challenging schools, but still only for relatively high performing schools with lower proportions of disadvantaged children. Such incentives are more successful in attracting young female teachers, but less so for older or male teachers. Also, the impact of monetary incentives is temporary, and lasts only while the incentive is still active – there is no residual benefit. Once the money stops teachers then leave at the same rate as before. It is also necessary to consider the negative impact of such incentives on other schools. Where incentives are used to try and attract teachers to specific local areas or schools this could be at the expense of other schools, so may not benefit the system as a whole. There are also some suggestions from less robust correlational studies that financial incentives alone may not be enough to compensate for poor working conditions, issues with school leadership and school climate (Waters-Weller 2009, Fulbeck 2014).

There is no evidence that widely advocated approaches, like Grow Your Own where teachers are trained and recruited from the local community, actually increase the number of teachers in hard-to-staff schools. This does not mean that such ideas do not work. It is just that almost all of the relevant studies are based on teachers' or principals' anecdotal reports of successful practice in their own school or district. Therefore, without a clear counterfactual it is not possible to be sure if this strategy leads to increasing the number of teachers, or if something else is happening. For example, economic events like a rise in unemployment can encourage people to go into teaching, which has nothing to do with any concurrent initiative to attract teachers.

There is also no good evidence that making it easier for people to enter into teaching by offering different pathways helps improve recruitment. This is largely because there is so much variation in the different routes in terms of who they are targeted at, and the extent to which they are actually different from the "traditional" routes on offer.

Most promising approaches to retain teachers

As for retention, financial incentives do not seem to be even as effective as for recruitment. Although many studies do show positive results, the more robust studies which control for context suggest that teachers only stay while the incentive is available. Such short-term results are not useful in solving the chronic shortage of teachers. In fact, the evidence suggests that the use of what are seen as discriminatory incentives may even worsen overall retention. Eligibility for an incentive, or a small incentive, seems to make little difference. Where incentives are used, they need to be substantial.

In many cases, monetary incentives work only because teachers are required to commit for a specified period or teach certain subjects in specified schools or areas as part of the contract agreement. These conditional incentives often entail a penalty for breaking the contract, raising questions about the value of such an approach, and the potential for a kind of enforced retention where teachers may feel "tied-in" to a role that they no longer wish to do.

Our review tentatively points to the importance of improving school cultures and ethos for recruitment and retention. Very few rigorous studies robustly evaluated interventions related to issues such as accountability, teacher stress, working conditions, behaviour, workload or levels of support from teachers/leaders, but some of the correlational and survey-based studies indicate that these could be valuable areas to explore further.

Many of the interventions also seemingly address the symptoms rather than the cause of teacher shortages. As shown in our accompanying analysis of secondary data, government policies that aim to improve the situation have actually led to a reduction in the number accepted into teacher training (See and Gorard 2019). Manipulating the number of teachers trained in higher education institutions, opening new kinds of schools, and reducing school funding, all have ramifications for the number of teachers in schools. A more coherent and long-term approach to policies is therefore needed.

Summary

It seems that incentives can encourage teachers to take up posts in disadvantaged areas and schools (Clotfelter et al. 2005; Feng 2014), but incentives do not usually help to retain them there, especially if the funding ceases or reduces. So, directing the funding to pay for more or better teachers is not a particularly promising avenue in richer countries, in order to improve the attainment of disadvantaged students. Note that this is different to the idea of paying for more teachers and school places in countries with less than 100% school enrolment (Chapter 4). It is not clear that teachers, even with a degree in a STEM subject, could earn more in an occupation outside of teaching (Fullard 2019). In fact, teachers who leave the profession tend to end up in lower paid occupations.

In summary, our substantive review findings suggest that monetary incentives, such as bursaries and scholarships are effective only in attracting those who are already considering teaching. Other kinds of financial incentives alone, including wage compensation, and higher salaries, are not effective in attracting teachers to challenging schools and areas. They are not particularly useful in retaining teachers as they work only because of the tie-in, which may encourage teachers to stay reluctantly. Our review, like almost all reviews in any area of education research, reveals both that many key areas have not been properly researched (such as workload), and that most of the research in any area is not fit for purpose (having no context, or having partial coverage). This is an issue for funders, universities, and governments to address.

Most of the research we found was very weak, and all of the higher quality work involved easier-to-measure, more concrete strategies (such as financial incentives).

More research with the kind of designs needed to address causal issues is urgently required to cover mentoring, support, training for teaching in difficult schools, and a host of other alternative approaches that could be combined with financial interventions to attract good teachers and then keep them where they are needed most. This is an ethical issue about the use of public funding and opportunity costs as much as anything else.

In the medium to longer-term a more comprehensive approach would be to change school allocation and economic policies so that there were no longer such clearly defined schools and areas with high levels of poverty (Gorard 2018), meaning that these schools would not be as hard to staff, even though some would remain geographically isolated.

Conclusion

As in prior chapters, the lessons from this chapter as a whole differ for more and less developed school systems. In less developed systems specific resources for schools and classrooms, and measures to encourage teacher attendance, can help improve attainment. In more developing countries maybe nothing that appears in this chapter is as effective as cash transfers (but see Chapter 15). Structural reforms to improve the allocation of school places for poorer children might be even better (see Chapter 11).

References

Banerjee, A., Cole, S., Duflo, E. and Linden, L. (2007a) Remedying education: Evidence from two randomized experiments in India, *The Quarterly Journal of Economics*, 122, 3, 1235–1264, (part 1).

Banerjee, A., Cole, S., Duflo, E. and Linden, L. (2007b) Remedying education: Evidence from two randomized experiments in India, *The Quarterly Journal of Economics*, 122, 3, 1235–1264, (part 2).

Clotfelter, C., Ladd, H. and Vigdor, J. (2005) Who teaches whom? Race and the distribution of novice teachers, *Economics of Education Review*, 24, 4, 377–392.

Dee, T. and Wyckoff, J. (2015) Incentives, selection, and teacher performance: Evidence from IMPACT, *Journal of Policy Analysis and Management*, 34, 2, 267–297.

Dillon, M., Kannan, H., Dean, J., Spelke, E. and Duflo, E. (2017) Cognitive science in the field: A preschool intervention durably enhances intuitive but not formal mathematics, *Science*, 357, 6346, 47–55.

Duflo, E. and Hanna, R. (2005) *Monitoring works: Getting teachers to come to school*, National Bureau of Economic Research, NBER Working Paper No. 11880.

Feng, L. (2014) Teacher placement, mobility, and occupational choices after teaching, *Education Economics*, 22, 1, 24–47.

Fulbeck, E. (2014) Teacher mobility and financial incentives: A descriptive analysis of Denver's ProComp, *Educational Evaluation and Policy Analysis*, 36, 1, 67–82.

Fullard, J. (2019) Relative wages and pupil performance, Evidence from TIMSS, Work In Progress: Institute for Social and Economic Research, 2021-07.pdf (essex.ac.uk).

Glewwe, P., Kremer, M. and Moulin, S. (2009) Many children left behind? Textbooks and test scores in Kenya, *American Economic Journal: Applied Economics*, 1, 1, 112–135.

Glewwe, P., Kremer, M., Moulin, S. and Zitzewitz, E. (2004) Retrospective vs. prospective analyses of school inputs: the case of flip charts in Kenya, *Journal of Development Economics*, 74, 1, 251–268.

Gorard, S. (2018) *Education policy: Evidence of equity and effectiveness*, Bristol: Policy Press.

Levy, D., Sloan, M., Linden, L. and Kazianga, H. (2009) *Impact evaluation of Burkina Faso's BRIGHT Program*, Final Report.

Loyalka, P., Liu, C., Song, Y., Yi, H., Huang, X., Wei, J., Zhang, L., Shi, Y., Chu, J. and Rozelle, S. (2013) Can information and counseling help students from poor rural areas go to high school? Evidence from China, *Journal of Comparative Economics*, 41, 4, 1012–1025.

Marchionni, M. and Vazquez, E. (2018) The causal effect of an extra year of schooling on skills and knowledge in Latin America. Evidence from PISA, *Assessment in Education*, https://www.tandfonline.com/doi/full/10.1080/0969594X.2018.1454401

McKay, H., Sinisterra, L., McKay, A., Gomez, H. and Lloreda, P. (1978) Improving cognitive ability in chronically deprived children, *Science*, 200, 4339, 270–278.

Nguyen, T. (2008) *Information, role models and perceived returns to education: Experimental evidence from Madagascar*, Unpublished manuscript, 6.

Powell, C., Walker, S., Chang, S. and Grantham-McGregor, S. (1998) Nutrition and education: a randomized trial of the effects of breakfast in rural primary school children, *The American Journal of Clinical Nutrition*, 68, 4, 873–879.

See, B.H. and Gorard, S. (2019) Why don't we have enough teachers? A reconsideration of the available evidence, *Research Papers in Education*, https://emxpert.net/sageedit/journals/?token=B1F8DD12-621A-4C30-B

See, B.H., Gorard, S., Lu, B., Dong, L. and Siddiqui, N. (2021b) Is technology always helpful? A critical review of the use of education technology in supporting formative assessment in schools, *Research Papers in Education*, https://doi.org/10.1080/02671522.2021.1907778

See, B.H., Gorard, S., Morris, R. and el-Soufi, N. (2020a) What works in attracting and retaining teachers in challenging schools and areas?, *Oxford Review of Education*, https://doi.org/10.1080/03054985.2020.1775566

See, B.H., Gorard, S., Siddiqui, N., El Soufi, N., Lu, B. and Dong, L. (2021a) A systematic review of technology-mediated parental engagement on student outcomes, *Educational Research and Evaluation*, Full article: A systematic review of the impact of technology-mediated parental engagement on student outcomes (tandfonline.com).

See, B.H., Morris, R., Gorard, S., Kokotsaki, D. and Abdi, S. (2020b) Teacher recruitment and retention: A rigorous review of international evidence of most promising interventions, *Education Sciences*, 10, 10, p. 262, https://www.mdpi.com/2227-7102/10/10/262/pdf

Simeon, D., Grantham-McGregor, S., Callender, J. and Wong, M. (1995) Treatment of Trichuris trichiura infections improves growth, spelling scores and school attendance in some children, *The Journal of Nutrition*, 125, 7, 1875–1883.

Tao, L., Li, H., Rozelle, S. and Zhang, L. (2010) Cash incentives, peer tutoring, and parental involvement: A study of three educational inputs in a randomized field experiment in China. 3ie, Cash Incentives, Peer Tutoring, And Parental Involvement: A Study Of Three Educational Inputs In A Randomized Field Experiment In China (3ieimpact.org).

Walker, S., Chang, S., Powell, C. and Grantham-McGregor, S. (2005) Effects of early childhood psychosocial stimulation and nutritional supplementation on cognition and education in growth-stunted Jamaican children: prospective cohort study, *The Lancet*, 366, 9499, 1804–1807.

Watanabe, K., Flores, R., Fujiwara, J. and Tran, L. (2005) Early childhood development interventions and cognitive development of young children in rural Vietnam, *The Journal of Nutrition*, 135, 8, 1918–1925.

Waters-Weller, C. (2009) Attracting veteran teachers to low socioeconomic status schools: Initiatives and considerations, US, *ProQuest Information and Learning*, 69, 2979–2979.

ISSUES IN EVALUATING PUPIL PREMIUM POLICY

8

THE PUPIL PREMIUM FUNDING POLICY IN ENGLAND

Introduction

This section of the book moves to considering in more detail a particular policy of cash transfers to schools. This chapter describes the Pupil Premium funding policy in England, what it is, what it was supposed to achieve, how schools are using the money, and what some of the earlier evidence has suggested about its impact. This policy is a kind of cash transfer, conditional not on any measure or outcome but on how it is used (as audited by the Department for Education and the school inspectors Ofsted). The next section of the book looks at how we assessed the impact of this policy in an innovative way, and what the results were. The final section returns to the more general lessons from all of the evidence in the book, for schools worldwide.

Background to Pupil Premium policy

Pupil Premium funding is by no means the first policy that has directed additional funding to raise the attainment of disadvantaged students in England (Hutchinson et al. 2016). One early attempt to address educational inequality brought about by social and economic deprivation was based on Educational Priority Areas, introduced following the Plowden Report in 1967 (Central Advisory Council for Education 1967). This was based on the principle of positive discrimination where certain geographical areas were designated to receive special educational resources to try and compensate for poor environmental conditions, and intended to increase teacher pay and expand nursery provision (Smith 1987).

DOI: 10.4324/9781003287353-12

Educational Priority Areas were eventually phased out in the 1980s and replaced with the Additional Need funding included in the notional schools component of local authority funding. Local authorities were not obliged to spend this money on the additional needs of schools nor on deprived schools (West 2009). Two new strands of funding were later developed to ensure that funding for schools reached the intended recipients (1984), and that compensatory funding was targeted at schools and pupils with the greatest needs (1990).

In England, numerous policy initiatives, all aimed at narrowing the attainment gap between disadvantaged children and their more privileged peers, were introduced when the New Labour government came to power in 1997. These initiatives included the introduction of Sure Start, and area-based interventions like Education Action Zones, Excellence in the Cities and the London Challenge, the creation of the National Strategies for Numeracy and Literacy, and the implementation of an Every Child Matters agenda (Whitty and Anders 2014). Other potentially relevant initiatives included increasing use of teaching assistants, improving school leadership training, the creation of academies and specialist schools, and the use of more personalised targeted interventions such as Reading Recovery and Fresh Start.

In 1998, the Standards Fund was introduced, which involved as many as 30 separate grants totalling £1.6 billion per year. The Standards Fund targeted disadvantaged areas and schools, funding priority projects like school lunches, one-to-one tuition, extended schools sports and music provision. But there were concerns throughout the 1990s about the degree of redistribution of funding to deprived schools. In 2003, local authorities had to include a deprivation factor in their funding formulae. Because there was no minimal level to be distributed based on the deprivation factor, few authorities used this factor fully.

According to the Child Poverty Review (DfES/HMT 2005) local authorities often allocated funding to schools for deprivation based on their historical knowledge of the school rather than any recent assessment of the needs of schools. And there were wide variations in the processes used by local authorities in assessing their funding needs. Deprivation funding was not accurately and consistently applied to schools in deprived areas. The review suggested that the funding was most effective when targeted at the most deprived schools, and to help children eligible for free school meals.

In 2006 the Dedicated Schools Grant was re-introduced to ring-fence education funding, and many of the specific grants were streamlined under a single School Standards Grant, which was later mainstreamed into the Dedicated Schools Grant in 2011 under the subsequent Coalition Government. In 2007, several of the Standards Fund Grants, including the Education Action Zones and Excellence in Cities programmes, aimed at deprivation and low achievement, were rationalised. The Ethnic Minority Achievement Grant remained until 2011 when the Standards Fund was subsumed into the Dedicated Schools Grant.

Most of these policies had never been robustly evaluated, and their individual effectiveness is difficult to ascertain due to lack of appropriate comparators or different comparators used over time, different objectives and outcome measures, and the complications of many other initiatives happening at the same time, along with annual changes in the socio-economic status of pupil intakes to schools. Analysis by the National Audit Office (2015) suggested that the attainment gap between advantaged and non-disadvantaged pupils (the poverty attainment gap) has remained large despite these initiatives.

When the Conservative-led Coalition Government came to power in 2010, they made a commitment to closing the attainment gap as part of an attempt to improve social mobility, which they claimed had actually worsened under the New Labour government (HM Government 2010), even though there was no evidence that it had (Gorard 2008). In 2011 a targeted grant was introduced, allocated to schools based on the number of deprived pupils in the school. This was the beginning of Pupil Premium funding.

These kinds of measures were implemented at least partly because of worries about school segregation (see Chapter 2), and partly because of the poverty attainment gap. For example, by Key Stage 4 (KS4) at around age 16, pupils eligible for free school meals (FSM) in England gained an average of 243 points (in GCSE and equivalent qualifications) compared to 319 for non-eligible pupils. This is a considerable attainment gap with an "effect" size of 0.78 (Gorard 2018). Almost twice as many non-eligible as FSM-eligible pupils then continued with academic study after the age of 16, gained at least the equivalent of two A-levels at grade E in KS5, and entered higher education at a traditional age. This is a big difference in outcomes and prospects.

What is the Pupil Premium?

In April 2011, the Coalition government introduced Pupil Premium funding for schools in England. It was allocated to all state-funded schools, in proportion to their intake of disadvantaged pupils (Roberts et al. 2021). The schools involved were infant, junior, primary, middle, secondary, high schools, special schools and pupil referral units. It included eligible pupils in independent special schools where full tuition fees were paid for by the local authority.

The policy differed from one based on giving money to poorer families on condition that their children attend school (see Chapter 3), and it differed from a policy based on extra funding for schools themselves that is not tied to their intake, such as the original Specialist Schools and then the Academies programmes in England (Gorard 2005).

Disadvantage for a child was defined as coming from a low-income family, known to be currently eligible for free school meals (FSM), and a much smaller number of children who had been looked after by the state continuously for more than six months (Education and Skills Funding Agency 2018). In 2012/13, the funding was extended to include pupils known to have been FSM-eligible in any of the previous six years (EverFSM6). A smaller premium was also paid for pupils having parents in the armed forces, and for pupils whose parent(s) had died while in the armed forces (Foster and Long 2020). Subsequently, similar policies have been introduced in the other home countries of the UK, including Pupil Equity Funding (PEF) in Scotland.

The premium was described as "additional" funding on top of the normal grant that schools received, but this does not necessarily mean that any more funding was provided. It was linked to the introduction of the National Funding Formula for schools (Roberts et al. 2021). Rather, it might mean that existing planned funding was redistributed slightly towards schools with poorer intakes, and certainly means that some of the previous streams were reduced or replaced.

In 2011, £430 was paid for any child who had been looked after by the local authority for at least six months. In 2014 this was increased to £1,900, and extended to children looked after for one day or more, and children adopted from care or who had left care on a special guardianship or child arrangements (previously known as a residence order). By 2020, the funding was £2,435. Similarly, in 2011, children eligible for free school meals attracted £430 whether in primary or secondary school. In 2012, this was raised to £530 and given for children who had been eligible for free school meals at any point in the prior six years. From 2014 onwards, children of primary age started attracting more funding than those of secondary age. By 2020, the figures were £1,345 per EverFSM6 pupil at primary school, and £955 at secondary. The funding for pupils from armed forces families was £200 in 2011, rising to £310 by 2020. For some primary schools, the overall funding amounted to well over £150k per annum, and for some secondary schools well over £300k.

The main element of recurrent annual funding for schools is the Age Weighted Pupil Unit, which was worth £2,747 per pupil at primary school in 2019/20 (The Secret Headteacher 2020). So, Pupil Premium provided about half as much again for disadvantaged students – a very substantial difference. Other funding includes cash for pupils with low prior attainment, or English as an additional language (EAL), a school deprivation (low household income) factor, plus a lump sum and a devolved formula capital grant which has to be spent on building work or ICT hardware. Schools are funded to provide free school meals for all infants (not means-tested), plus perhaps a Sports Premium, top up funds to cover teachers' pay and pension rises, and of course top up to support resources and activities for pupils with Special Educational Needs (SEN). Schools might also try to generate their own funds from parents, properties, offering placements for student teachers and applying for external grants. Most funds other than the Age Weighted Pupil Unit are for specified and audited expenditure. Therefore, the Pupil Premium funding (above) can make a substantial difference to the running of schools.

As the eligibility criteria expanded, the total number of pupils benefitting from Pupil Premium and the total amount of funding also increased. The most substantial increase in total Pupil Premium funding was between 2011/12 and 2014/15 from £623 million to £2.41 billion. This is reflected in the increase in the total number of pupils counted for Pupil Premium, largely the result of an increase in the number of children eligible for free school meals (see Table 8.1).

TABLE 8.1 Number of pupils eligible for Pupil Premium (2011/12 to 2020/21)

Year	Deprivation	Looked after and previously looked after	Service family	Total
2011–2012	1,217,560	40,560	45,070	1,303,190
2012–2013	1,831,130	41,420	52,370	1,924,920
2013–2014	1,917,270	42,540	57,940	2,017,750
2014–2015	1,919,260	86,370	64,390	2,070,020
2015–2016	1,920,360	86,150	68,900	2,075,410
2016–2017	1,906,480	93,720	73,470	2,073,670
2017–2018	1,892,300	99,380	75,270	2,066,950
2018–2019	1,865,320	105,670	76,320	2,047,310
2019–2020	1,850,310	111,710	77,150	2,039,170
2020–2021	1,831,950	116,100	79,340	2,027,390

Associated with the introduction of Pupil Premium, a new school performance measure was introduced through which schools were accountable for the attainment of their Pupil Premium pupils (relative to other students), and thereby indirectly for how the new funding was spent.

In 2020/21, the government made available additional one-off funding known as the "Recovery Premium" to provide further support for disadvantaged pupils impacted by Covid-19. And the DfE extended Pupil Premium to children with "no recourse to public funds" after a legal challenge (Whittaker 2021). In 2021 the key census date for registering disadvantaged pupils was moved by the government, which might have reduced or delayed Pupil Premium payments for the most mobile pupils (Coughlan 2021). None of the most recent changes is relevant to the analyses presented in the next section of the book, which only go up to 2019, because the Covid-19 lockdown led to disruption of national assessment systems and school record-keeping, as explained in Chapter 10.

What is Pupil Premium funding for?

Reducing segregation between schools

When some of the original planning took place to introduce what became the Pupil Premium, it was clearly intended to address the problem of social and economic "segregation" between school intakes. This concern emerged partly from evidence given to successive House of Commons Select Committee investigations into school admissions and segregation – about how less segregated school systems perform better and how, if school admissions could address this, it could help to reduce the tail of low achievement in England (House of Commons 2004).

In proposing the Pupil Premium, Freedman and Horner (2008) suggested that it would "act as an incentive for schools to stop cream-skimming children from wealthier areas as they will lose out financially" (p.41), and "give their neighbouring schools located in more disadvantaged communities the resources to attract middle-class parents" (p.9). The idea was still there in 2010 just before the launch, with the new coalition government stating that it had the intention of "reducing any disincentive that schools might have to recruit such pupils" (Gov.UK 2010). The then Education Secretary said "What we wanted to do is see how we could give priority in admissions to children from poorer homes" and "historically, we haven't achieved as well as we should, particularly given the nature of Britain's stratified and segregated education system" (The Guardian 2014).

One objective of the funding from the outset was therefore to reduce social and economic segregation between school intakes. The idea was for schools to prioritise disadvantaged pupils in some way, to encourage them to take a fairer share of the local poorer children in each area, and so reduce socio-economic segregation between secondary schools (Gov.UK 2010). The funding provided assistance and interventions to decrease the apparent unattractiveness of disadvantaged students (during the allocation of school places) who might need more resources to achieve expected levels of attainment (Freedman and Horner 2008).

To some extent, this emphasis on reducing the "tail" of low achievement by incentivising schools for admitting disadvantaged pupils has subsequently been rather lost. Instead, the emphasis has tended to be on direct involvement in raising the attainment of disadvantaged pupils, wherever they attend school. There were doubts originally about whether the premium was large enough to reduce any disincentive that schools may have for attracting lower attaining and disadvantaged pupils, and whether it could reduce social segregation between schools (Chowdry et al. 2010). Radical changes to the intake of schools might also have been hindered by the Schools Admissions Code. However, in December 2014 the government published a revised admissions code that permitted all admission authorities in England to prioritise disadvantaged children in their admission arrangements (Foster and Long 2020).

The attainment gap

DfE (2015) stated that the objective of the Pupil Premium funding was:

> to address inequality by giving every school and teacher the resources they need to help their most disadvantaged pupils, allowing them the freedom to respond appropriately to individual circumstances.

From the outset, a key purpose of the funding was to improve the attainment of poorer pupils, and so help reduce the "achievement gap" between children coming from richer and poorer families (Gov.uk 2010, NASEN 2014, Copeland 2019). School performance tables in England now include separate results for the attainment of pupils who attract Pupil Premium funding, and the national school inspection body Ofsted looks at how effectively schools are using their funding to increase the achievement of disadvantaged pupils (DfE 2019a). Ofsted and the Department for Education (DfE) can suggest that a school must review its provision for disadvantaged pupils, where this is considered unsatisfactory.

This aim emerged from the fact that disadvantaged pupils are more likely to be struggling, and have challenges or other priorities while at school (Rolle et al. 2008). Pupil Premium provides schools with the funds to support low-income low attaining pupils with additional resources and interventions (Copeland 2019). Pupil Premium is a kind of catch up or even remedial policy for disadvantaged pupils, to reduce the poverty attainment gap, and schools are increasingly judged in terms of the results for their Pupil Premium pupils compared to the rest (DfE 2019a).

How is the funding used?

It is crucial for any funding scheme intended to improve education for disadvantaged groups that the funding reaches its correct "target", and that the funding is then used effectively. The funding allocation must be fair, which largely depends on having high quality administrative data (Baker et al. 2014), otherwise some intended recipients can miss out on the benefits (Minorini and Sugarman 1999). Good intentions and extra money are not enough in themselves. We will consider further who is best identified as being disadvantaged in Chapter 10.

Pupil Premium funding is paid directly to schools because the government has stated that schools are best placed to identify and assess the needs of their eligible children (DfE 2015). Although schools are given the freedom to use the funding in ways they deem best to benefit their pupils, they do remain accountable for its use. They are accountable through the DfE published school performance tables, which include data on the attainment of pupils eligible for the funding, the progress made by these pupils, and the gap in attainment between these pupils and their peers. Schools that have made significant improvements in the attainment of the eligible pupils had, until recently, been rewarded with Pupil Premium Awards.

Schools are also accountable via Ofsted – the national school inspection regime. Ofsted inspectors report how schools are using the funding to support the academic attainment of disadvantaged pupils, how much was spent, what it was spent on, how schools decide on the strategies to fund, and the perceived impact of this spending on the academic performance of Pupil Premium pupils. School governors are expected to be kept informed of how the funding has supported the attainment of disadvantaged children, and to question the senior leadership where there are important variations in achievement between different groups (Anilkumar 2021). How effectively the governing body are seen to handle this could affect the grade that Ofsted inspectors give to schools for their leadership and management. A third form of accountability is the requirement for schools to publish on their website how they use the funding and the perceived impact this had on the attainment of disadvantaged pupils (Gorard et al. 2020).

Where funding is paid to local authorities for looked-after children, the responsibility for managing the fund falls on Virtual School Heads, who will work with neighbouring schools to ensure that the funding is used to support the educational needs of the children. They can either pass all of the funding to schools or retain some for activities that benefit looked-after children in the authority.

Schools are required to use the extra funding to support low-income and other target pupils, but they can choose how to do this. This even includes spending it for the benefit of such pupils at other maintained schools, or via community facilities. The National Governance Association reported that schools do not always ring-fence Pupil Premium funding (NGA 2018). Schools do not have to spend Pupil Premium directly on teaching activities, and can introduce programmes related to attendance, behaviour, personal development or parental engagement, for example. As long as the focus is on the identified disadvantaged pupils, other pupils, perhaps especially low attainers can benefit as well. Interestingly, schools have reported using a range of criteria to define disadvantage. These include EAL children, refugee/asylum seeker children, families in receipt of state benefits, single parent families, children from areas designated as deprived and those excluded from mainstream schools.

There has up to now been some rather specialist and sometimes esoteric research on how schools have responded to the new policy (e.g. Craske, 2018, Barrett 2018, Yaghi 2021). We found no research studies reporting evidence that using the funding to address segregation between schools was a concern, perhaps because this can never be assessed in a single school. An early study, commissioned by the DfE, reported that the many schools reported that they had already been doing what the Pupil Premium required anyway (Carpenter et al. 2013). Most schools (90%) said that they relied on their own experience of what works when making decisions about what to do with the funding. They also used ideas from other schools (70%), while less than half (45%) said used research evidence, including from the DfE website, and the EEF Teaching and Learning Toolkit (see below). The biggest areas for expenditure tended to be on curriculum learning and on behavioural, social and emotional support.

At the same time as the Pupil Premium was announced, the Coalition government also set up the Education Endowment Foundation (EEF) as a charity, initially funded by DfE, in order to create, accumulate and communicate robust evidence on how the Pupil Premium money could best be used to reduce the attainment gap. The Educational Endowment Foundation has now had eleven years to help generate and disseminate secure evidence for schools on how best to use funding to reduce the attainment gap. Although the effects of their work will be muted when looking at the whole school system, there ought to be signs of its impact.

EEF has so far commissioned hundreds of evaluations, mostly based on randomised control trials, and reviews of best practice, identified what they term "promising approaches", and published a Teaching and Learning Toolkit summarising the strengths and weaknesses of many common interventions used in the classroom. The idea is that schools and teachers should use this evidence, and more like it from other key sources, to select valid programmes for their chosen purposes. Valid approaches would be those that had been demonstrated to have worked in reducing the attainment gap, while raising general attainment, and which could be considered the "best bets" to do so again. Many schools now report using these resources or something like them (Education Endowment Foundation 2021).

While inspecting schools Ofsted (2012) found that most of the funding was being spent on staff – including teaching assistants, new or existing teachers, mentors, behaviour support workers, counsellors and attendance workers. The next most popular, and related, area of use was for small group or individual tuition. In descending order of frequency, school heads reported to Fellows and Barton (2018) that they saw the funding as being intended to raise the attainment of disadvantaged pupils, close the attainment gap in their school, improve engagement with parents of poor pupils, and the attendance of poor pupils, to close the attainment gap nationally, and reduce exclusions from school for Pupil Premium pupils. A survey by the Sutton Trust (2012) suggested that the only a small proportion of the £1.25 billion was spent on activities specifically to raise attainment.

The DfE has published information and advice for schools on how the funding should be spent (DfE 2019b). While the funding is designed to raise the attainment of disadvantaged groups, strategies that do not address attainment directly, but can have a positive impact on their education, can be supported through the funding. For example, the funding could be used to address challenges relating to persistent absence, behaviour, access to technology and educational materials and the high mobility of some pupils. Schools can use the funding to support children with identified needs, such as those who have or had a social worker, or who act as a carer themselves.

DfE (2021) guidance to schools suggested that a tiered approach may be the most effective, focusing on:

- *Teaching* (e.g. training of teachers, professional development, recruitment and retention and early career support for teachers, use of teaching assistants, mentoring)
- *Targeted academic support* (e.g. one-to-one tuition, small group tuition, language/speech therapy)
- *Wider support* (e.g. breakfast clubs, counselling, enrichment activities such as educational trips and visits, sports, drama and arts clubs, music lessons, summer schools, garden/environment based projects).

Greenshaw Research School (2022) reported using the EEF Tiered Model of School Improvement, with the majority of planned activities focusing on improving teaching and learning. Less attention was paid to targeted academic interventions and wider school approaches.

Prior evidence on the impact of Pupil Premium

The Pupil Premium is perhaps most like the additional funding that schools in England have long received for individual pupils with statements of special educational needs (SEN) or a disability. Both funds are intended to assist those pupils facing long-term challenges in accessing the curriculum. The SEN funding is not tied to compliance standards or other criteria. It is simply based on the needs of individuals attending schools. And its spending is directed by professional guidance and statements of needs/entitlement. This should reduce the chances of failure of implementation, as has happened previously with more complex schemes elsewhere (Bastagli 2010). This record is promising for a scheme such as Pupil Premium funding, which is also based on individuals attending each school but its expenditure is not tied to the individual in the same way as for SEN. The evidence on the impact of using funding for poorer pupils is mixed but reasonably promising overall (Jenkins et al. 2008, Henry et al. 2010). Holmlund et al. (2010), using what they term a "back-of-envelope calculation", report that increased expenditure on schools is linked to improved school outcomes (and see Chapter 6).

The widespread and expensive Pupil Premium policy was implemented in England without prior robust evaluation. Subsequent research has been limited by being very early (Carpenter et al. 2013), or weak and small scale (e.g. Craske 2018, Copeland 2019). And because the policy applies to all schools it is no longer possible to design an evaluation with a clear counterfactual group which does not receive Pupil Premium funding. Instead researchers have to rely on before-and-after time series analyses, coupled with attempts to factor out other changes to the law, to the economy and to assessment, that have taken place over the same period.

Until the work we describe in Chapter 11, there had been no robust prior studies of the impact of Pupil Premium funding on SES segregation between schools. In fact, we have found no other studies on this at all. We have only found studies on Pupil Premium and the attainment gap.

These prior studies still have several problems. Some only look at data since 2011 which cannot portray a change since the policy was introduced. For example, DfE (2018a, 2018b) used a version of the attainment gap that had not been used before 2011, and so any changes they portray cannot be attributed to a policy change in 2011 (there is no comparator). They cannot genuinely say that any trend was not already in existence beforehand.

Jenkins and Sneider (2019) analysed the impact of Pupil Premium in reducing the attainment gap between disadvantaged pupils and their non-disadvantaged peers over a 12-year period (from 2008 to 2019) across 22 local authorities in Wales. The attainment gap was defined in terms of the Level 2 qualification (i.e. 5 GCSEs at A*-C including a grade A*-C in English/Welsh and maths). From 2017 onwards there were changes to the GCSE maths, English, Welsh and maths qualifications and the Level 2 thresholds were revised so that no more than two of the five subjects in Level 2 could be vocational (StatsWales 2020). While the size of the gap remained fairly constant over the period as overall attainment rose, the analysis showed that the Pupil Premium period was correlated with a reduction in the attainment gap, defined as the proportional difference between disadvantaged pupils and others. The authors noted that data on GCSE results were recorded only if the student is eligible for FSM at the time of the examination. This means that data for students eligible at any point in the last six years are missing.

Hutchinson et al. (2016) used a progress gap rather than an attainment gap, in England. A progress gap is defined as the additional months' progress made by non-disadvantaged pupils compared to their disadvantaged peers. But in 2014, the first entry rules for GCSE were introduced. This meant that only the first entry counts towards the performance measures for core subjects (DfE 2013). The progress and attainment gaps in 2014 and 2015 could be exacerbated as a result. Analysis by Cambridge Assessment (Rodeiro 2014) suggested that there is a positive effect of multiple entries on GCSE maths and English language grades for pupils who have lower than expected attainment at KS2 compared to single entrants. The abolition of the multiple entry rules, therefore, has the potential to widen the attainment gap.

Work on the raw-score attainment gap suggests that it has been declining to some extent since 2011, but perhaps no more than it declined before 2011 in some accounts. According to the Education Policy Institute (2017), the gap has been reducing very slowly and erratically since at least 2007, with no clear difference before and after 2011 The Social Mobility Commission (2019) also reported that the gap has been falling slowly, but again not necessarily more so since 2011.

However none of these prior studies takes account of changes over time in the economy, the legal definitions of indicators of disadvantage, the introduction of Universal Credit, the impact of the incentive to register pupils as FSM-eligible because of the Pupil Premium, or the amount of missing data, and so the prevalence of disadvantage (see Chapter 9). Economic and policy changes matter because they will change the proportion and nature of the group officially labelled as disadvantaged in any year. And this will then alter the apparent attainment gap between pupils labelled disadvantaged and the rest in a way that is unrelated to the impact of the Pupil Premium, or the work of schools. Analyses are also complicated by changes in the metrics used, the curriculum, and in the way attainment has been assessed and scored.

The DfE (2014) have attempted to deal with abrupt changes in the nature of assessment and grading by using national rankings of attainment scores rather than the raw scores themselves when assessing the poverty attainment gap. Using the DfE ranked measure, the attainment gap at KS2 appeared to have dropped from 3.34 in 2011 to 2.90 in 2018 (DfE 2018b), and at KS4 from 4.07 in 2011 to 3.66 in 2017 (DfE 2018c). However, this drop cannot simply be attributed to the Pupil Premium because the same metric was not used before 2011, and the DfE have not gone back before 2011 to recalculate the gap using the newer method, and there is therefore no evidence in these reports of what would have happened in the absence of Pupil Premium (i.e. there is no counterfactual result). The DfE ranking approach does not address economic and legal changes over time, and anyway has been shown to produce the same substantive findings as using raw scores (Gorard 2022a, 2022b).

Conclusions

It is traditionally accepted by analysts that socio-economic inequality in education cannot be addressed simply by enacting equality laws (Gorard 2018), just as with any policy legislation (Cerna 2013). The Pupil Premium policy, however, is both a law giving duties to schools and teachers, and a way of channelling funding to at least some of the most needy pupils in England (Barrett 2018), alongside providing a growing body of evidence on how that funding is best spent, through the EEF and other bodies (see Chapter 15).

Although it was welcome, the Pupil Premium was not as ambitious as originally planned. The level of funding was smaller than originally envisaged by the Liberal Democrats (Whitty and Anders 2014). It was introduced at a time when there were severe expenditure cuts, so schools may not have felt the immediate impact of the funding, and this may have offset any improvements in the attainment gap.

Until the work presented in the next section of this book we really did not know whether Pupil Premium funding was effective in overcoming socio-economic segregation between schools, or reducing the poverty attainment gap. How did we evaluate this robustly?

References

Anilkumar, A. (2021) *Ofsted pupil premium accountability 2021: Guidance for schools.* London: Third Space Learning. https://thirdspacelearning.com/blog/pupil-premium-ofsted

Baker, B., Sciarra, D. and Farrie, D. (2014) *Is school funding fair? A national report card,* Education Law Center, Rutgers Graduate School of Education, https://edlawcenter.org/assets/files/pdfs/publications/Is_School_Funding_Fair_7th_Editi.pdf

Barrett, D. (2018) The effective design, implementation and enforcement of socio-economic equality duties: Lessons from the pupil premium, *Journal of Social Welfare and Family Law,* 40, 1, 57–77.

Bastagli, F. (2010) Poverty, inequality and public cash transfers: lessons from Latin America, Background Paper for the *European Report on Development (ERD) 2010 on Social Protection for Inclusive Development,* European University Institute, Florence, http://eprints.lse.ac.uk/36840

Carpenter, H., Papps, I., Bragg, J., Dyson, A., Harris, D., Kerr, K., Todd, L. and Laing, K. (2013) *Evaluation of Pupil Premium,* London: DfE, http://dera.ioe.ac.uk/18010/1/DFE-RR282.pdf

Central Advisory Council for Education (1967) *Children and their primary schools,* The Plowden Report. London: HMSO.

Cerna, L. (2013) The nature of policy change and implementation, OECD, The Nature of Policy Change and Implementation.pdf (oecd.org).

Chowdry, H., Greaves, E. and Sibieta, L. (2010) *The Pupil Premium: assessing the options,* IFS Commentary C113, https://www.ifs.org.uk/comms/comm113.pdf

Copeland, J. (2019) A critical reflection on the reasoning behind, and effectiveness of, the application of the Pupil Premium Grant within primary schools, *Management in Education,* 33, 2, 70–76.

Coughlan, S. (2021) School poverty cash at risk in date switch, *BBC News,* https://www.bbc.co.uk/ne

Craske, J. (2018) 'You can't show impact with a new pair of shoes': negotiating disadvantage through Pupil Premium, *Journal of Education Policy,* 33, 4, 526–557.

DfE (2013) *Multiple entry to GCSEs. Memorandum to the education select committee,* London: Department for Education.

DfE (2014) Measuring disadvantaged pupils' attainment gaps over time (updated): Statistical Working Paper, https://assets.publishing.service.gov.uk/government/uploads/system/uploads/attachment_data/file/398657/SFR_40_2014_Measuring_disadvantaged_pupils_attainment_gaps_over_time__updated_.pdf

DfE (2015) *2010–2015 government policy: Education of disadvantaged children.* London: Department for Education. https://www.gov.uk/government/publications/2010-to-2015-government-policy-education-of-disadvantaged-children/2010-to-2015-government-policy-education-of-disadvantaged-children

DfE (2018a) *Revised GCSE and equivalent results in England,* 2016 to 2017, SRF 01/2018, https://assets.publishing.service.gov.uk/government/uploads/system/uploads/attachment_data/file/676596/SFR01_2018.pdf

DfE (2018b) *National curriculum assessments at key stage 2 in England,* 2018 (revised), https://assets.publishing.service.gov.uk/government/uploads/system/uploads/attachment_data/file/764135/Key_stage_2_text_v6.pdf

DfE (2018c) *Revised GCSE and equivalent results in England,* 2016 to 2017, SRF 01/2018, https://assets.publishing.service.gov.uk/government/uploads/system/uploads/attachment_data/file/676596/SFR01_2018.pdf

DfE (2019a) *Pupil premium: funding and accountability for schools,* https://www.gov.uk/guidance/pupil-premium-information-for-schools-and-alternative-provision-settings?utm_source=2e5c52b2-c00c-4268-82c5-e809ff49194dandutm_medium=emailandutm_campaign=govuk-notificationsandutm_content=immediate#measuring-the-effectiveness-of-your-approach

DfE (2019b) *Using pupil premium: Guidance for school leaders,* London: Department for Education. https://www.gov.uk/guidance/pupil-premium-effective-use-and-accountability

DfE (2021) *Using pupil premium: guidance for school leaders,* Using pupil premium: guidance for school leaders - GOV.UK (www.gov.uk).

DfES/HMT (2005) Review of deprivation funding for schools" publication statement, London: DfES/HMT, https://councillors.herefordshire.gov.uk/documents/s8751/07.06.06%20social%20deprivation%20treasury%20annex%202.pdf

Education Endowment Foundation (2021) *Using your pupil premium funding effectively: Steps for developing an effective pupil premium strategy.* London: Education Endowment Foundation. https://educationendowmentfoundation.org.uk/guidance-for-teachers/using-pupil-premium

Education Policy Institute (2017) *Closing the gap? Trends in educational attainment and disadvantage,* Closing the Gap? Educational Attainment and Disadvantage - Education Policy Institute (epi.org.uk).

Education and Skills Funding Agency (2018) *Pupil Premium grant 2018 to 2019,* https://www.gov.uk/government/publications/pupil-premium-conditions-of-grant-2018-to-2019/pupil-premium-2018-to-2019-conditions-of-grant

Fellows, T. and Barton, M. (2018) *Spotlight on Disadvantage,* National Governance Association, https://www.nga.org.uk/About-Us/Campaigning/Spotlight-on-Disadvantage.aspx.

Foster, D. and Long, R. (2020) *The Pupil Premium,* House of Commons Library Briefing Paper 6700, file:///C:/Users/pjxx25/Downloads/SN06700.pdf

Freedman, S. and Horner, S. (2008) *School funding and social justice,* Policy Exchange, https://www.policyexchange.org.uk/wp-content/uploads/2016/09/school-funding-and-social-justice-oct-08-3.pdf

Gorard, S. (2005) Academies as the 'future of schooling': Is this an evidence-based policy?, *Journal of Education Policy,* 20, 3, 369–377.

Gorard, S. (2008) Research impact is not always a good thing: a re-consideration of rates of 'social mobility' in Britain, *British Journal of Sociology of Education,* 29, 3, 317–324.

Gorard, S. (2018) *Education policy: Evidence of equity and effectiveness*, Bristol: Policy Press

Gorard, S. (2022a) Segregation and the attainment gap for permanently disadvantaged pupils in England, *Educational Review*, https://doi.org/10.1080/00131911.2021.2007055

Gorard, S. (2022b) What is the evidence on the impact of Pupil Premium funding on school intakes and attainment by age 16 in England?, *British Educational Research Journal*, What is the evidence on the impact of Pupil Premium funding on school intakes and attainment by age 16 in England? - Gorard - British Educational Research Journal - Wiley Online Library.

Gorard, S., Wardle, L., Siddiqui, N. and See, B.H. (2020) Engagement and impact in addressing and overcoming disadvantage, pp. in Gorard, S. (2020 Ed.) *Getting evidence into education: Evaluating the routes to policy and practice*, London: Routledge.

Gov.uk (2010) Government announces pupil premium to raise achievement, https://www.gov.uk/government/news/government-announces-pupil-premium-to-raise-achievement

Greenshaw Research School (2022) *Through the lens of disadvantage*, Through the Lens of disadvantage | Greenshaw Research School.

Henry, G., Fortner, C. and Thompson, C. (2010) Targeted funding for educationally disadvantaged students: A regression discontinuity estimate of the impact on high school student achievement, *Educational Evaluation and Policy Analysis*, 32, 2, 183–204.

HM Government (2010) *The coalition: our programme for government*. London: Cabinet Office, http://programmeforgovernment.hmg.gov.uk/

Holmlund, H., McNally, S. and Viarengo, M. (2010) Does money matter for schools? *Economics of Education Review*, 29, 6, 1154–1164.

House of Commons Education and Skills Committee (2004) *Secondary Education: School Admissions Fourth Report of Session 2003–04 Volume II*, https://publications.parliament.uk/pa/cm200304/cmselect/cmeduski/58/58ii.pdf

Hutchinson, J. and Dunford, M. with Treadaway, M. (2016) *Divergent Pathways: the disadvantage gap, accountability and the pupil premium*, London: Education Policy Institute, https://democracy.kent.gov.uk/documents/s80605/Divergent%20Pathways%20Report.pdf

Jenkins, B. and Sneider, A. (2019) *The impact of pupil premium on the attainment gap in Wales*, Bachelor of Economics thesis, Småland, Swedeon: Jönköping University.

Jenkins, S., Micklewright, J. and Schnepf, S. (2008) Social segregation in secondary schools: how does England compare with other countries?, *Oxford Review of Education*, 34, 1, 21–37.

Minorini, P. and Sugarman, S. (1999) School finance litigation in the name of educational equity: Its evolution, impact, and future, pp. 34–71 in Ladd, H., Chalk, R. and Hansen, J. (Eds.) *Equity and adequacy in education finance: Issues and perspectives*, Washington DC: National Research Council.

NASEN (2014) *The Pupil Premium. A quick guide to maximising the impact of additional funding for disadvantaged pupils*, file:///C:/Users/czwc58/Downloads/pupil_premium.pdf.

National Audit Office (2015) *Funding for disadvantaged pupils*, London: National Audit Office.

NGA (2018) *Characteristics of the most effective pupil premium strategies revealed in research report*, National Governance Association, https://www.nga.org.uk/News/NGA-News/July-2018-Sept-2018/Characteristics-of-the-most-effective-pupil-premiu.aspx

Ofsted (2012) *The Pupil Premium: How schools used the funding*, https://www.gov.uk/government/publications/the-pupil-premium-how-schools-used-the-funding

Roberts, N., Foster, D. and Long, R. (2021) *The Pupil Premium. House of Commons Briefing Paper*, Number 6700, London: House of Commons Library.

Rodeiro, C. (2014) *Multiple entries in GCSE/IGCSE qualifications*, Cambridge: Cambridge Assessment.

Rolle, A., Houck, E. and McColl, A. (2008) And poor children continue to wait: An analysis of horizontal and vertical equity among North Carolina school districts in the face of judicially mandated policy restraints 1996–2006, *Journal of Education Finance*, 75–102.

Smith, G. (1987) Whatever happened to educational priority areas?, *Oxford Review of Education*, 13 (1), 23–38.

Social Mobility Commission (2019) *State of the Nation 2018–19*, https://assets.publishing. service.gov.uk/government/uploads/system/uploads/attachment_data/file/798404/ SMC_State_of_the_Nation_Report_2018-19.pdf

StatsWales (2020) *Key Stage 4 Interim Measures by FSM, from 2018/19*, https://statswales.gov. wales/v/Ha7F

Sutton Trust (2012) *The use of the Pupil Premium, NFER Teacher voice omnibus 2012 Survey*, Slough: National Foundation for Educational Research.

The Guardian (2014) State schools may prioritise poorest pupils in admissions revamp, *The Guardian* 22nd July 2014, https://www.theguardian.com/education/2014/jul/22/ state-schools-prioritise-disadvantaged-pupils-admissions-reform

The Secret Headteacher (2020) *A Guide to School Finance*, A Guide to School Finance – The Secret Headteacher.

West, A. (2009) Redistribution and financing schools in England under Labour: Are resources going where needs are greatest? *Education Management, Administration and Leadership*, 37, 2, 158–179.

Whittaker, F. (2021) DfE extends Pupil Premium to children with "no recourse to public funds" after legal threat, *Schools Week*, 9/6/21, Pupil premium extended to children with 'no recourse to public funds' (schoolsweek.co.uk).

Whitty, G. and Anders, J. (2014) (How) did New Labour narrow the achievement and participation gap? *LLAKES Research Paper*, *46*, 1–57. http://www.llakes.org

Yaghi, B. (2021) The Pupil Premium and policy transfer in English standalone and system leader multi-academy trust academies, *Research Papers in Education*, https://doi.org/10.10 80/02671522.2021.1961298

9

PROBLEMS IN ASSESSING THE IMPACT OF PUPIL PREMIUM POLICY

Introduction

As foreshadowed at the end of the last chapter, this chapter describes problems faced by researchers attempting to evaluate the impact of the Pupil Premium Policy. The chapter is mainly about confounds. The Pupil Premium Policy was introduced to all state-funded schools in one step in April 2011. There was and remains no chance to randomise schools or areas to receive the extra funding or not, and so a randomised control trial or similar is not possible. There is not even a reasonable comparison group of schools with which we can compare the progress of schools in England. We cannot use matched pairs, instrumental variables, difference in difference calculations, or regression discontinuity – the usual alternatives when an RCT is not feasible (Gorard 2013). The best available design for this evaluation is an interrupted time series analysis.

On first consideration this sounds relatively simple. For the poverty attainment gap, for example, we can just look at the standardised difference between the attainment of disadvantaged and not disadvantaged pupils for several years before and after 2011. If the Pupil Premium Policy has an impact on the attainment gap then we should see a change after 2011 that was not predictable from the pattern up to 2011, and cannot be simply explained by anything else.

In order to assess whether disadvantaged and non-advantaged pupils are getting more evenly mixed in schools since 2011, or whether the attainment of the two groups is growing closer, it is necessary to first identify pupils as belonging to one of these two groups – disadvantaged or not. The definition for receipt of Pupil Premium is relatively straightforward (Chapter 8). However, identifying the two groups in any year, and tracking any changes in attainment/segregation for the two groups over time, is not straightforward as it first appears.

DOI: 10.4324/9781003287353-13

There are several practical problems in implementing this time series approach. The nature of pupil assessments might change over time, and so affect the gap. The economy could worsen, pushing families just above the relative poverty threshold into relative poverty, thereby increasing the proportion of the age cohort in any year who are registered as disadvantaged. And the opposite could happen when the economy improves. The economic cycle can also affect the proportion of each age cohort attending private fee-paying schools, adding or removing their results to/from the calculation of the official poverty attainment gap. Other policy, legal, and practice changes over the same time period can also create confounds for any time series analysis of the impact of the Pupil Premium Policy.

Pupil Premium status for pupils in England is based mostly on socio-economic disadvantage as represented by FSM eligibility, but it also includes pupils living in care, and there is a smaller Service Premium for those from Service families (see Chapter 8). For most of the analyses in the ensuing results chapters, we do not use either living-in-care or having family in the armed forces as an indicator. This is because the data on these has only been systematically available in NPD for more recent years (crucially it does not predate the triggering of Pupil Premium funding in 2011). It also only represents a very small fraction of each eligible cohort.

None of the studies of the attainment gap prior to ours have taken into account confounding factors such as economic changes, new definitions of disadvantage, and non-educational policies such as the introduction of Universal Credit. Economic and policy changes matter because they will change the proportion and nature of the group officially labelled as disadvantaged in any year. And this will then alter the apparent attainment gap between pupils labelled disadvantaged and the other pupils, in a way that is unrelated to the impact of the Pupil Premium, or the work of schools. And there have been no studies at all, other than ours, which have looked at the link between Pupil Premium funding and the levels of socio-economic segregation between schools.

Put simply, as this chapter demonstrates, the standard poverty attainment gap and the extent to which disadvantaged pupils are segregated between schools can be influenced by a number of powerful factors that are nothing to with the Pupil Premium Policy. This chapter describes the problems and the Chapter 10 presents our methodological solutions to these problems.

As an aside, the Covid-19 pandemic may have further increased the number of FSM-eligible pupils in England (Carr 2021). However, this is not relevant here, other than being another example of how volatile the number of FSM-eligible pupils is. The school closures and associated disruption to school-age formal assessments in England, caused by Covid-19 from 2020 onwards, mean that our analyses only go up to 2019. Other than that our results predate, and are unaffected by, Covid-19.

Changes in the nature of assessment

The first, and perhaps the simplest, confound lies in changes to the assessment system in England, in the years before or after 2011. The many and rapid education reforms in England have made the measurement of attainment gaps over time difficult. Changes in performance measures complicate any analysis of the seeming impact of the Pupil Premium Policy because test scores are no longer so comparable over time. Where this alters the differential difficulty of assessments for different groups of pupils, then it can affect the apparent size of the official poverty attainment gap. Some, but far from all, of these issues can be addressed by using standardisation of scores and the use of "effect" sizes (as described in Chapter 10). Here we outline some of the major changes to national assessments in England from just before the onset of Pupil Premium funding onwards.

Changes to KS1 and KS2

Key Stage 1 (KS1, statutory attainment at age 7) and KS2 (statutory attainment at age 11) outcomes at primary school in England were reported nationally using a standard scale until 2015/16. This was based on levels 1 to 8, with level 2 being the expected level at age 7 for KS1, and level 4 the expected level at age 11 for KS2. Each level was sub-divided into categories a, b and c, and each category was given a notional point score. Level 1c was scored as 7, level 1b as 9, 1a as 11, 2c as 13, and so on. KS1 levels were based on teacher assessment, and KS2 levels were based more on statutory tests. Both used numeracy and elements of literacy such as reading, grammar or spelling. In some earlier years science was also included.

In 2016, levels were replaced at KS1 with descriptor categories assessed by teachers for reading, writing and maths (which can be mapped onto the old point scores with some adjustments), and scaled scores from 85 to 115 from tests (with 100 being the expected standard). Pupils who do not achieve at least the lowest scaled score on the test would be assessed by the teacher using one of the new categories for pre-KS1 standards. Teacher assessment in English was revised for 2018, with new criteria for tasks that pupils have shown that they can do. Teacher assessments for all subjects were revised for 2019. For these reasons, the analyses in the following chapters present KS1 scores (not levels) as standardised z-scores, to assist comparisons over time. In fact, z-scores are used for all such comparisons at every Key Stage, and using every indicator, for the same reasons.

There was a widespread teacher boycott of KS2 tests in 2010, and many results are missing nationally from the dataset. For these reasons, the attainment scores for 2010 should be largely disregarded in the following chapters; otherwise they may make results after 2010 look misleadingly different. This boycott may have affected other assessments in the same year as well. Until 2014, the preferred official metric used at KS2 to create the poverty attainment gap was the difference between the percentage of FSM-eligible and non-eligible pupils achieving level 4 or above in reading, writing and maths.

The KS2 curriculum changed in 2014, and the relevant age cohort faced new tests in 2016 (DfE 2016a). In 2016, KS2 students were assessed using scaled scores matched against new curriculum levels (DfE 2018b, Fellows and Barton 2018). These scores range from 80, the lowest possible scaled score, to 120, the highest possible scaled score. A scaled score of 100 or more means that the child has met the expected standard in each KS2 standard attainment test (SAT). A scaled score of 99 or less means they have not reached the expected standard.

As with KS1 we present the key results in later chapters in terms of z-scores for all years 2006 to 2019, in an attempt to even out these changes in metrics, to some extent.

Changes to KS3 and KS4

Key Stage 3 (KS, statutory assessment at age 13/14) levels were abolished in 2014/15, and so it is not possible to consider KS3 results for many years after 2011. KS3 is therefore ignored in the chapters that follow.

At KS4 (statutory assessment at age 16), unlike KS2, there is a wide range of qualification types (BTEC, NVQs, Diplomas, and so on) and subjects taken (history, arts, vocational subjects, and so on). To cope with this and provide a summary value, the National Pupil Database records a KS4 total points score based on converting all grades, subjects and types of qualification into a common aggregated total. The majority of qualifications are based on the GCSE. There is also a capped point score limited to the best 8 GCSE grades or their equivalent, which addresses the issue that some schools and families can afford to enter students into a very large number of examinations. There have been other summary measures, but only the total and the Best 8 (or "capped") equivalent are available in the same format for all years 2006 to 2019, and so these are the scores used in our analyses.

The "English Baccalaureate" (EBacc) was created in 2010. The EBacc is not really a qualification but a kind of performance measure, as schools are judged by the percentage of pupils achieving high grades in a combination of EBacc subjects (including English, maths, science, a humanity subject, and a language). Associated with this was a reduction in the number of qualifications allowed in school performance tables as alternatives to the GCSE qualifications – leading to a greater emphasis on what are considered to be traditional academic subjects. Some commentators observed that this may have had an adverse effect on disadvantaged pupils because they are more likely to take vocational subjects of a kind that do not lead to university entrance (Whitty and Anders 2014).

From 2014 to 2016 some qualifications began to be ignored in the official points scores – including where a pupil sat more than one qualification with considerable overlap, perhaps by entering through more than one awarding body, or type of qualification. Such qualifications were no longer double-counted (DfE 2016b). This can influence apparent changes in attainment, especially for disadvantaged students who might be more likely to take non-traditional qualifications.

Until 2014, the preferred official metric used to create the attainment gap was the difference between the percentage of FSM-eligible and non-eligible pupils achieving five A★-C GCSE grades (or equivalent) including English and maths at KS4, or achieving level 4 or above in reading, writing and maths at KS2. This metric was used by Hutchings et al. (2012) to evaluate the London Challenge impact on the attainment gap, for example, and by the think tank Demos (Exley 2015), the National Audit Office (2015), the Public Accounts Committee (2015), EEF (2017), and the DfE (2018a, Table 10) to look at the impact of Pupil Premium. None of their claims about changes over time take account of changes in the scale of the attainment figures from which the gap emerged – creating what is termed the "politician's error" (Gorard 1999).

Until 2016, GCSEs (and so the points scores based on them) were graded from G (the lowest pass grade) to A★ (the highest). From 2017 onwards the grades were reversed in order, an extra category added, and were presented as numbers (from 1 as the lowest to 9 as the highest). These numeric grades do not map neatly onto exact letter grades, but the DfE has created a conversion so that the new grades can also be summarised in point scores. In 2017 the results included these new grades for English and maths, and the other subjects used new grades in 2018 and 2019. There was a deliberate attempt by policy-makers to stop what they saw as annual grade inflation and so, although equivalents were stated, the KS4 scores after 2016, perhaps even after 2014, are on a different scale. As a result of the change in grading to numeric scores (9 to 1), the Best 8 scores in 2017 for state-funded schools saw a decrease from an average of 49.9 points per pupil in 2016, to 46.3 in 2017 (a drop of 3.6 points).

From 2015/2016 onwards, new metrics were used to judge attainment at KS4 – Attainment 8 (the total score in the best 8 GCSEs or equivalent, as above) and Progress 8 (the value-added progress score based on Attainment 8).

In an attempt to overcome discrepancies in the time series created by these changes in scores from 2014 onwards, DfE (2014) started using the mean rank difference between the scores of disadvantaged (FSM-eligible) pupils and the rest, for computing the poverty attainment gap. Note that they did not raise or address the economic and legal changes discussed in the following sections of this chapter. DfE (2014) claimed their new approach was intended to be resilient to changes in grading systems, such as the addition of new top grades, and resilient to changes to assessments and curricula, because the gap is only about the order of results, and not the metric used to create the order. They say in their summary –

> While there is still a possibility of reform effects which do not reflect changes in underlying ability, and regular robustness assessments of the Index would be needed, the risk of substantial non-comparability due to changes to GCSEs appears to be small.

The DfE (2018a) compared the performance of disadvantaged pupils (defined as pupils eligible for free school meals in the last six years (year 6 to year 11), looked after children and previously looked after children or in care, and the other children using a Disadvantage Gap Index (DGI). The DGI is calculated by using the average rank order of disadvantaged children and that of the others multiplied by 20. The gap is measured on a scale from 0 to 10 (or minus 10 if disadvantaged pupils performed higher). Analysis suggested that the gap decreased from 10% overall since 2011 (the year Pupil Premium was introduced) to 3.2% in 2016. We consider this approach further in Chapter 12.

All of these changes to attainment could influence the apparent level of the official poverty attainment gap, if the changes make more difference to high- or low-attaining pupils, or to poorer pupils especially. The next sets of confounding changes that we discuss are even more clearly problematic for computing the attainment gap.

Changes in related policy

Pupil Premium funding is based on pupils in each school with families in the armed forces, who have lived in care, or are eligible for free school meals (FSM). FSM-eligibility is by far the most prevalent of these, and is the only one that has been recorded consistently since at least 1992. Assessing the impact of the Pupil Premium involves comparing the attainment gap for years before 2011 when there was no Pupil Premium with later years when there was. FSM is the only measure possible to use here as a long-term criterion, because pupils living in care and Service children were not officially or consistently recorded in the NPD until relatively recently. Since 1989, the proportion of pupils registered as eligible for (or taking) FSM has varied with extremes from just above 10% of the school population to just above 20%. This is a considerable variation over time. Because FSM-eligibility varies so much over time, in some years the disadvantaged group would be much larger than in others. This section of the chapter looks at why the proportion varies so much, and what it means for calculating the attainment gap.

Although the purpose and legal definition of FSM entitlement has remained reasonably constant over decades, there have been some changes in the law. Most recently, in November 2017, all recipients of Universal Credit qualified as eligible for FSM (and so for Pupil Premium funding) which changed the number eligible, And arrangements introduced to assist the transition to Universal Credit increased the number eligible even further (Foster and Long 2020, Julius and Ghosh 2022). According to the latter authors, and as we pointed out (Gorard et al. 2019), it will become increasingly hard to tell whether apparent changes to the attainment gap are being driven by changes to the composition of the disadvantaged group or by true changes to the underlying levels of attainment (see below).

Changes in registration for FSM-eligibility

Complicating the problem of the identification of Pupil Premium pupils is missing data. Every year the NPD has shown that about 4% of pupils in state-maintained schools are missing any value for their FSM-eligibility which is therefore actually a three-way value – yes, no, and don't know (Gorard 2012). The "don't know" pupils tend to be even more disadvantaged than the FSM-eligible pupils, more likely to have special educational needs, to be in special schools, recent arrivals at school, and/or to be from some ethnic minority groups such as Travellers. They are entered for fewer formal examinations, and gain lower qualifications at every stage of education (Gorard 2018). These pupils missing FSM data are not evenly spread across the school system, but clustered both by area and school. Because they are missing data they are either ignored in the official attainment gap calculation, or treated as not disadvantaged. Either compromise distorts the results. For example, treating them as non-disadvantaged, as the DfE usually does, makes the computed attainment gap appear smaller than it should be, because these lower average attaining pupils are mixed in with the non-disadvantaged and generally higher attaining group of pupils. This reduces the average attainment for the purportedly not disadvantaged group and so makes the poverty attainment appear smaller. But ignoring the missing cases instead also artificially reduces the scale of the real gap, because the missing cases tend to be disproportionately highly disadvantaged and lower attaining.

A slight variation on this problem is where pupils are living in relative poverty but are not known to be FSM-eligible, and so are recorded as not disadvantaged (Campbell and Obolenskya 2021). This may have been made more problematic (for research) by the introduction of universal infant free school meals which reduces schools' incentives to register pupils as being eligible for free school meals.

Based on HMRC (UK tax office) household income figures, it is estimated that 11% of pupils in 2013 who ought to be entitled for FSM in terms of their household income were not officially registered (Lord et al. 2013). This represents a drop from 14% in 2012. This drop may be because schools then had more of an incentive, in terms of extra funding via Pupil Premium, to identify disadvantaged pupils among those that they taught. If so, this figure is likely to continue falling. In 2012, schools and local authorities were encouraged by the DfE to persuade parents to register for FSM, even if they did not want the meals, because of the funding the school would then attract. Registering more of these pupils in order to attract more Pupil Premium funding will reduce the amount of missing data, and so increase the recorded prevalence of disadvantage, thereby influencing the apparent poverty attainment gap.

Local authorities were also allowed to check data held by HMRC and other government offices to see if any of their pupils who qualify had not registered (Foster and Long 2020). However, some schools have reported a reluctance to chase up missing data, in case publicising the Pupil Premium upset other struggling families who were not eligible, or encouraged Pupil Premium families to insist that their child had the precise amount of funding spent on them only (Carpenter et al. 2013). The DfE has suggested that around 100,00 pupils are still not registered for free schools despite being eligible in theory, and that this leads to schools missing out on a total of £93m per year in Pupil Premium (Speck 2019). More research is needed on how these pressures have changed the numbers registered, but it is understandably difficult to gain permission to access HMRC data, and even more difficult to link it to individual pupil data, within the constraints now created by UK GDPR (individual data protection) legislation.

Changes in economic indicators

As well as being an indicator of relative disadvantage, eligibility for FSM can also tell us something about the state of the economy in England. As shown clearly in Chapter 10, the proportion of pupils registered as eligible for FSM in England is highly sensitive to things like economic recessions. The proportion of pupils registered as FSM-eligible obviously changes as economic conditions change. In general, a growth in GDP reduces the proportion of FSM-eligible pupils, and a reduction in GDP leads to more FSM-eligible pupils.

This complicates comparisons over time because the FSM-eligible group in some years will contain pupils who would not have been eligible in prior years, and *vice versa*. Any change in the definition or prevalence of those known to be disadvantaged will change the apparent attainment gap even without any actual change in attainment. The number and proportion of pupils registered for FSM will affect the measurement of the attainment gap, and any assessment of how segregated disadvantaged pupils are, between areas and schools. Ignoring the kinds of factors discussed so far will make local and national changes in the economy, law, and handling of FSM, appear as changes in the attainment gap (even though the actual level of attainment for either group might remain constant). But taking them into account makes the calculation of a simple attainment gap between disadvantaged pupils and the rest more complex than is usually portrayed in a comparison just between those known and not known to be disadvantaged in each year (or area or school).

Use of private schools

Similar things also happen when economic or educational changes lead to more or fewer families in England using the minority of private schools. The roughly 6.5% of private pupils are not generally included in official estimates of the attainment gap based on the National Pupil Database, and are not often FSM-eligible. If the pupils on the cusp of using private schools are, on average, slightly higher attaining than the remaining pupils in the state-funded system, then in years when they are in the state-funded system they will be included in the calculations, and so the attainment gap will appear larger. The official gap will appear smaller in years when such pupils are in private schools and omitted from the gap calculation. Again this is nothing, directly, to do with the impact of Pupil Premium funding. It will just confuse the conclusions drawn from a simple time series analysis (such as those cited in Chapter 8, including all official versions of the attainment gap in England).

The duration of poverty

The main reason why the volatility of numbers in the proportion of each annual cohort registered as FSM-eligible matters is that more marginally disadvantaged students have higher average attainment than the most disadvantaged students, as this section illustrates.

To recap, receipt of Pupil Premium is mostly defined on the basis of eligibility for FSM, which is a categorical measure based on something like a threshold of income for entitlement. This means that there is variation within the FSM-eligible category (and outside it), both in terms of how far below that threshold any pupil's family income is, and for how long pupils have been FSM-eligible during their school career. This has important implications for computing the attainment gap at local and school levels, as will be illustrated.

Figure 9.1 shows that the attainment gap ("effect" size), for FSM-eligible pupils compared to pupils never eligible for FSM, is substantially greater for every year that pupils are known to be eligible for FSM, during their schooling up to the end of KS4. For those interested, the methods and dataset are explained in Gorard (2018). The "effect" size for pupils only eligible for a year or two, compared to never-FSM, is around -0.5 but it is -1 for pupils who are eligible throughout their schooling, again compared to never-FSM. In fact, the difference in the "effect" size between the longest-term and shortest-term FSM-eligible pupils is greater than the difference between short-term FSM-eligible pupils and those who were never eligible. Put simply the temporarily disadvantaged pupils are more like the never disadvantaged than they are to the long-term disadvantaged.

Therefore, simply dividing pupils into currently or EverFSM6 as disadvantaged and not or never-FSM as not disadvantaged in order to calculate the attainment gap ignores important variation in levels of disadvantage relating to attainment, and will

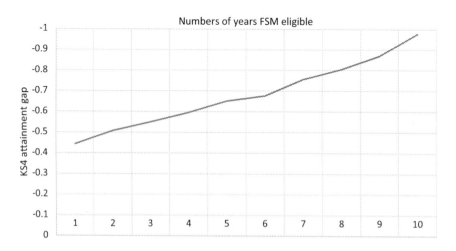

FIGURE 9.1 Comparison of attainment gap by years FSM, England, KS4 capped points, 2015 cohort

give a misleading picture of the true attainment gap in any school or local area. Put another way, the attainment gap should be expected to be lower in areas, schools, or years, with more FSM pupils known to be only temporarily eligible, because this sub-group will have higher average attainment than other FSM-eligible pupils.

The link between the duration of poverty and attainment shows that comparing eligible with non-eligible pupils using raw scores, as in many studies looking at the attainment gap, can be misleading. Yet this is the kind of evidence that the Pupil Premium Awards used in praising or rewarding schools for having low or declining Pupil Premium attainment gaps (Gov.uk 2016). The Pupil Premium Awards also used the value-added Progress 8 scores, as a supposedly fairer measure of pupil progress and school performance, which is purportedly independent of the raw level of attainment. What Figure 9.2 shows is that the problems in Figure 10.1 cannot be avoided by using value-added or Progress 8 scores. Despite value-added being intended to be independent of the underlying raw-scores, it is not (nor is it stable, Gorard 2018). This flaw in value-added scores creates a situation where the only group that has average positive value-added progress in England consists of those pupils who are never eligible for FSM. All groups of pupils ever eligible for FSM for any amount of time have negative progress scores, and these scores are substantially lower for every year that a pupil is known to be eligible (just as with Attainment 8). The longest term disadvantaged pupils have very low progress scores indeed, and therefore years, areas or schools with proportionately more of this group of pupils will tend to have lower progress, and therefore create higher attainment gaps as well.

Just like pupils with missing data, the longer-term FSM-eligible pupils with much lower average attainment and progress are not evenly spread between areas and schools (and will also vary over time with the economy). For example,

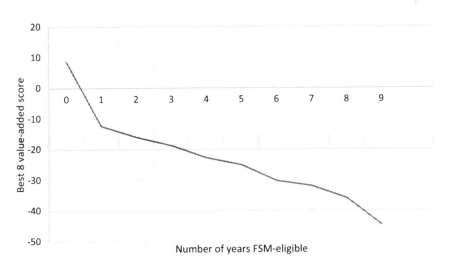

FIGURE 9.2 Comparison of Best 8 value-added scores by years FSM, England, KS4 capped points, 2015 cohort

EverFSM6 pupils in the relatively poor authority of Middlesbrough tend to have been eligible for over four times as long as the supposedly equivalent EverFSM6 pupils in relatively rich Buckinghamshire (Gorard 2018). This example from our prior work has now been picked up the by the Social Mobility Commission to illustrate the mistakes being made in policy (Speck 2019). Since average attainment is lower for long-term FSM-eligible pupils, this means that simply computing an attainment gap between Ever- and never-FSM pupils will seriously misrepresent the challenges faced by poorer areas, and by schools with poorer intakes, and the chances of their pupils making good progress. The Pupil Premium Awards, London Challenge, Ofsted reports and many other real-life judgements are being inadvertently unfair here. The DfE (2019) advice to schools, that they should compare their disadvantaged pupils' performance with the national average for non-disadvantaged pupils, would lead to the same misrepresentations.

Figure 9.3 shows what a difference this issue could make to the results. Using the EverFSM6 attainment gap at a local level, it is clear that local authorities in England with high attainment gaps tend to have fewer EverFSM6 pupils who have only been eligible for one year in their school, and proportionately more long-term FSM-eligible pupils. This is because these temporarily eligible pupils, while labelled disadvantaged, have higher average attainment than pupils with longer-term eligibility (as shown above).

If this factor is not taken into account, the official attainment gaps will partly or perhaps mostly represent the pre-existing duration of relative disadvantage in any area, school, or year, rather than something directly attributable to the schools or teachers there. Therefore, to be fair, comparisons between schools, regions, and

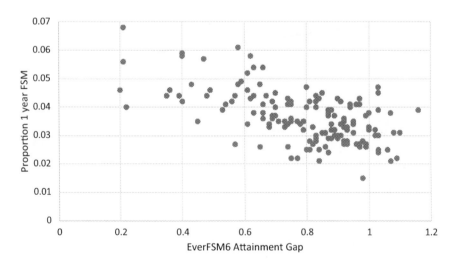

FIGURE 9.3 Comparison of local authority EverFSM6 attainment gap by proportion of pupils FSM-eligible for only one year, KS4 capped points, 2015

years should take into account the depth and duration of poverty of the pupils involved.

Another factor that is ignored in presentations of the attainment gap at any level of aggregation over time is the proportion of pupils in any area or year not in state-maintained schools. If the pupils attending private provision are not included in the attainment gap calculation, because it is not clear whether they are FSM-eligible or not, this may distort the result. Figure 9.4 shows that there is wide variation in private schooling by local authority (from 0 to almost 50% of local pupils). These figures will also vary from year to year and with the economy. If the kinds of pupils attending private school tend to have higher than average attainment for their area, then the skimming effect will make it look as though areas with high private school use have lower attainment gaps. The relatively high attaining private pupils will not appear in the non-disadvantaged group, artificially reducing the average for that group, and so reducing the apparent gap compared to disadvantaged pupils. The picture in the graph is messy, but it shows that the areas with the highest gaps do tend to have low private school attendance, and several areas with especially high private attendance have relatively low attainment gaps.

A simple regression model, using only three variables (the proportion of pupils in each local authority attending private schools, the proportion FSM-eligible for one year, or for two years only) explains about 55% (R= 0.74) of the variation in the EverFSM6 attainment gaps between local authorities. But none of the these explanatory variables is a measure of attainment, so this suggests that well over half of the variation in the official attainment gap is *nothing* to do with how well equivalent disadvantaged pupils are doing in any area or school. Nor is it to do with the impact of any educational initiative or the efforts of teachers. And there may

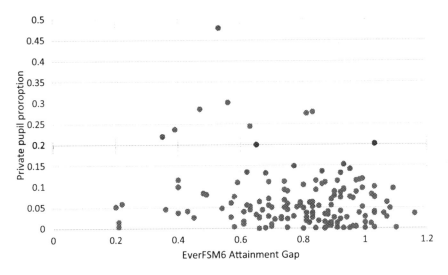

FIGURE 9.4 Comparison of local authority EverFSM6 attainment gap by proportion of pupils in private schooling. KS4 capped points. 2015 cohort

be other factors than these that are also not measures of attainment that can help explain these gaps. The coefficients for the model are in Table 9.1, showing that the size of the attainment gap in any area is negatively related to the local number of privately educated and shorter-term FSM-eligible pupils. Each factor tends to reduce the apparent size of the gap – either by removing pupils with a higher average attainment from the calculation, or by treating everyone who ever registered for FSM as being equally disadvantaged. The same kind of differences would occur across years, as the economy changes, and none of these differences would be to do with changes in measures of attainment, or with the impact of the Pupil Premium for example.

Using the simple, commonly used, EverFSM6 attainment gap, official results suggest that the poverty gradient is the lowest in most of the London and inner-London authorities, and highest in areas further north like Lincolnshire, Cumbria, Hartlepool, and Cheshire. Using instead the residuals from this new regression model as an estimate for the attainment gap, accounting for private school intakes and shorter-term disadvantage does not completely transform the picture. But it does change the emphasis considerably. For example, both Leicestershire and Warrington have relatively high raw attainment (EverFSM6) gaps, higher than average for England, and might be considered therefore to be failing their disadvantaged pupils to some extent (Table 9.2, column 1). Leicestershire has fewer short-term than long-term disadvantaged pupils, and about the same proportion of private pupils as the national average (6%). Warrington has fewer short-term disadvantaged pupils and almost no private pupils. Both areas therefore end up with substantial negative residuals from the regression model, meaning that their attainment gaps can actually be considered as much lower than the overall average for England, once

TABLE 9.1 Non-attainment predictors of the local attainment gap

Coefficients	EverFSM gap
Percentage of private pupils	−0.11
Percentage only FSM-eligible for one year	−0.22
Percentage only FSM-eligible for two years	−0.33

TABLE 9.2 Examples of authorities from London and the north of England, 2015

Local authority	EverFSM6gap	Percentage only one year FSM	Percentage only two years FSM	Percentage in private school	Residual attainment gap
Leicestershire	0.83	0.04	0.03	0.06	−0.98
Warrington	0.84	0.04	0.03	0.00	−0.83
Westminster	0.47	0.06	0.06	0.29	+1.06
Lambeth	0.62	0.06	0.06	0.06	+1.56
ENGLAND	0.82	0.05	0.04	0.06	0.00

these other explanatory variables are accounted for. There is therefore an argument that, far from failing their disadvantaged pupils, both authorities might be doing relatively well in this regard, given more precise information about the nature of their local school intakes.

Westminster and Lambeth in central London, on the other hand, show the opposite pattern. Both have low raw attainment gaps, noticeably lower than the national average of 0.82, but considerable short-term, as opposed to long-term, disadvantage. Lambeth has 6% of pupils eligible for only two years, compared to 4% nationally, and 3% in Warrington. In addition, Westminster has very high private school attendance (29%). Once these factors are accounted for, the residuals suggest that the attainment gaps for these two London boroughs are actually higher than might be expected from the raw figures, and well above the average for England. Taking long-term disadvantage seriously matters. The illustrative analysis here is based on only one year group, and is used to make the key point. It is crucial to take variation over time and place into account because of its link to the attainment gap. A much more detailed and longer-term analysis appears in Chapter 12.

A substantial part of the apparent change in the official attainment gap in any year, area or school is linked to factors such as changes in assessments, private school attendance, the economy, changes in the definition of poverty, other policy changes, and the duration of poverty. None of these are strictly anything to do with attainment levels, but they become confounding variables unless accounted for. These problems arise whether the gap is based on current FSM-eligible pupils and the rest, or pupils who have ever been FSM-eligible and the rest. If anything, the EverFSM indicator is even more sensitive to such concurrent non-educational changes than simple eligibility is.

All prior attempts at evaluating the impact of Pupil Premium funding have been found wanting in several crucial respects (Gorard et al. 2019). There have been no evaluations of the impact on socio-economic segregation between schools, until a study of primary schools by Gorard et al. (2021). There have been some studies of the attainment gap which only looked at the picture since 2011, when Pupil Premium started, and so they cannot genuinely say that any trend was not already in existence beforehand. None of the prior studies of the attainment gap have taken into account confounding factors such as economic changes, new definitions of disadvantage, non-educational policies such as the introduction of Universal Credit, and changes in the nature and scoring of assessments. These changes matter because they will change the proportion and nature of the group officially labelled as disadvantaged in any year. And this will then alter the apparent attainment gap between pupils labelled disadvantaged and the rest in a way that is unrelated to the impact of the Pupil Premium, or the work of schools.

Analyses like those of Exley (2015,) National Audit Office (2015), Public Accounts Committee (2015), EEF (2017), Education Policy Institute (2017), and Social Mobility Commission (2019), outlined in Chapter 8, are misleading because what they are portraying as changes in the attainment gap are at least partly just changes in the economy (plus other changes in policies and assessment).

We need a better way of assessing the attainment gap, and so judging the impact of Pupil Premium funding. In order to evaluate Pupil Premium impact directly we need a definition of disadvantage that can be used for the analysis of all cohorts, including those before and after 2011. We also need a dataset that contains common variables and measures available over all of that time. We need to identify a sub-set of pupils who would have been eligible for Pupil Premium funding in any era, even when there was no funding, and under any legal, economic, or other conditions. The solution is presented in the next chapter.

References

Campbell, T. and Obolenskya, P. (2021) *No such thing as a free lunch? Exploring the consistency, validity, and uses of the 'Free School Meals' (FSM) measure in the National Pupil Database*, CASE Paper 225, Centre for Analysis of Social Exclusion, London School of Economics, https://sticerd.lse.ac.uk/dps/case/cp/casepaper225.pdf

Carpenter, H., Papps, I., Bragg, J., Dyson, A., Harris, D., Kerr, K., Todd, L. and Laing, K. (2013) *Evaluation of Pupil Premium*, London: DfE, http://dera.ioe.ac.uk/18010/1/DFE-RR282.pdf

Carr, J. (2021) More than 1 in 5 pupils on free school meals after Covid surge, *Schools Week*, 17/6/21, DfE: 1 in 5 pupils now eligible for free school meals (schoolsweek.co.uk).

DfE (2014) Measuring disadvantaged pupils' attainment gaps over time (updated): Statistical Working Paper, https://assets.publishing.service.gov.uk/government/uploads/system/uploads/attachment_data/file/398657/SFR_40_2014_Measuring_disadvantaged_pupils_attainment_gaps_over_time__updated_.pdf

DfE (2016a) *Key Stage 2 assessment and reporting arrangements*, https://www.gov.uk/guidance/2016-key-stage-2-assessment-and-reporting-arrangements-ara/section-2-key-changes#:~:text=2.1%20New%20testsandtext=There%20will%20only%20be%201,replaced%20with%20an%20arithmetic%20test

DfE (2016b) Revised GCSE and equivalent results in England, 2014 to 2015: Quality and methodology information, https://assets.publishing.service.gov.uk/government/uploads/system/uploads/attachment_data/file/493295/SFR01_2016_QualityandMethodology.pdf

DfE (2018a) *Revised GCSE and equivalent results in England, 2016 to 2017*, SRF 01/2018, https://assets.publishing.service.gov.uk/government/uploads/system/uploads/attachment_data/file/676596/SFR01_2018.pdf

DfE (2018b) *National curriculum assessments at key stage 2 in England*, 2018 (revised), https://assets.publishing.service.gov.uk/government/uploads/system/uploads/attachment_data/file/764135/Key_stage_2_text_v6.pdf

DfE (2019) *Pupil premium: funding and accountability for schools*, https://www.gov.uk/guidance/pupil-premium-information-for-schools-and-alternative-provision-settings?utm_source=2e5c52b2-c00c-4268-82c5-e809ff49194dandutm_medium=email andutm_campaign=govuk-notificationsandutm_content=immediate#measuring-the-effectiveness-of-your-approach

Education Endowment Foundation (2017) *The attainment gap*, https://education endowmentfoundation.org.uk/public/files/Annual_Reports/EEF_Attainment_Gap_Report_2018_-_print.pdf

Education Policy Institute (2017) *Closing the gap? Trends in educational attainment and disadvantage*, Closing the Gap? Educational Attainment and Disadvantage - Education Policy Institute (epi.org.uk).

Exley, S. (2015) Pupil premium 'has failed to close attainment gap', thinktank claims, *Times Educational Supplement*, 4, 9, 15.

Fellows, T. and Barton, M. (2018) *Spotlight on Disadvantage*, National Governance Association, https://www.nga.org.uk/About-Us/Campaigning/Spotlight-on-Disadvantage.aspx

Foster, D. and Long, R. (2020) *The Pupil Premium*, House of Commons Library Briefing Paper 6700, file:///C:/Users/pjxx25/Downloads/SN06700.pdf

Gorard, S. (1999) Keeping a sense of proportion: the "politician's error" in analysing school outcomes, *British Journal of Educational Studies*, 47, 3, 235–246.

Gorard, S. (2012) Who is eligible for free school meals? Characterising FSM as a measure of disadvantage in England, *British Educational Research Journal*, 38, 6, 1003–1017.

Gorard, S. (2013) *Research design*, London: SAGE.

Gorard, S. (2018) *Education policy: Evidence of equity and effectiveness*, Bristol: Policy Press.

Gorard, S., Siddiqui, N. and See, B.H. (2019) The difficulties of judging what difference the Pupil Premium has made to school intakes and outcomes in England, *Research Papers in Education*, 36, 3, 355–379.

Gorard, S., Siddiqui, N. and See, B.H. (2021) Assessing the impact of Pupil Premium funding on primary school segregation and attainment, *Research Papers in Education*, https://doi.org/10.1080/02671522.2021.1907775

Gov.uk (2016) *Pupil Premium Awards*, Pupil Premium Awards finalists announced - GOV.UK (www.gov.uk).

Hutchings, M., Greenwood, C., Hollingworth, S., Mansaray, A. and Rose, S. with Minty, S. and Glass, K. (2012) *Evaluation of the City Challenge programme*, https://www.gov.uk/government/uploads/system/uploads/attachment_data/file/184093/DFE-RR215.pdf

Julius, J. and Ghosh, A. (2022) *Investigating the changing landscape of pupil disadvantage*, Slough: NFER, Investigating the changing landscape of pupil disadvantage - NFER.

Lord, A., Easby, J. and Evans, H. (2013) *Pupils not claiming Free School Meals*, DfE, https://assets.publishing.service.gov.uk/government/uploads/system/uploads/attachment_data/file/266339/DFE-RR319.pdf

National Audit Office (2015) *Funding for disadvantaged pupils*, London: National Audit Office.

Public Accounts Committee (2015) *Funding for disadvantaged pupils*, HC 327, Funding for disadvantaged pupils report publication - Committees - UK Parliament.

Speck, D. (2019) Schools lose £93m a year in pupil premium, TES, 7/6/19, https://www.tes.com/news/exclusive-schools-lose-ps93m-year-pupil-premium

Social Mobility Commission (2019) *State of the Nation 2018–19*, https://assets.publishing.service.gov.uk/government/uploads/system/uploads/attachment_data/file/798404/SMC_State_of_the_Nation_Report_2018-19.pdf

Whitty, G. and Anders, J. (2014) (How) did New Labour narrow the achievement and participation gap? *LLAKES Research Paper*, 46, 1–57. http://www.llakes.org

10

EVALUATING PUPIL PREMIUM POLICY THROUGH CONSIDERATION OF LONG-TERM DISADVANTAGE

Introduction

This chapter explains in more detail how our new research on the impact of Pupil Premium funding addresses the problems identified in Chapter 9. It starts by looking at possible indicators of disadvantage, and continues to the methods section, describing the datasets used and outlines the major analyses to be presented in Chapters 11 to 14. The chapter ends by showing how the confounds described in Chapter 9 can be largely removed when analysing changes over time or place, by focusing only on the pupils known to have been permanently disadvantaged over their entire school career. These pupils would presumably have been labelled as disadvantaged in any era or year, and under any economic or policy circumstances.

Is FSM eligibility a good indicator of disadvantage?

Under current conditions in England it is not possible to use actual measures of household income. HMRC have repeatedly refused access to us and other researchers. Where household income is available from other datasets such as Next Steps, the quality is poor and over half of the cases are missing data (Siddiqui et al. 2019). In the US, free and reduced-price lunch status has been found to capture elements of educational disadvantage that IRS-reported household income data do not (Thurston et al. 2018). The equivalent in England is eligibility for free school meals, an official and verifiable measure of low income (often state benefits) that is recorded by all state-funded schools. Our previous work has shown that, despite concerns about its threshold nature (Taylor 2018), it is the most suitable proxy most easily and fully available in England for household income (Gorard 2018, Siddiqui et al. 2019). At the end of this chapter, we show how it can be improved for the purposes of this book.

DOI: 10.4324/9781003287353-14

We need to identify pupils who would have been eligible for Pupil Premium funding in any era, had it been available. For the age cohort ending KS4 in 2019, used as an example, 0.7% came from designated Service families. Very, very few of these Service families were long-term poor, and only 0.003% had been living in state care. Whatever issues Service families face they represent a different problem for education to the long-term poor. This indicator is therefore ignored hereon in this book.

Around 0.9% of the age cohort had lived in state care for the past six months. Of those living in care, 10.4% of looked after pupils were also long-term poor (higher than the overall 4.4% of the age cohort who are long-term poor pupils, see below). This confirms that the two issues are linked to some extent, and that the small number of looked after pupils are represented in the disadvantaged group used in our subsequent analyses. We occasionally present snapshot figures including for those in care but not labelled as being long term poor, to illustrate that they make no overall difference to the main findings being reported. However, the living-in-care data has not been recorded consistently enough over time, unlike free school meal status, to be used to create a strong time series.

Methods

National Pupil Database

Our main data source is the combined National Pupil Database (NPD), held by the DfE, for the Key Stage 4 (KS4) cohorts completing their KS4 school years at age 16 in 2005/06 to 2018/19, and for the KS2 cohorts completing KS2 over the same period. All pupils in state-maintained schools are included, regardless of school type, including Pupil Referral Units (PRUs) and special schools, but only those in the correct age band for that school year. Only the variables that appear for all year cohorts are used, for consistency. The records, containing some sensitive data, were accessed via a secure area set up by the Office for National Statistics (ONS).

Table 10.1 shows the total number of all pupils in each cohort with reasonably complete records. The latest year is 2019 because there was no statutory attainment data for England in 2020 (or 2021). There is some variation over time, with a growth in numbers for the most recent years.

There was a widespread boycott of KS2 assessment in 2010, and this seems to have affected more than the recorded KS2 scores. The values for 2010 are therefore sometimes out of alignment with 2009 and 2011, and so should be treated with great caution. The 2006 primary cohort is the earliest we can use with reasonably complete information about their prior KS1 characteristics and outcomes. Even so, this cohort has incomplete information about their FSM status in the first year. We could ignore this year, and start with 2007. However, given that the 2010 attainment data is affected by the boycott, this would give us only three clear cohorts before 2011 (2007–2009). All analyses have been run without 2006 as well. The results are substantively the same.

TABLE 10.1 Number of pupils in each cohort

Cohort	Total in cohort (valid NPD records)
End of KS4 in 2006	56,1257
End of KS4 in 2007	55,5097
End of KS4 in 2008	56,6604
End of KS4 in 2009	55,2397
End of KS4 in 2010	53,5453
End of KS4 in 2011	53,1924
End of KS4 in 2012	51,9179
End of KS4 in 2013	51,5745
End of KS4 in 2014	55,2848
End of KS4 in 2015	57,0562
End of KS4 in 2016	58,3981
End of KS4 in 2017	59,7466
End of KS4 in 2018	61,7272
End of KS4 in 2019	64,2189

New and derived indicators

Using the variables in NPD we created new ones, and we also added some new data. From outside the NPD, we added data for each year on GDP and GDP annual growth (ONS 2020), as an indicator of economic change over time, and on annual private school attendance from DfE (2020). We also grouped the cases into nine official Economic Areas, and 148 local authorities.

We created new values from the existing datasets, including:

- how many years each pupil had been FSM-eligible for, for each year and Key Stage
- the number of years that knowledge of FSM-eligibility was missing, for each year and Key Stage
- a new category of missing, for any key categorical variables that had missing values
- a new flag variable representing "missing or not", for any key numeric variables that had missing values
- the national rank of each pupil in terms of their points scores at every Key Stage
- standardised z-scores from points scores for every Key Stage
- value-added residuals for each pupil based on simple regression models linking their KS1 and KS2 scores, and their KS2 and KS4 scores (the models for each cohort predicted later attainment with R at or above 0.7)
- a Gorard Segregation residual for each pupil.

Our approach to missing data means that no cases were lost to analysis, and so the N is each table is the same as reported in Table 11.1. It also means that the missing data can be used in any analysis to assess if its "missingness" affects the substantive findings (Gorard 2020). The amount of data was so small relative to the dataset that it made no discernible difference.

Analyses

Segregation residuals were computed as the number of FSM-eligible pupils in an individual's school, divided by the number of FSM pupils in all maintained schools in England. From this we subtracted the number of all pupils in the schools, divided by the number of pupils in all schools. We use these residuals to assess national, regional and local authority figures for the segregation of long-term socio-economic disadvantage between schools (Gorard 2018). The sum of these absolute values for any area is termed the (Gorard) Segregation Index.

We ranked all pupils in each year by their KS2 and KS4 average points, and computed the difference between the average rank for long-term disadvantaged pupils and the rest. This is the approach used by the DfE from 2014 onwards, which is claimed to overcome abrupt changes in metrics, caused by changes in grading and assessment formats. For each year we also computed the percentage of long-term disadvantaged pupils who were at or above the average national score for KS2 or KS4 points.

We have run separate analyses looking at the pupils who were FSM-eligible only for the six years at primary school (Gorard et al. 2021), or for the five years at secondary school (Gorard 2022), which allowed us to use KS4 cohorts 2006 to 2019 for all 11 years at school. This book presents the first set of results for these most stably disadvantaged comparison groups, and so provides the most accurate assessment so far of whether Pupil Premium had any impact on between school segregation or the poverty attainment gap.

Where appropriate, including for attainment gaps and when comparing the segregation index between two sub-groups of disadvantaged pupils, we created "effect" sizes, computed as the difference between the means for disadvantaged groups and the rest, divided by their overall standard deviation.

To aid comparison, all effect sizes are presented in line graphs as positive (absolute) values. This becomes clearer when explained in the text. Strictly, line graphs are not the most appropriate for 14 years of data points, but they are more readable. Readers just have to remember that the graphs are based on 14 points and are not continuously measured. Times series graphs are presented for GDP change over time, the percentage of long-term FSM-eligible pupils, and the percentage in private schools and so excluded from NPD and the official attainment gaps. These are used as context for changes in segregation and the attainment gap.

For some analyses, the data for all 14 cohorts was combined into one dataset representing 7,895,115 pupils. This large dataset was used to create summaries of the characteristics of long-term disadvantaged pupils. We looked at the characteristics of permanently disadvantaged pupils in terms of their sex, ethnicity, and special educational need status (SEN). SEN status was aggregated with codes A (school action), P (school action plus) and S (statemented) treated as SEN, and N (no SEN) or missing as not SEN. This was to create larger cell sizes, especially for comparisons. ONS/GDPR rules do not allow the publication of findings based on small cell sizes. We use only the major ethnic groups – Asian, black, Chinese, mixed, other, and white – for the same reason. Of course, it would have been preferable to have results for separate south Asian groups such as Indian and Pakistani origin, and for separate black groups such as black African and black Caribbean origin. These sub-groups may well have produced disparate findings. We looked at the gaps in mean segregation indices and KS2 score outcomes, for each of these groups. We also looked at the same outcomes in terms of the Economic Areas of England.

In order to assess the impact of the Pupil Premium policy more formally, two multivariate regression models were created – with outcomes represented by the annual attainment gap, and average segregation of long-term disadvantage pupils. The predictor variables were entered in two blocks. The first block consisted of GDP change, the percentage of long-term FSM-eligible pupils, and the percentage of pupils in private schooling. The second block was one variable, representing whether any year was before (up to 2010) or after (2011 onwards) the introduction of Pupil Premium.

Further information comes from the School-Level Annual Schools census (SLASC) available via the DfE. This dataset is valuable here, despite being at school- rather than individual-level, because it is easily available for many years. It includes the proportion of pupils eligible for FSM in each school, and the proportion of pupils registered as having special educational needs (SEN), for each year from 1989 onwards. These are used to create indices of national segregation (the extent to which FSM or SEN pupils were clustered in schools with others like them) using the Gorard Segregation Index (GS) (see above, and Gorard 2009, 2018). National figures are also computed from SLASC for each year, including the proportion of SEN and FSM-eligible pupils in the system. From 1989 to 1992, eligibility for FSM was not registered, and so actual take-up of FSM is used instead for those years, and dealing with this kind of abrupt change of measurement is one of the advantages of using GS (Gorard and Taylor 2002).

The results are used in two further regression models. These models had the GS index for FSM-eligibility and SEN as outcomes, from 1989–2018. The predictors were the prevalence of FSM (or SEN) in each year, annual changes in GDP, and whether the year was before 2011 or not (when PP was introduced). Each model has two steps, with the second step adding only whether the year was before 2011 or not. These analyses were used to assess the possible impact of PP, net of economic and other factors. The school-level figures do not have the detail of the individual level data from 2015/16 (above), but they do span nearly 30 years and so they directly address issues of change over a longer time.

Stability of permanent disadvantage

In order to assess any educational (rather than economic or other) changes over time caused by Pupil Premium funding, it is important to compare outcomes for a non-disadvantaged group with a disadvantaged group that would have been identified as such in any era. The group of pupils in any cohort who have been permanently FSM-eligible by the time they reach the end of KS4 is relatively stable over time (the lower line in Figure 11.1). This group of just over 4% of all pupils, who would go on to complete KS4 in 2019, is largely unaffected by economic, political and legal changes. Therefore, we argue, they would have attracted Pupil Premium funding had it been available in any year, and under any conditions. The much larger group of temporarily FSM-eligible pupils (the middle line in Figure 10.1), who would have been eligible for some years while at school but not others, is much less stable. In the nine years for which we have full cohort data, their percentage ranges from around 24% to over 28%. This reflects changes in the legal definition of FSM-eligibility and in the economy (as discussed above). It means that some or even most of the annual variation in segregation and attainment gaps, as officially calculated, is attributable to changes in the proportion of the cohort attracting Pupil Premium, and nothing to do with the work of pupils, teachers and schools, or the impact of Pupil Premium funding. This temporary group cannot be used to make a fair assessment of the poverty attainment gap over time.

The even larger group of pupils who have never been FSM-eligible by the end of KS4 (the top line in Figure 10.1) is a mirror image of the proportion of temporarily eligible (because the small group of always eligible is so stable over time). Therefore, this group is not a suitable comparator for assessing the poverty

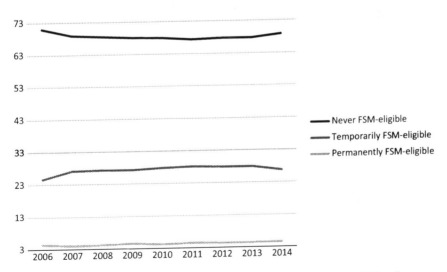

FIGURE 10.1   Percentage of all pupils of each FSM status, 2006 to 2014 KS2 cohorts

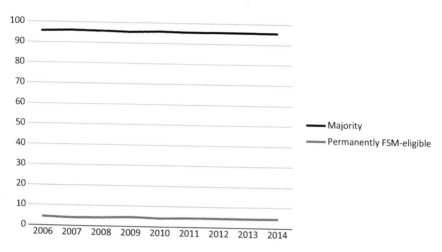

FIGURE 10.2 Percentage of all pupils of each FSM status, 2006 to 2014 KS2 cohorts

attainment gap either, because its size is affect by factors beyond schools' control and largely unrelated to Pupil Premium funding. Comparing the never eligible pupils to all others is misleading because both groups will then have a size linked to economic and other non-educational changes. However, comparing the always eligible to only the never eligible is equally problematic, because the latter group also changes so much. Instead, what we did, as suggested in Gorard et al. (2019), was to compare the always eligible to everyone else. This creates two groups for comparison that are fairly stable over time (Figure 10.2). The top line combines the never- and the only temporarily eligible pupils. It means that we can look at the impact of Pupil Premium funding largely unaffected by changes in legal definitions and economic fluctuations, because the smaller group would be labelled disadvantaged in any era and under any circumstances.

Of course, adding the temporarily disadvantaged group to the majority comparator does not imply that they are not disadvantaged at all, or should not attract Pupil Premium funding. Nor does it suggest that the attainment gap should always be computed in this way. It will reduce the apparent size of the "real" gap. But it is a device used here for the purposes of scientific research, to create a fair comparison group for assessing policy impact, given that an experiment or similar evaluation is no longer possible.

This is the empirical basis for the argument that long-term disadvantage is a better definition for use in assessing changes in segregation and the attainment gap over time. The size of this long-term group is substantially less affected by legal, economic and other changes over time, than the temporary or never eligible groups. If segregation and/or the attainment gap has improved for this long-term disadvantaged group in the Pupil Premium era specifically then that would be an indication of impact that could not be so easily explained by changes in the proportion (and so the average characteristics) of pupils labelled FSM-eligible in any year.

A recent study by Hutchinson et al. (2020) took our advice on this, and looked at outcomes for what they called "persistently disadvantaged" pupils. They compared results for these long-term FSM-eligible pupils with the results of pupils who had never been eligible (excluding from analysis those who had ever been eligible in the past six years, but not persistently so). This is an advance on prior work, but as shown above it still has the problem of sensitivity to legal, economic and other changes over time that are nothing to do with schools, teachers, or attainment. It is safer to compare a stable disadvantaged group (however defined) with the equally stable group of all of the remaining pupils in any cohort.

Hutchinson et al. (2020) also excluded non-standard schools like PRUs from their figures, even though PRUs are part of the Pupil Premium scheme, and the number of pupils in PRUs can also change over time according to policy, practice and the prevalence of pupils needing PRUs. This affects the apparent attainment gap because potential PRU students tend to have lower average attainment, and be more likely to be disadvantaged. In years when more of such pupils are in mainstream settings their scores will increase the estimated gap. The same kind of thing happens over time with intakes to special schools and hospitals.

Table 10.2 illustrates further why the focus on length of disadvantage in this chapter is important, and crucially why it is important for segregation as well as the attainment gap (as argued in Chapter 9). There is a clear difference, of course, between the average attainment scores for the never FSM-eligible pupil group (zero years at secondary school spent as FSM-eligible) and the rest. But there is also a clear gradient of scores linked to the number of years a student has been known to be FSM-eligible by the end of KS4. The students facing the longest-term disadvantage tend to have the worst attainment scores, by some margin. They have lower total and capped point scores, and they even have worse value-added progress scores (which are meant to be independent of raw-score attainment). They also attend schools with the highest clustering of long-term disadvantage students like them (higher segregation residuals). So, in years when more pupils become temporarily FSM-eligible, the apparent attainment gap between FSM-eligible and the rest (the official gap) will tend to reduce, because these short-term disadvantaged pupils have higher average attainment than the core group of long-term disadvantaged

TABLE 10.2 Outcome measures by length of FSM-eligibility, all years 2006–2019 combined

Years FSM-eligible by KS4	KS4 Total points z-score	KS4 Capped points z-score	KS4 VA Residual	KS4 Segregation
0 years	+0.15	+0.16	+0.10	−0.02
1 years	−0.40	−0.43	−0.29	+0.04
2 years	−0.50	−0.54	−0.37	+0.05
3 years	−0.57	−0.63	−0.43	+0.06
4 years	−0.64	−0.70	−0.48	+0.09

N = 7,895,115

pupils. If this is not taken into account, changes in the apparent attainment gap due to economic events or changes in the law will be mistakenly attributed to the work of schools. This problem appears in all previous analyses (above) including official figures.

Conclusion

The analyses in this book are focused on the most stably disadvantaged group of pupils, who were known to be FSM-eligible for every year while at school, or phase of schooling. This group – the long term FSM-eligible – would presumably have been labelled disadvantaged in any year and under any economic conditions. This group is then compared to all of the other pupils in the cohort, including those who had been temporarily FSM-eligible. In the absence of a randomised control trial (RCT) or similar, this is perhaps the strongest way to test the impact of Pupil Premium, unaffected by economic and legal changes. We are glad to note that other commentators are now citing our work, and proposing the use of long-term measures of disadvantage (e.g. Pattaro et al. (2019). Having outlined the methods used, the book now moves to the important substantive findings, starting with the impact of Pupil Premium funding on socio-economic segregation between schools.

References

Gorard, S. (2018) *Education policy: Evidence of equity and effectiveness*, Bristol: Policy Press.

Gorard, S. (2020) Handling missing data in numeric analyses, *International Journal of Social Research Methods*, 23, 6, 651–660.

Gorard, S. (2022) What is the evidence on the impact of Pupil Premium funding on school intakes and attainment by age 16 in England?, *British Educational Research Journal*, What is the evidence on the impact of Pupil Premium funding on school intakes and attainment by age 16 in England? – Gorard –British Educational Research Journal – Wiley Online Library.

Gorard, S. and Taylor, C. (2002) What is segregation? A comparison of measures in terms of strong and weak compositional invariance, *Sociology*, 36, 4, 875–895.

Gorard, S., Siddiqui, N. and See, B.H. (2019) The difficulties of judging what difference the Pupil Premium has made to school intakes and outcomes in England, *Research Papers in Education*, 36, 3, 355–379.

Gorard, S., Siddiqui, N. and See, B.H. (2021) Assessing the impact of Pupil Premium funding on primary school segregation and attainment, *Research Papers in Education*, https://doi.org/10.1080/02671522.2021.1907775

Hutchinson, J., Reader, M. and Akhal, A. (2020) *Education in England: Annual report 2020*, Education Policy Institute.

Pattaro, S., Bailey, N. and Dibben, C. (2019) Using linked longitudinal administrative data to identify social disadvantage, *Social Indicators Research*, 147, 865–895.

Siddiqui, N., Boliver, V. and Gorard, S. (2019) Assessing the reliability of longitudinal social surveys of access to higher education: The case of the *Next Steps* survey in England, *Social Inclusion* Special Issue, 7, 1, https://doi.org/10.17645/si.vXiX.1631

Taylor, C. (2018) The reliability of free school meal eligibility as a measure of socio-economic disadvantage: Evidence from the millennium cohort study in Wales, *British Journal of Educational Studies*, 66, 1, 29–51.

Thurston, D., Pharris-Ciurej, N., Penner, A., Penner, E., Brummet, Q., Porter, R. and Sanabria, T. (2018) Is Free and Reduced-Price Lunch a valid measure of educational disadvantage? *Educational Researcher*, http://journals.sagepub.com/doi/abs/10.3102/001 3189X18797609

KEY FINDINGS FOR PUPIL PREMIUM POLICY

11

CHANGES IN SOCIO-ECONOMIC SEGREGATION BETWEEN SCHOOLS

Introduction

We now turn to the results of our analysis of the impact of Pupil Premium funding. Our first set of substantive results concern the extent to which long-term disadvantaged pupils are clustered in schools with other long-term disadvantaged pupils. As might be expected, long-term disadvantaged pupils tend to go to schools in England with more pupils like themselves. And the not-disadvantaged and only temporarily disadvantaged pupils tend to go to schools with more not-disadvantaged and only temporarily disadvantaged pupils than would be expected if these characteristics were independent of schools' allocation of pupil places. The extent to which pupils eligible for free school meals (FSM) are clustered together in schools with others like them is termed socio-economic segregation between schools. We discussed the dangers and disadvantages of such segregation in Chapter 2. And we explained in Chapter 8 that one of the main purposes of Pupil Premium funding in England was to try to reduce the level of poverty segregation between schools. In this chapter, we assess the changes over time for cohorts arriving in school from 1989 and reaching the end of Key Stage 4 in 2019. Further details are available in Gorard et al. (2019, 2021) and Gorard (2022a, 2022b).

Segregation and the duration of poverty

In Chapter 9 we showed how attainment and the poverty attainment gap were strongly linked to the duration of individual student disadvantage. Students who had been disadvantaged for the longest had the lowest average attainment, and areas or schools with the most such students had the highest poverty attainment gaps. Using a dataset of 8 million pupils for all KS2 cohorts from 2006 to 2019 combined,

DOI: 10.4324/9781003287353-16

TABLE 11.1 Key Stage scores, value-added, and segregation linked to length of known disadvantage

	Never FSM-eligible	FSM-eligible for 1 year	FSM-eligible for 2 years	FSM-eligible for 3 years	FSM-eligible for 4 years	FSM-eligible for 5 years
KS1 Points	16.2	14.7	14.4	14.2	13.9	13.5
KS2 Points	51.9	55.3	47.8	51.9	49.9	42.9
KS2 VA Residual	0.04	−0.06	−0.07	−0.07	−0.10	−0.13
FSM segregation	−0.04	0.05	0.06	0.07	0.09	0.12

we now show that a similar picture emerges for the segregation gap and that the achievement and segregation gaps are linked in this respect.

Table 11.1 shows the average test scores, value-added progress scores, and FSM segregation residuals for pupils nearing the end of primary school, separated into those never labelled disadvantaged, and those classified by the number of years at primary school known to be disadvantaged. It is clear that outcomes are worse with every year of known disadvantage at school. The gap between never FSM-eligible pupils and rest is large, with only the never-eligible having a positive value-added score for KS2 (i.e. all of the other pupil groups make differentially negative average progress at primary school). Nevertheless, the temporarily disadvantaged pupils have scores that are closer to the never disadvantaged than they are to the always disadvantaged. These are very different groups, and should not be treated the same in standard calculations of the attainment gap. Using current FSM status or EverFSM6, as happens in official analyses and even much academic research, does not provide a fair picture of the situation.

More importantly for this chapter, only the never-eligible pupil group generally attend schools with fewer than their fair share of disadvantaged pupils (segregation). As with attainment, the position worsens with every year of disadvantage. The most disadvantaged pupils are attending schools with the most pupils who are like them, and the "effect size" compared to all other pupils (never and only temporarily disadvantaged) is a massive 0.97. This worrying concentration of pupils with potential problems for teaching and learning in specific schools (and all of the damage noted in Chapter 2) is then linked to the attainment gap (see Chapter 13).

Longer-term school-level segregation

A key question for this book is whether the Pupil Premium is linked to a reduction in SES segregation between schools. The question faces many of the same problems as the attainment gap – in terms of defining the two groups (disadvantaged and the rest) in a consistent way over time. However, as with the attainment gap, it may be possible to make some progress in addressing the segregation question by considering first the other determinants of segregation (as explained, for example, in Gorard 2015). This is possible using SLASC data as far back as 1989.

The possible determinants discussed in Chapter 2 include diversity of school types, rules for allocating school places, and local residential segregation. But all of these are relatively minor in impact. For any indicator of disadvantage the biggest determinant of segregation is its prevalence. All other things being equal, the scarcer any pupil characteristic is the more segregated between schools it has been shown to be.

For example, segregation by Special Educational Need (SEN) has fallen nationally since 1989 (starting at near 0.5 in Figure 11.1). It reached a low of around 0.22 in 2006, and then began to rise slightly again. This trend correlates at $R = -0.86$ with the increase and the plateau of pupils identified as having SEN in mainstream schools over that historical period (Gorard 2018). The changes are probably partly the result of a policy of inclusion from the 1990s onwards in which special schools were closed and many students with statements of special needs were included in mainstream schools. They are also probably partly the result of increasing identification and labelling of special needs leading to more SEN pupils in total, especially with non-visible challenges or disabilities such as dyslexia. If so, then the changes are less to do with more general changes in the way mainstream school places were allocated.

Segregation between schools by poverty (FSM) has a more cyclic pattern over time, moving up and down several times over 26 years (from a high of around 0.35 in 1989 to a low of about 0.28 in 2018 (the top line in Figure 11.2). This cyclic pattern means that the (linear) correlation between prevalence and segregation is

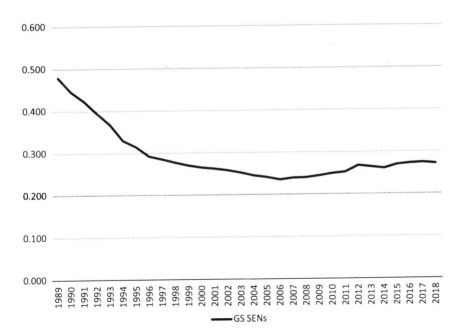

FIGURE 11.1   Segregation by SEN and FSM, England 1989 to 2018

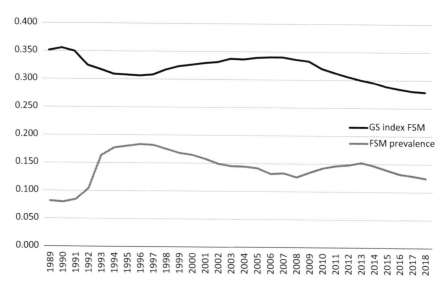

FIGURE 11.2 Segregation by FSM, and FSM prevalence, England 1989 to 2018

Note: Figures are for FSM takeup until 1992 and for FSM eligibility thereafter.

lower for FSM (R = -0.41) than for SEN (-0.86). But there is just as strong a pattern, at least until 2011. Figure 12.2 (the lower line) also shows the trend for the prevalence of FSM pupils in England, defined as the proportion of pupils known to be eligible for free school meals. This figure has also varied in an up and down manner, being lowest at around 8% in 1989 and peaking at around 18% in 1996, and again at around 15% in 2014.

More importantly, and as first reported in Gorard et al. (2019), the two trends mirror each other closely over time. When the proportion of FSM-eligible pupils is lower, as it was in 2008 just before the economic recession, the segregation index representing how evenly they are distributed between schools is higher. Put simply, when there are fewer poor children they tend to appear more clustered in specific schools. Conversely, when the proportion of poorer children is higher, as in 1996, then segregation tends to appear lower. As with SEN, this does not mean that school places are necessarily being allocated differently or that pupils are moving schools. It may simply mean that at a time of economic recession, some pupils not previously considered as being disadvantaged are now being labelled as eligible for FSM – which, as already shown in Chapter 9, is an important factor to take into account both in assessing segregation and computing the "attainment gap" over time. The changes in prevalence are related to the economy and GDP growth; there was an economic recession after 2008, for example. It has been observed before that prevalence of poverty is a likely determinant of poverty segregation (e.g. Gorard et al. 2003, Gorard 2015).

It means that at a time of economic recession, some pupils not previously considered as being disadvantaged are labelled as eligible for FSM-eligible, where their

families have lost income or may even have lost their job and require state benefits. And the reverse happens when the economy recovers. Family income might
increase, and people on benefits could find jobs or better jobs. The changes in FSM-
eligibility may also be related to changes in operational definition, other policies
such as the introduction of Universal Credit, and any push to register more pupils
as FSM-eligible including the incentive to register created by the Pupil Premium
funding. All of these possible confounds were discussed in Chapter 9.

However, from 2012/2013, Figure 11.2 shows that this mirroring pattern of
prevalence and segregation ceased, for the first time for all of the years for which
data is available. Both the prevalence of FSM-eligibility and its clustering within
schools have been declining ever since. By 2018, segregation reached its lowest
figure since the recording of eligibility started in 1992.

This could be an indication that the Pupil Premium introduced in 2011 started
to change how strongly the poorer pupils were clustered in schools, and that the
policy is therefore being successful in these terms. This suggestion is strengthened
by the fact that whatever is happening with FSM-eligibility after 2011 is not also
happening with SEN (where segregation is still going up slightly). The change for
FSM is not a general decrease of clustering of pupils of specific types because it is
not happening for SEN (or other indicators such as ethnicity, or having a first language other than English).

However, without taking account of legal changes and other factors in some
way, and using more detailed individual-level data, it is too early to conclude
that something unusual did indeed occur after 2011, that was linked to the Pupil
Premium policy.

Overall though, the cycle of FSM prevalence appears to be key to understanding
changes in FSM segregation (and the attainment gap) over time. This means that
prevalence must be taken into account when attempting to judge the impact of the
Pupil Premium policy on how evenly poor pupils are distributed between schools.
We are looking for a change in segregation, net of changes in FSM prevalence. This
is modelled as follows.

Modelling school-level segregation

Table 11.2 summarises two similar regression models, each with two steps. The
first model has an estimate of FSM segregation for each year as the predicted outcome variable, based on the GS index (see methods). The second model has SEN

TABLE 11.2 R values from two stepped regression models predicting between-school
segregation, 1989–2018

	GS for FSM	GS for SEN
GDP change and FSM prevalence	0.42	0.55
PP era or not	0.89	0.60

TABLE 11.3 Coefficients from two regression models predicting between-school segregation, 1989–2018

	GS FSM	GS SEN
FSM prevalence	−0.48	-0.57
PP era or not	−0.79	-0.24

segregation as the predicted variable, and this is used to check for spurious patterns in the FSM segregation result. SEN pupils already received extra funding and were not specifically addressed by Pupil Premium, and therefore the pattern for them should be different to that for FSM, if Pupil Premium were effective. Of course, the two indicators are correlated to some extent (poorer children are more likely to have SEN), and so we might expect some similarities in their changes over time. The initial predictors for each model are FSM prevalence and GDP changes for each year, in the first step, and then whether the Pupil Premium policy is in effect (i.e. whether the year is before 2011 or not) in a second step.

In the first model, the majority of variation is explained by whether the year is before or after 2011 and the onset of Pupil Premium funding. This suggests again that Pupil Premium may have had an impact on the level of between-school segregation. The suggestion is confirmed by the second model, in which Pupil Premium should be less relevant, and where appropriately very little variation is explained in the second step. Having accounted for economic factors, the years after the Pupil Premium do indeed seem to have bucked the historical trend for segregation, however measured, and as portrayed in Figure 11.2.

Nevertheless, in both models a considerable amount of variation is predictable from the economic/prevalence factors in Step 1. This must be taken into account when comparing trends in segregation and other possible determinants. For completeness, Table 11.3 shows the coefficients for each model. In each model FSM prevalence is related to the outcome. Using GDP change if FSM prevalence is available does not improve the model at all, so it is omitted as an explanatory variable here. Net of these influences, and as also shown in the R scores from Table 11.2, there is still a role for whether the date is after the Pupil Premium was launched or not. The link to the Pupil Premium is much greater for FSM segregation than for SEN (although, as noted, the two variables do correlate to some extent).

Primary school segregation

The rest of this chapter is based on individual pupil estimates of segregation, using much more detailed data which has only been available in official datasets since around 2006.

Looking first at the difference ("effect" size) between the gap in the average segregation between schools attended by FSM-eligible pupils and their peers, when they first arrive at school, Figure 11.3 shows that the gap remains about the same

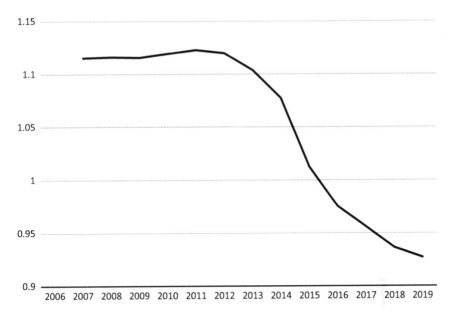

FIGURE 11.3 Change in "effect" size for the gap between FSM-eligible pupils and the rest, FSM Segregation Year 1, 2006–2019

from 2006 to 2011 (just over 1.1). This is a large "effect" size. Poorer children are certainly attending schools with more social segregated intakes than the majority of children do. The difference is substantial, and worthy of policy attention. These are not necessarily long-term disadvantaged children. The figures here are simply for those FSM-eligible or not in Year 1 at primary school (aged around 5).

Then, from 2011 onwards, for as long as we have figures, pupils arriving in the first year of primary school are clearly less clustered by poverty every year (as suggested already by Figure 11.2). This would be what would be expected if the Pupil Premium funding, introduced in 2011, was linked to a change in the "attractiveness" of disadvantaged pupils to schools, when new school places are being allocated. This change occurs at exactly the right time for it to be Pupil Premium impact, and is otherwise unexpected according to the prior trend (for as many years as are available). There is also a feasible model of how this "impact" could take place.

The impact of the funding incentive on Year 1 school places could have been immediate. The 2011 entry cohort, for the first time, brought additional funding to their schools if the pupils were registered as coming from families living in poverty. Coming from a poor family is not necessarily an indication that a child will be harder to teach than average – the link between SES and attainment at school is only ever on average. This means that schools could take more poor children in Year 1, gain extra funding and face no more problems in teaching the new cohort than any previous ones. Alternatively, where some disadvantaged pupils are harder to teach, the new funding can provide the resources to cope with this better, making such pupils "less unattractive". Finally, as noted in Chapter 8, for the first time changes to the law on allocating school places allowed FSM-eligibility to be a criterion used by admission authorities when deciding how to allocate over-subscribed places. The combined effect of all three factors could help explain the otherwise dramatic changes in Figure 11.3.

It has been noted before that when a change of policy is linked to changes in segregation, the biggest changes occur while each school is filling up with pupils arriving since the change in policy (Gorard 2015). Perhaps something similar is happening here. By 2017, a full six cohorts had arrived in their schools during the Pupil Premium era, and the graph shows some signs of flattening out.

Turning now to a consideration of longer-term disadvantage, Figure 11.4 shows the trend for the segregation gap between Year 6 pupils who had been recorded as FSM-eligible for every year at primary school, and their peers who had only been temporarily, or never, eligible. This analysis addresses at least part of the confounding nature of changes in prevalence, because long-term disadvantage is more stable over time, than simple eligibility or not (see Chapter 10).

In most respects, Figure 11.4 illustrates the same trend as Figure 11.3. The segregation gap was volatile within a narrow range from 2006 to 2010, and then declined annually from 2011 onwards. By 2019, the extent to which long-term FSM-eligible pupils were differentially clustered in schools with others like them was at a historic low. This is good news, and this drop in segregation may well then be linked to a decrease in the attainment gap for the later pupils (Chapter 12), and to a number of other benefits for the individuals and the school system as a whole (see Chapter 2).

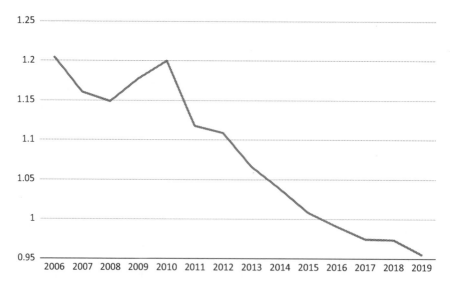

FIGURE 11.4 Change in "effect" size for the gap between long-term disadvantaged pupils and the rest, FSM Segregation by KS2, 2006–2019

The key drop here, as with Figure 11.3, is uniquely associated with the Pupil Premium era starting in 2011. However, it is not quite as easy to see how any incentive effect from Pupil Premium funding would have affected the composition of long-term disadvantaged Year 6 pupils in primary schools almost as quickly as it may have done with Year 1 pupils. The majority of pupils arrive in their primary school for Year 1. We might therefore expect to see the most impact from the Pupil Pupil on segregation (if there is any) to show up for Year 6 pupils in 2016 (five years later).

However, the gaps illustrated in Figure 11.4, of around 1 to 1.2, are based on residuals that are the percentage of disadvantaged pupils that would have to change schools for all schools to have their precise share of disadvantaged pupils. Given an average cohort size of around 580,000 pupils, and perhaps only 4% labelled as being disadvantaged throughout their primary school (see Chapter 10), this means we are talking about the possible exchanges involving only 23,000 pupils nationally, in addition to those happening at the end of primary school.

Previous studies have found figures of around 4.4% of all pupils making a non-enforced change of school in any academic year (Machin et al. 2006). This figure is larger in London, perhaps as high as 6% and higher for disadvantaged pupils (Sharma 2016). So, every year from Year 1 to Year 6 a disproportionate number of disadvantaged pupils might have changed schools. In the Pupil Premium era, these changes of schools would have involved the new regulation that disadvantage can be used as a factor when deciding on a school place, and any incentive effect of the Pupil Premium funding.

Given the relatively small number of long-term disadvantaged pupils who would have had to exchange schools to produce the decline in Figure 11.4 (and others), it is feasible (but not proven) that the drop in the segregation gap started for _every_ year group in 2011.

Finally in this section, we look at the changes over time for the very long-term disadvantaged – those who would go on from their primary school to be FSM-eligible for the full 11 years from Years 1 to 11. We can only present figures up to the 2014 cohort because for this analysis we need to know what happened to the Year 6 pupils in their subsequent secondary schooling phase. This analysis, while using fewer cohorts, is the least sensitive to economic and other changes over time (see Chapter 10).

For pupils in primary school in Year 6, the gaps in the extent of socio-economic segregation between permanently disadvantaged and the rest was again relatively stable 2006–2010. It then declined quite dramatically for the cohort that reached the end of KS2 from 2011 onwards (Figure 11.5). These pupils would have been the first year groups to do so after the Pupil Premium policy in 2011.

So, in summary, it is clear that the segregation of long-term disadvantaged pupils from their peers declined specifically and unexpectedly (in terms of historical trends) in primary schools in England from 2011 onwards. It is possible to envisage this happening, at least partly, as a consequence of the Pupil Premium, when pupils start school or move between schools. We will consider in later chapters what other explanations there could be.

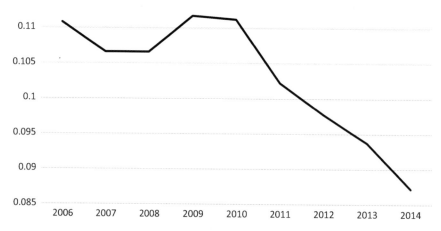

FIGURE 11.5 Change in "effect" size for the gap between permanently (11 year) disadvantaged pupils and the rest, FSM Segregation by KS2, 2006–2014

Secondary school segregation

We now present the same kinds of figures for secondary schools as for primary (above). Figure 11.6 illustrates the gap in segregation between secondary schools for FSM-eligible pupils when they first arrive in Year 7. This is when the majority arrived in their secondary school. There is some volatility from 2006 to 2010 (with a peculiar spike in 2008), and then a steady decline from 2011 onwards. The gap in segregation for Year 7 school intakes is at the lowest level ever recorded by 2019. As with the primary school intakes, it is feasible that secondary school intakes started to desegregate almost as soon as disadvantaged pupils were known to bring additional

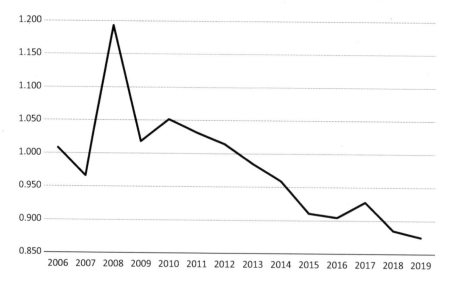

FIGURE 11.6 Between school segregation of Year 7 FSM-eligible pupils, KS4, 2006–2019

funding to schools, so making them "less unattractive to schools" to use the official phrasing. Most school leaders have reported that the new funding immediately affected their activities, although only a few felt that it had affected their admissions (Ofsted 2012). However, Freedman and Horner (2008) envisaged a kind of unconscious bias in the process of allocating school places, even within the existing guidelines. And wanted to give "schools located in more disadvantaged communities the resources to attract middle-class parents" (p.9). In 2014, the government published a revised admissions code that permitted all admission authorities in England to prioritise disadvantaged children in their admission arrangements (Foster and Long 2020). The Pupil Premium funding may have provided the incentive for such prioritisation. As with primary schools then, these changes in segregation could therefore be the result of the Pupil Premium, making poorer pupils seem "less unattractive" both consciously and unconsciously.

The pattern of decline in the segregation gap is not quite as clear for the long-term disadvantaged pupils (who had been FSM-eligible for every year while at secondary school) who reached the end of KS4 in Year 11. The gap does drop after 2011 to reach a historic low in 2019, but the drop is somewhat erratic (Figure 11.7). The picture from 2006 to 2011 is flatter than in Figure 11.6 but still slightly erratic. As with Year 6 pupils in primary schools, the decline might be considered rather soon to be a reaction to a 2011 policy given that these figures are for the cohorts in Year 11. However, everything that has been said about changes in school place allocation criteria, possible bias, the incentive effect of new funding, and the rate of school turnover by pupils, make the onset of Pupil Premium a possible explanation here. We will consolidate all of the evidence first and then discuss the possible explanations further in later chapters.

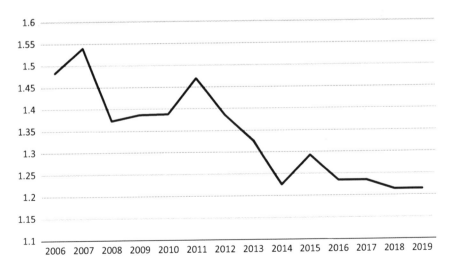

FIGURE 11.7 Between school segregation of Year 11 long-term disadvantaged pupils, KS4, 2006–2019

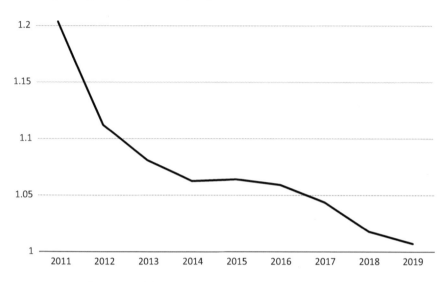

FIGURE 11.8 Change in "effect" size for the gap between permanently (11 year) disadvantaged pupils and the rest, FSM Segregation by KS4, 2011–2019

Figure 11.8 shows the segregation gap in Year 11 for pupils known to be FSM-eligible for all 11 years over their combined primary and secondary schooling period – the permanently disadvantaged. Because the figures track back to the start of each pupil's schooling, cohorts are only available from 2011 onwards, and so none predate the Pupil Premium policy. However, the figure does show that since 2011 this most chronically disadvantaged group are less likely each year to be clustered in schools with others like themselves, compared to the remaining pupils. The Pupil Premium era is linked with a clearly continuing national decline in the gap in the economic segregation of pupils between schools at KS4, just as was happening at KS2.

Conclusion

Whether looked at in terms of pupils arriving for their first year in primary or secondary school, or those reaching the final year of KS2 or KS4, and looking at pupils who were permanently labelled as disadvantaged, there is a clear overall pattern. The segregation gap between FSM-eligible pupils was higher in the period 2006 to 2010 than it was later, and the gap declined in a substantive way from 2011 onwards. The most recent year of data, 2019, shows the segregation gap at its lowest ever recorded level, for all phases. As discussed, these changes could be explained by the onset of Pupil Premium funding.

These results are analysed further after a consideration of the equivalent results for the attainment gap over time, in the next chapter.

References

Foster, D. and Long, R. (2020) *The Pupil Premium*, House of Commons Library Briefing Paper 6700, file:///C:/Users/pjxx25/Downloads/SN06700.pdf

Freedman, S. and Horner, S. (2008) *School funding and social justice*, Policy Exchange, https://www.policyexchange.org.uk/wp-content/uploads/2016/09/school-funding-and-social-justice-oct-08-3.pdf

Gorard, S. (2022a) Segregation and the attainment gap for permanently disadvantaged pupils in England, *Educational Review*, https://doi.org/10.1080/00131911.2021.2007055

Gorard, S. (2022b) What is the evidence on the impact of Pupil Premium funding on school intakes and attainment by age 16 in England? *British Educational Research Journal*, What is the evidence on the impact of Pupil Premium funding on school intakes and attainment by age 16 in England? – Gorard – British Educational Research Journal – Wiley Online Library.

Gorard, S. (2015) The complex determinants of school intake characteristics, England 1989 to 2014, *Cambridge Journal of Education*, 46, 1, 131–146.

Gorard, S. (2018) *Education policy: Evidence of equity and effectiveness*, Bristol: Policy Press.

Gorard, S., Siddiqui, N. and See, B.H. (2019) The difficulties of judging what difference the Pupil Premium has made to school intakes and outcomes in England, *Research Papers in Education*, 36, 3, 355–379.

Gorard, S., Siddiqui, N. and See, B.H. (2021) Assessing the impact of Pupil Premium funding on primary school segregation and attainment, *Research Papers in Education*, https://doi.org/10.1080/02671522.2021.1907775.

Gorard, S., Taylor, C. and Fitz, J. (2003) *Schools, Markets and Choice Policies*, London: RoutledgeFalmer.

Machin, S., Telhaj, S. and Wilson, J. (2006) *The mobility of English school children*, Centre for the Economics of Education, Estimating Pupil Mobility with PLASC Data (lse.ac.uk).

Ofsted (2012) *The Pupil Premium: How schools used the funding*, https://www.gov.uk/government/publications/the-pupil-premium-how-schools-used-the-funding

Sharma, N. (2016) *Pupil mobility*, A London Council members briefing, Pupil Mobility Member Briefing.pdf.

12

CHANGES IN THE ATTAINMENT GAP

Introduction

As explained in Chapter 8, one of the purposes of Pupil Premium funding in England was to try to reduce the "gap" in attainment at school between poor (disadvantaged) children and the rest. In this chapter, we present our next set of substantive results looking at the changes over time in the poverty attainment gap, for cohorts arriving in primary school from 2006 and for those reaching the end of Key Stage 4 in 2019. The poverty attainment gap is defined here (unless otherwise stated) as the difference between the average attainment scores for disadvantaged pupils and their peers, standardised by dividing the difference by the overall standard deviation of both sets of scores.

Key stage 1 outcomes

KS1 assessments in literacy and maths have taken place at the end of Year 2 in primary schools up to 2019. These are teacher assessed, which may be influenced by genetic and other differences between children unrelated to their work at school (Morris et al. 2018), and may not be as robustly validated and moderated as occurs with many subsequent assessments at school. But they can provide a good indication of children's level of skill in these areas so far. In 2020 they were replaced by a new Reception Baseline Assessment, which is another reason why our analysis ends in 2019.

Figure 12.1 shows a pattern over time for the KS1 attainment gap (for pupils who would be disadvantaged for all six years while at primary school) that is very similar to changes in the segregation gap in primary schools (see Chapter 11). The figures show a period of slight volatility from 2006, with no overall pattern until 2010. There was a widespread boycott of KS assessments by teachers in 2010, and

DOI: 10.4324/9781003287353-17

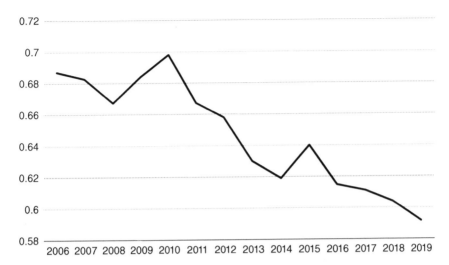

FIGURE 12.1 Change in "effect" size for the gap between long-term disadvantaged pupils and the rest, KS4 Points, 2006–2019

so the result (a sudden apparent growth in the gap) for this year may not be directly comparable with others. Nevertheless, after 2010 there is a substantial decline in the attainment gap, with the gap at its lowest ever level in 2019. As with the pattern for segregation, this is consistent with the era of Pupil Premium funding.

This improvement in equity occurred at the same time as an improvement in KS1 scores for both groups, which is important. It represents levelling up, not down. The changes to the nature of assessment (Chapter 9) may have created a blip in 2015, but after that the annual decline in the attainment gap continues.

Looking at this long-term disadvantaged group, who would presumably have attracted Pupil Premium funding in any era, whatever the conditions in place, it is clear not only that they have improved their level of attainment but also that they are slowly catching up with those pupils who have only been temporarily FSM-eligible and with the pupils who have never been eligible. For KS1 cohorts, it looks as though the Pupil Premium funding era is linked to success in meeting its two objectives – reduced segregation of school intakes, _and_ a lower poverty attainment gap.

KS2 outcomes

The picture for the attainment gap at KS2, based on pupils who were FSM-eligible for all six years at primary school, is less clear than at KS1 and for the segregation gap at the same stage (Figure 12.2). The attainment gap in 2019 is substantially lower than in 2006, indeed much lower than in 2010 or before (again the figures for 2010 are very likely to have been affected by the teacher boycott of KS2 tests in that year). There is a sudden drop in the attainment gap after 2010 and the introduction of Pupil Premium funding, just as with KS2 segregation, and the attainment gap at

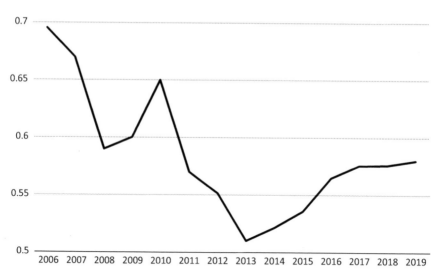

FIGURE 12.2 Change in "effect" size for the gap between long-term disadvantaged pupils and the rest, KS2 Points

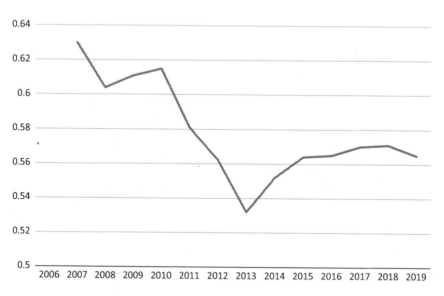

FIGURE 12.3 Change in ranking gap between long-term disadvantaged pupils and the rest, KS2 Points

KS1. However, the gap grew in 2014, and then again from 2016 with the changes made to KS2 assessment and scoring (Chapter 9). After that time there is no clear trend of improvement. In fact, the gap continues to rise.

Figure 12.3 is based on the approach used by DfE (2014) and subsequently, to try to overcome abrupt changes in assessment (see Chapter 9), by comparing the average ranking of attainment for disadvantaged pupils and the rest, rather than computing a difference between scores. It shows that this approach does not overcome the change in difficulty in 2014. Figure 12.3 is very similar in trajectory to Figure 12.2. Maybe the true gap has started to decline again. The use of ranking is an interesting idea but it has not apparently solved any problems.

Looking at the picture for the permanently FSM-eligible pupils, who would go on to be labelled disadvantaged for every year up to Year 11, clarifies the earlier period somewhat (Figure 12.4). There was a sudden drop in the attainment gap in 2008, and then again in 2012/13. The earlier drop is clearly unrelated to the Pupil Premium policy. The drop from 2012 could be linked to the Pupil Premium. The curriculum for KS2, and so the nature of the assessment, began changing in England in 2014, and this could account for the attainment gap flattening out for the most recent cohort (for whom we have 11 years of school data).

By the time pupils reach KS2 it is also possible to try and compute the progress they have made since KS1, and compare the average progress made by disadvantaged and other pupils. Progress here is measured in terms of predictions of KS2 scores based on prior KS1 scores. The value-added residual is the difference between the average KS2 score predicted for every individual's KS1 score, and their actual KS2 score. The gap in the average residuals for long-term disadvantaged pupils and the rest declined markedly from 2006 to 2012, plateaued for one year, and then started rising again (Figure 12.5). In all important respects, the picture after 2013 is the same as for the raw-score attainment gap, whether expressed as an effect size, or in terms of ranking.

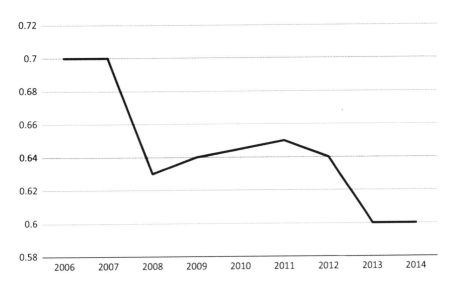

FIGURE 12.4 The attainment gap between pupils FSM-eligible for 11 years, and the rest, KS2 points, 2006–2104

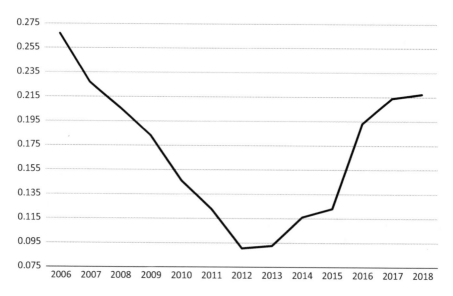

FIGURE 12.5 Change in "effect" size for the gap between long-term disadvantaged pupils and the rest, KS2 VA Residual

The changes to assessment in 2014 and again in 2016 may be linked to the reversal of a historic trend in Figure 12.5. Now, the most disadvantaged groups face an increasing attainment gap, with long-term FSM-eligible pupils making less and less relative progress at primary schools. Insofar as value-added scores are meaningful, they suggest that the reforms to scoring for KS2 have disproportionately affected long-term disadvantaged pupils, and undone much of the progress in reducing the attainment gap since 2006. Two government policies, of reducing the attainment gap and preventing the "inflation" of exam results, appear to be working against each other here. We revisit this issue in Chapter 15.

However, as has been shown many times previously, value-added scores do not really work. They are meant to be independent of the raw scores on which they are based, and to portray progress instead. In fact, they are heavily correlated with raw scores (Gorard 2010). They are also very unstable.

Also, because progress is measured between one Key Stage and the next, these KS2 value-added scores may be worsened by the very improvement noted for KS1 (above). It is a further flaw of the whole value-added model that more progress at one stage of education must translate into less progress, on average, at the next stage. Amusingly, using "value-added" models to estimate the "effects" of teachers on their students' height, Bitler et al. (2021) find results as convincing for teacher effects on height as on student attainment. This is, of course, ridiculous, because teachers cannot plausibly have an impact on height. The model shows that value-added attainment results are really nothing of the sort, and so could be dangerously misleading.

KS4 outcomes

The attainment gap as KS4 has so far had a different pattern to segregation at any stage of schooling and to the attainment gap at primary school level (Figure 12.6). Historically the gap had been falling from 2006 to 2013, as assessed in terms of both total and capped point scores (best 8 GCSE scores or equivalent). The gap in total point scores, influenced by how many examinations pupils are entered for, and so by the need for funds to pay for subject entries, is always higher than for capped point scores. Put simply, the poorer pupils who are recorded as FSM-eligible for their five years at secondary school are entered for fewer qualifications on average. However, the trends over time are the same. The remainder of this chapter considers only capped point scores.

The decline in the attainment gap 2006–2013 was historical, and predated Pupil Premium funding. The gap grew suddenly in 2014 at around the same time as new scores for KS4 were devised, grades were changed, and marking became harder. It dropped again after 2015 when the first Pupil Premium era cohort in secondary schools reached the end of KS4.

One explanation for the abrupt rise in 2014 lies in the changes to assessment at KS4 at that time. To explore the possible impact of the changes to assessment at KS4 in 2014, we did several additional analyses. The first analysis used the DfE (2014) approach of expressing the attainment gap as the difference in the mean rank of the KS4 scores for disadvantaged and other pupils for each year. This, the DfE suggested, would even out changes caused by the nature of the assessment. Here, we used long-term disadvantaged pupils and others so that the results would be less affected by economic and legal changes over time than the DfE model

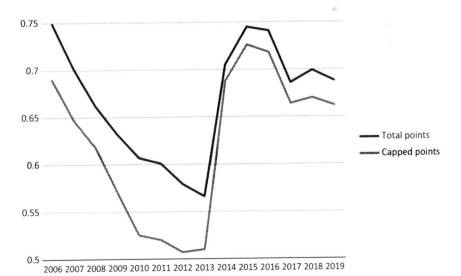

FIGURE 12.6 Change in "effect" size for the gap between long-term disadvantaged pupils and the rest, KS4 Points, 2006–2019

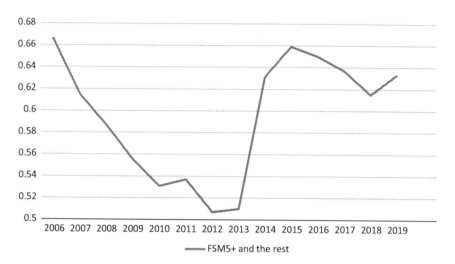

FIGURE 12.7 Change in ranking gap between long-term disadvantaged pupils and the rest, KS4 Capped Points, 2006–2019

(Figure 12.7). The result shows that the attainment gap is stubborn and that, whatever this ranking approach does, it does not overcome the changes in KS4 assessment from 2014 onwards. The pattern in Figure 12.7 is effectively the same as in Figure 12.6.

The next attempt to look at the attainment gap net of changes in assessment and scoring involved the percentage of long-term disadvantaged pupils who scored above the national mean for all pupils. In a sense, this is the inverse of the figures above. If disadvantage were unrelated to attainment then around 50% of long-term disadvantaged pupils would be above (and below) the national mean score at KS4. By 2012 the figure had grown from 36% to 42% of long-term disadvantaged pupils gaining qualification better than the national mean (Figure 12.8). This is a reasonably impressive figure for equity, and perhaps something that should have been treasured more. But from 2014 this figure plummeted to only 25% before rising again annually after 2017. Something very serious seems to have happened in and after 2013/14 that undid all of the previous progress and more, making the system more polarised by disadvantage than it had ever been at KS4.

Over and above the confusion created by the 2014 to 2016 changes to assessments, there are now signs that the attainment gap, looked at in this way, may be reducing somewhat for cohorts completing their secondary education.

As with KS2, we can also consider the gap in the progress made by both groups of pupils from KS2 to KS4 (Figure 12.9). Value-added residuals are supposedly independent of raw-score attainment, and so the gap would be zero if KS4 attainment was solely attributable to KS2 attainment or to noise, and unrelated to poverty. In fact, the gap shows a sudden drop after 2010, too early to be strongly associated with Pupil Premium funding, and then a sharp increase in 2014. Whatever

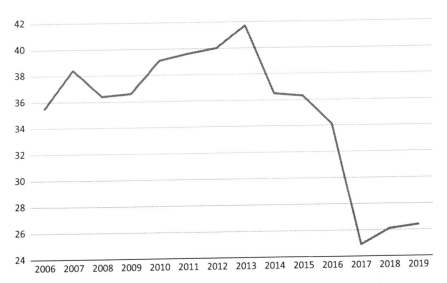

FIGURE 12.8 Percentage of long-term FSM-eligible pupils scoring above national mean, KS4 Capped Points scores, 2006–2019

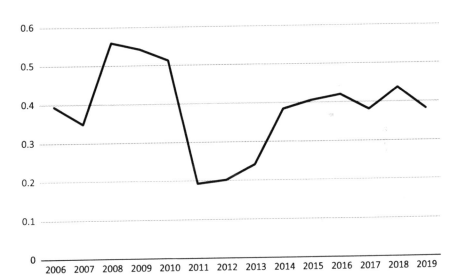

FIGURE 12.9 Change in "effect" size for the gap between long-term disadvantaged pupils and the rest. KS4 VA Residual, 2006–2019

happened in 2014 it seems to have made assessment markedly harder for poorer pupils and so led to a larger attainment gap, even as assessed by these value-added scores which are supposedly independent of raw-score levels. As at KS2, two or more government policies appear to be in tension. The Pupil Premium is intended to reduce the attainment gap. But the pressure to make assessment harder, prevent grade inflation, and have greater differentiation among higher attaining pupils, is linked to a sudden large increase in the gap. All of our analyses for the attainment gap, however computed, show the same thing.

Conclusion

Focusing on pupils who have been FSM-eligible for long term, there is strong evidence of a decline in the attainment gap at KS1 following the introduction of the Pupil Premium Policy, slightly weaker evidence at KS2, and much more mixed evidence for KS4. When reforms were made to the assessments, mostly from 2014, they seem to have made the tests harder. This is linked to a rapid increase in the attainment gap, and even in the value-added gap, where it has been possible to compute this. Adjusting the analyses to consider gaps in terms of national rankings, or the percentage of disadvantaged pupils above the national mean, still shows the same pattern. We examine the situation further in Chapter 14.

References

Bitler, M., Corcoran, S., Domina, T. and Penner, E. (2021) Teacher effects on student achievement and height: A cautionary tale, *Journal of Research on Educational Effectiveness*, https://doi.org/10.1080/19345747.2021.1917025

DfE (2014) Measuring disadvantaged pupils' attainment gaps over time (updated): Statistical Working Paper, https://assets.publishing.service.gov.uk/government/uploads/system/uploads/attachment_data/file/398657/SFR_40_2014_Measuring_disadvantaged_pupils_attainment_gaps_over_time__updated_.pdf

Gorard, S. (2010) Serious doubts about school effectiveness, *British Educational Research Journal*, 36, 5, 735–766.

Morris, T., Davies, N., Dorling, D., Richmond, R. and Davey Smith, G. (2018) Testing the validity of value-added measures of educational progress with genetic data, *British Educational Research Journal*, https://doi.org/10.1002/berj.3466

13

THE CHARACTER AND GEOGRAPHY OF LONG-TERM DISADVANTAGE

Introduction

This chapter illustrates further some of the trends and patterns in this section of the book so far, by considering what else is known about long-term disadvantaged pupils in England, including links to their background characteristics and where they live. We consider outcomes for pupil sub-groups such as those identified as having a special educational need (SEN), from different ethnic origins, and in different areas of England. The composition of the long-term FSM-eligible group can change over time in terms of such sub-group characteristics, and so the analyses for these sub-groups do *not* have the same stable comparator as for the national figures. First, we look at missing values, and what we know about cases with missing values.

Missing cases

Using the overall dataset for all KS2 cohorts combined from years 2006 to 2019, with around 8 million cases, it is clear that the tiny number of pupils missing FSM data have attainment scores more like the majority not-disadvantaged pupils at KS1, and more like the disadvantaged pupils at KS2 (Table 13.1). In fact, their KS2 scores are worse than the disadvantaged groups, forming a kind of super-disadvantaged group, as shown previously at KS4 (Gorard 2012). Given that the dataset is based on complete KS2 cohorts, the missing values at KS1 are most likely for those pupils coming to primary schools in England later, after Year 1, from other home countries, overseas, private schools, or home tutoring. Those missing FSM data at KS2 (but having KS2 scores) may be more mobile pupils such as recent immigrants or those from Traveller families.

DOI: 10.4324/9781003287353-18

TABLE 13.1 Comparing KS1 and KS2 scores for pupils missing FSM data with the rest

	Not FSM-eligible	FSM-eligible Year 6	Missing FSM data
KS1 Points	15.92	13.55	15.09
KS2 Points	52.31	47.52	37.40

Note: 12,340 cases, or less than 0.2% of cases, are missing KS2 FSM data

Characterising the permanently disadvantaged pupils

As might be expected, permanently disadvantaged pupils appear in about the same proportions as the majority of pupils in terms of many of their other characteristics, such as their reported sex, or age-in-year. And these proportions remain the same across the KS2 cohorts from 2006 to 2014.

Ethnic groups

Long-term disadvantaged pupils are somewhat less likely to report a white ethnic origin, and are somewhat more likely to be of Asian, black or mixed origin, than the remaining pupils (even including the short-term disadvantaged). They are also slightly less likely to have English as their first language. Historically, permanently disadvantaged pupils have been disproportionately from some ethnic minorities in England (especially Asian, black and mixed ethnicity), but this has declined markedly over time, alongside an increase in white permanently disadvantaged pupils (Figure 13.1). The proportion of white ethnicity pupils has increased slightly over

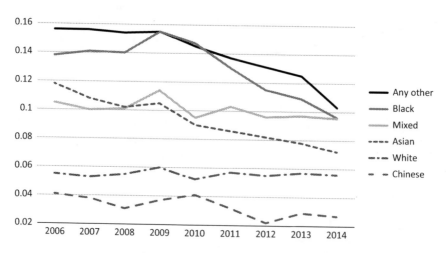

FIGURE 13.1 Percentage of each ethnic group also FSM-eligible for 11 years, 2007 to 2014 KS2 cohorts

Note: For all graphs in this chapter, the key on the right is in the same order as the appearance of the lines in 2014, from top to bottom, in order to aid readability.

time. Chinese are the ethnic group with the lowest proportion of permanent disadvantage, and this proportion has declined along with most other groups. These changes in composition mean that any comparisons over time between ethnic sub-groups are not based on stable comparators (as they are with long-term FSM-eligibility, in Chapters 11 and 12), and that the changes in prevalence alone could explain any differences over time in the segregation or attainment gap outcomes for any ethnic group (below).

The segregation between schools in England of long-term disadvantaged Asian, Black, Chinese and mixed origin pupils has declined visibly since 2011 (Figure 13.2). And this is despite them becoming a smaller proportion of the long-term disadvantaged group over time, which would normally (and all other things being equal) lead to an increase in estimates of segregation (Chapter 11). Therefore, this reduction in segregation may be, at least in part, an inadvertent result of Pupil Premium funding and its impact on poverty segregation figures. Overall, schools are becoming slightly more mixed in intakes, in terms of poverty, ethnicity and special needs, as already portrayed using school-level data (e.g. Gorard 2015). However, there is less of a decline in segregation (if any) for the majority white origin long-term poor pupils. If the Pupil Premium has helped reduce ethnic and poverty segregation between schools then it is the Asian, black, Chinese, mixed and other groups of pupils who have apparently been most affected so far.

The attainment gap at KS2 between permanently FSM-eligible pupils and other pupils of Asian origin is lower than the national average (Figure 13.3). The attainment gap for long-term poor black pupils compared to all other black pupils is even lower than for poor Asian pupils. But it has grown over time, even since 2011.

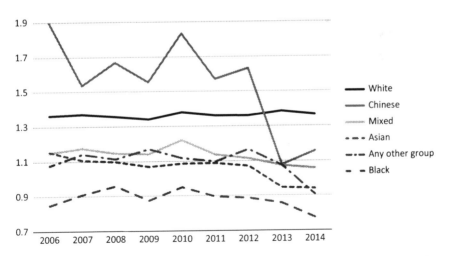

FIGURE 13.2 Segregation gap for pupils of each ethnic group who are permanently FSM-eligible, or not

Remember: these are not gaps between ethnic groups, but gaps between long-term poor students and others within each ethnic group.

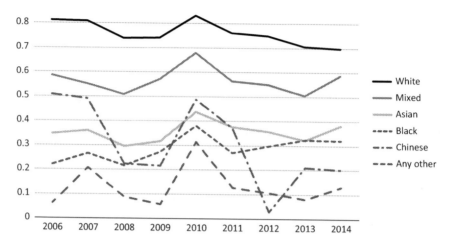

FIGURE 13.3 KS2 attainment gap for pupils of each ethnic group who are permanently FSM–eligible, or not

Whatever benefits a decrease in segregation for ethnic minorities might bring they are not obvious in this attainment gap yet. A national (overall) decline in the KS2 attainment gap is really only visible for Chinese and white origin poor pupils, and the decline occurs after 2007 and again after 2011.

Special educational needs (and disability)

The strongest link between other pupil characteristics and long-term disadvantage relates to SEN. Long-term disadvantaged pupils are far more likely to have any SEN recorded, than the majority of students, and over twice as likely to have a statement of SEN (Table 13.2). The educational and other challenges faced by pupils with additional needs or disability, and their preponderance in the economically disad-vantaged group, could help explain why the "poverty" attainment gap exists at all, and why it is worse for long-term disadvantaged pupils.

So, permanently disadvantaged pupils are more often reported as having a SEN or disability than the majority, and this disproportion has generally grown across cohorts (Figure 13.4). This growth is perhaps driven largely by growth in the national proportion of young people identified as facing a learning challenge

TABLE 13.2 Percentage of pupils, SEN status and long-term FSM–eligibility

	None	SEN no statement	SEN statement
Majority (not long-term FSM) pupils	83	15	3
Long-term FSM–eligible pupils	63	30	7

Note: "Statement" includes those with an Education, Health and Care Plan. "No statement" includes School Action, School Action Plus and SEN support.

(prevalence). Non-SEN but long-term economically disadvantaged pupils remain at about the same smaller proportion. The changes in composition of the long-term disadvantaged group mean again that the patterns for SEN segregation and attainment gaps over time are not based on stable comparisons in the same way as the national figures are.

The segregation gap between long-term disadvantaged SEN and non-SEN pupils is high, suggesting that these two groups attend rather different sets of schools. However, there is a long-term decline in the segregation gap (Figure 13.5).

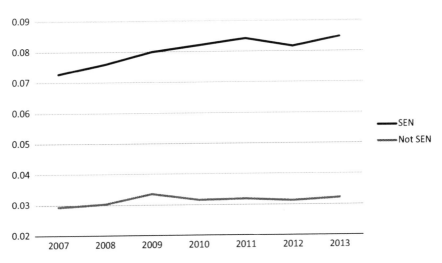

FIGURE 13.4 Percentage of SEN pupils also FSM-eligible for 11 years, 2007 to 2014 KS2 cohorts

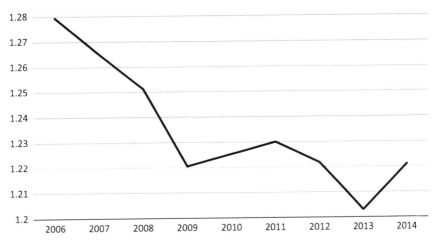

FIGURE 13.5 Segregation gap for SEN pupils who are permanently FSM-eligible or not

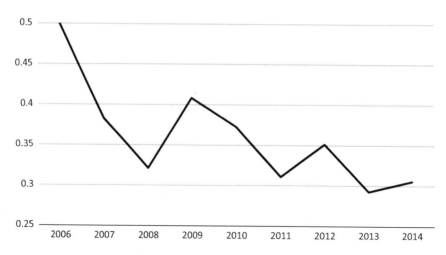

FIGURE 13.6 KS2 attainment gap for SEN pupils who are permanently FSM–eligible or not

This long-term decline could be linked to the increase in the prevalence of SEN reporting amongst the long-term disadvantaged pupils, perhaps especially in mainstream primary school settings in the years 2006 onwards. There is also a discernible drop after 2011, but overall its scale in unremarkable in historical terms.

The attainment gap between long-term disadvantaged SEN and non-SEN pupils is also quite high, and again shows a decline that is not specifically associated with the Pupil Premium era (Figure 13.6). The trend is also likely to be linked to the increase in SEN pupils who are also long-term poor.

The geography of disadvantage

We turn now to a consideration of where long-term disadvantaged pupils live within England.

Regional variations

There are quite large differences between Economic Areas of England in terms of the proportion of pupils who are long-term disadvantaged (FSM-eligible for all 11 years at school). Whether considered for KS2 (Figure 13.7) or KS4 pupils (Figure 13.8), the pattern is similar. The North East is the most deprived area, followed by London, the West Midlands and the North West. The South and East of England have the fewest long-term disadvantaged pupils. Not much has changed over nine years (although there is a suggestion that the regions are moving slightly closer to each other in these terms.

Prevalence matters. The gap in socio-economic segregation between schools, in terms of the most disadvantaged pupils, is lowest in areas where such pupils are

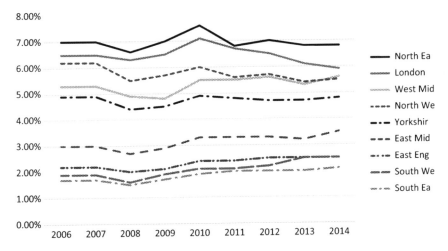

FIGURE 13.7 KS2 prevalence of 11 year FSM–eligible pupils by Economic Area

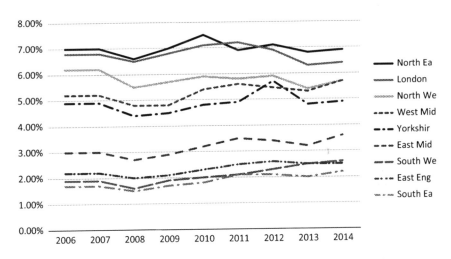

FIGURE 13.8 KS4 prevalence of 11 year FSM–eligible pupils by Economic Area

most prevalent such as London, the North East and West Midlands (Figure 13.9). It is highest in the South East, East, and South West of England. These areas have proportionately fewer long-term disadvantaged pupils. Segregation has declined slightly in all areas since 2011, sometimes erratically. It is most marked in East England and the West Midlands.

A similar picture is observed for the KS2 attainment gap, which again appears to be linked to the prevalence of long-term disadvantage (Figure 13.10). The gap is the highest in the South East and South West, and the lowest in London and the West Midlands. The gap has declined over time, more erratically than segregation,

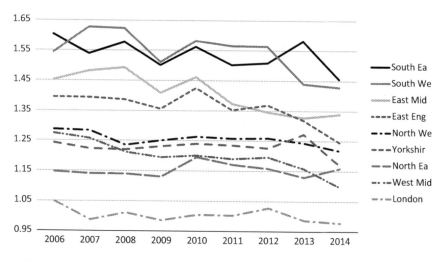

FIGURE 13.9 KS2 11 year FSM segregation gap by Economic Area

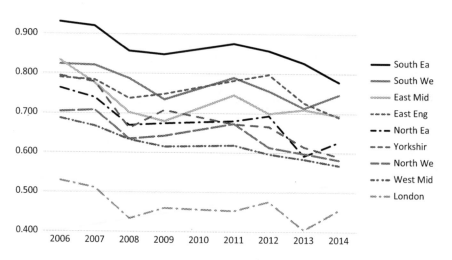

FIGURE 13.10 KS2 11 year FSM attainment gap by Economic Area

in all areas and generally in line with the drop in poverty segregation, as also shown nationally. The decline is most marked in South East, East, Yorkshire, and the West Midlands.

London appears to be an outlier, even given its share of long-term disadvantaged pupils. But as the next chapter shows, this may be due to another confounding variable. The high use of private schools in parts of London makes the poverty attainment gap appear smaller than it really is, and smaller than it should be to be compared fairly with the gap in areas like the North of England, or the West Midlands.

Conclusion

In this chapter, there is a suggestion of a link, at least geographically, between the patterns in the segregation and attainment gaps for pupil sub-groups and for areas of England. As schools become more mixed locally, their poverty attainment gap may also decline. We assess this idea further in the next chapter.

References

Gorard, S. (2012) Who is eligible for free school meals? Characterising FSM as a measure of disadvantage in England, *British Educational Research Journal*, 38, 6, 1003–1017.

Gorard, S. (2015) The complex determinants of school intake characteristics, England 1989 to 2014, *Cambridge Journal of Education*, 46, 1, 131–146.

14

COMBINING THE RESULTS ON PUPIL PREMIUM FUNDING

Introduction

Having established the trends over time for both the segregation and attainment gaps, this chapter looks further at the relationship between the two. Are the two patterns strongly linked, and could one be helping to create the other, or could they be mutually reinforcing? We begin to assess the answers by correlating the national figures over time, and then correlating the figures for one cohort by economic region, and then by local authority area.

The relationship between segregation and attainment gaps over time

As an example, the KS2 poverty segregation and attainment gaps for permanently disadvantaged pupils from 2006 to 2014 form an approximate straight line when plotted together (Figure 14.1). In general, years that have had higher levels of poverty segregation between schools also have higher poverty attainment gaps. And *vice versa*. As socio-economic segregation between schools has declined (Chapter 11) so has the attainment gap (Chapter 12), in a slightly erratic fashion. The two sets of figures are correlated with R of 0.75 (R-squared 0.56). Therefore, over 56% of the variation in one trend is predictable/explicable in terms of the other trend over time. Although the number of years is necessarily small, this is a strong relationship, suggesting that the two patterns are linked.

The relationship over place

A similar link is visible for the two gaps when examined over space. The geographical link between segregation and the attainment gap is very clear for the Economic Areas (even stronger than the link over time). If we cross-plot the figures for both

DOI: 10.4324/9781003287353-19

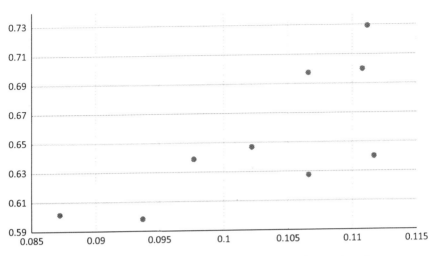

FIGURE 14.1   Scatterplot of long-term disadvantage segregation and attainment gaps, by year

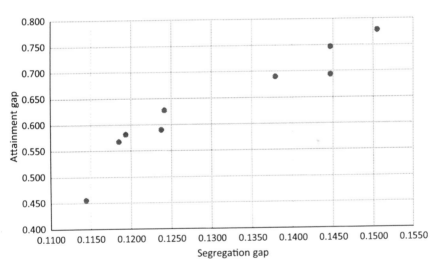

FIGURE 14.2   Scatterplot of segregation (y axis) by attainment gap (x axis) for Economic Areas

values for the 2014 KS2 cohort (or indeed any cohort) there is a strongly linear relationship (Figure 14.2). The figures correlate with R = +0.95 (R-squared of over 0.90). Clearly, areas with less segregation have correspondingly low attainment gaps between the long-term poor and the rest, and *vice versa*. This strengthens the finding for the relationship over time. Segregation appears to matter a lot for the spread of educational outcomes as well as for social reasons (Gorard 2018).

If we plot the scores for each local authority area, for segregation and the attainment gap (for any year), there is a weaker positive linear relationship (Figure 14.3).

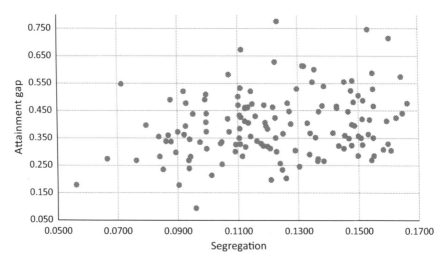

FIGURE 14.3 Scatterplot of segregation (y axis) by attainment gap (x axis) for local authorities

For 2014 the scores correlate with $R = +0.29$ (R-squared 0.08). So again, lower socio-economic segregation of pupils between schools in any area is linked to a generally lower poverty attainment gap.

Summary

In any year, region or local area, low poverty segregation is linked to a lower poverty attainment gap, especially at primary school level. Although some are based on a relatively small number of data points, these correlations over time and region are too strong to be considered as a coincidence. Both sets of figures, for the segregation and attainment gaps, could be the outcome of another, unobserved, factor. They could be mutually reinforcing, or one pattern could actually help to create the other. It is unlikely that a drop in the attainment gap is directly responsible for reducing segregation, although it may have a medium-term impact on parental preferences for schools, and so on the eventual intakes to schools. But the reverse relationship is much more plausible. A decline in segregation would mean that the most disadvantaged pupils were more evenly spread between schools. This would allow schools to focus help and interventions more easily for some of their pupils, such as those with the severest challenges or who could be seen as requiring more resource to reach any specified level of proficiency. Pupil Premium funding could then assist with the costs of such activity. We explore this idea further in Chapter 15.

Economic considerations

The focus on long-term disadvantage in this section of the book means that the results are less sensitive than prior studies have been to the confounding effects of economic and policy changes over time. As shown in Chapter 9, the proportion of long-term disadvantaged pupils is less volatile than the proportion of temporarily disadvantaged pupils. This protects the results in this section of the book, to a large extent, from changes unrelated to attainment that could confound the results in previous and official accounts of the attainment gap (and so of the impact of Pupil Premium funding). However, it is still worth considering whether there are links to the economy or other changes that are not captured by the analysis so far. We first look at economic and other changes over time, and then use these changes along with the onset of Pupil Premium funding as predictors of both the segregation and attainment gaps in any year.

There are reasons, other than Pupil Premium funding and changes in test severity, why the poverty attainment gap may change over time. One of these is changes in the economy. When the economy is weaker there are more FSM-eligible pupils, and so the apparent attainment gap between FSM-eligible and non-eligible pupils may reduce. Length of poverty is linked to lower average attainment, and so these newly FSM-eligible pupils will tend to have higher average attainment than other disadvantaged pupils (Chapter 9).

Also, in better economic times more students may attend private schools (which are largely excluded from NPD and official measures of the gap), which could have the same effect as a weakened economy by taking somewhat higher attaining scores out of the calculation (Gorard et al. 2019). This is a key reason why the emphasis in this section of the book is on long-term FSM-eligible pupils who would have been disadvantaged and not attending private schools in any era under almost any economic circumstances.

Private schools

Chapter 9 examined how, in principle, the proportion of pupils attending private schools in England could influence the apparent size of the official attainment gap. The use of private schools is likely to increase slightly when the economy is stronger. Pupils in private schools do not generally appear in the NPD (meaning that the data for them is weak or non-existent), and so are not included in official versions of the poverty attainment gap. This takes the somewhat higher attaining scores of private school pupils out of the calculation, so making the gap look smaller than it really is (Gorard et al. 2019). The inverse could apply when the economy is weaker. Because marginal attendees at private school are unlikely to be FSM-eligible and could have slightly higher than average attainment, they will make the national attainment gap appear smaller when in private schools, and larger when they are not. But these changes would be nothing to do with the impact of Pupil Premium funding, or the focus and work of schools in reducing the attainment gap.

So, what has happened to overall private school attendance over the period covered by the figures in Chapters 11 and 12 (years 2006 to 2019)? Figures from the DfE (2020) suggest that private school use has declined since around 2009, perhaps following the economic recession of 2007/8 (see below). But the slight downward

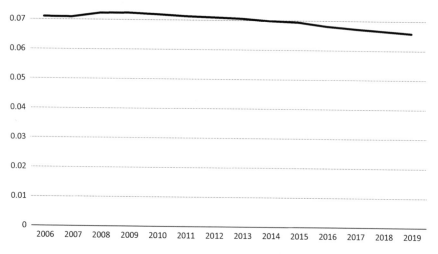

FIGURE 14.4 Percentage of pupils attending private schools, 2006–2019

trend has continued or even strengthened since then, so that private school attendance in England was at its lowest recorded level by 2019 (Figure 14.4).

This decline since 2009 in the use of private schools could mean that the attainment gap would appear to grow, as slightly higher attaining pupils, presumably almost all labelled as not disadvantaged, are included in the attainment gap calculation in a way that they would not be in a year when private school use was higher. Figure 14.4 means that any reduction in the segregation or attainment gaps since 2011 cannot be explained by this factor. This makes the positive findings in Chapters 11 and 12 even more robust. We assess the role of private school usage in the segregation and attainment gaps further via regression models (below).

Of course, use of private schools varies considerably across the country. With the exception of London, more pupils attend private schools in regions and local authorities that have fewer long-term disadvantaged pupils, thereby reducing the appearance of the poverty attainment gap there – by removing averagely higher attaining pupils from the state-funded pool. Similarly, areas with high levels of long-term poverty tend to have very few local pupils using private schools. This makes straight-forward un-contextualised comparisons between poor and not so poor areas very misleading.

For example, the following local authorities all have zero (or indistinguishable from zero) pupils attending private schools:

- Knowsley, North West England
- South Tyneside, North East England
- Redcar and Cleveland, North East England
- Thurrock, East of England
- Blackpool, North West England
- Hartlepool, North East England

The poverty attainment gap in each of these areas, and others like them, will not have private school usage as a confounding value, and so will tend to be valid, and comparisons over time will be valid, in this respect at least.

There are also areas that retain formal selection to grammar schools, via the 11+ entrance exam, such as Bexley or South Gloucestershire. For more on this, see Gorard (2018). These have lower than might be expected private school usage, only of the order of magnitude 0.3% of school population. This is presumably because grammar schools are seen by some parents as providing important (to them) elements of what private schools do. But grammar schools are free. By retaining more high attaining pupils in the state-funded sector, and so part of the official poverty attainment gap, grammar school areas intriguingly are like poor areas in yielding a valid attainment gap in this respect.

At the other extreme are areas, largely in London and the South East, such as:

- Lambeth, London, 33% private school usage
- Bracknell Forest, South East of England, 34%
- Islington, London, 37%
- Windsor and Maidenhead, South East of England, 38%
- Richmond Upon Thames, London, 58%
- Rutland, East Midlands, 66%

These authorities have very large proportions of their local pupils in private schools, over a third, and for some nearly two thirds of the school population (note these private pupils will not necessarily attend schools in their local areas). These figures mean that the official attainment gaps for these areas, even those presented in Chapter 13, will not make valid comparisons with areas in the North or West Midlands with effectively no private school usage, and high levels of long-term disadvantage.

This *caveat* is especially important when considering London. The apparent success of areas like Lambeth in terms of the poverty attainment gap, or of Islington in having some of the lowest between-school SES segregation in England, is illusory. Taking a third or more of the richest and highest attaining pupils (on average) out of the segregation or attainment gap calculations would make any part of England look "successful". For example, if we ignore the top third highest attaining pupils in South Tyneside (at KS4 in 2019), the poverty attainment gap there is zero. But that does not, in itself, mean that we should use South Tyneside as an exemplar of how to reduce the attainment gap. In the same way it would be wrong to use Lambeth or Islington as examples of how to reduce the attainment gap (except by sending a third or more of the richest students to private schools!).

Although the changes in national usage of private schools cannot help explain the national results in Chapters 11 and 12, local variations can help explain local patterns of segregation and the attainment gap, especially for London. This is important for consideration of the success of the Pupil Premium, the over-hyped and largely illusory results of the London Challenge, the work of Ofsted, how DfE judge schools' use of funding, and a host of other policy and practice issues (Gorard 2018).

Changes in GDP

Chapter 9 also explained how the economy could be directly linked to changes in the segregation and attainment gaps, as more families fall into poverty during a recession, or recover household income in better years. Historically, socio-economic segregation between schools in England has been largely the inverse of Gross Domestic Product (GDP). What has happened to the economy in the years 2006 to 2019 and how is this related, if it is, to the segregation and attainment gaps for permanently disadvantaged pupils?

Figure 14.5 shows the dramatic change for GDP in 2008 as part of a much wider worldwide economic recession. Since then, this economic indicator has improved until 2014, which would tend to increase both the segregation of poorer pupils, and the attainment gap somewhat, because pupils who had been labelled disadvantaged and had lower than average attainment would now be labelled as not disadvantaged. After 2014, the reverse is true. GDP lowered slightly, which historically would tend to increase the proportion of pupils labelled disadvantaged, reduce their apparent segregation between schools, and decrease the apparent attainment gap (as slightly higher attaining pupils would now be labelled as disadvantaged).

As with private school use, the pattern of change in GPD over time therefore does not match, or somehow provide a simple explanation for, the positive results in Chapters 11 and 12. The changes after 2011 neither match nor mirror the trends for segregation and the attainment gap. If the reason for any changes in the gaps is not economic, then some other reason such as the Pupil Premium policy is more likely to be behind them.

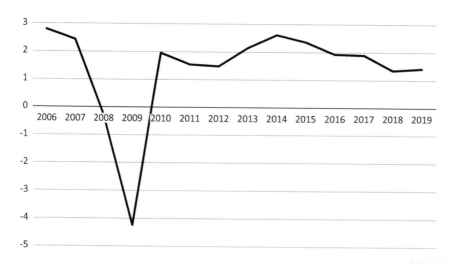

FIGURE 14.5 Annual changes in GDP, 2006–2019

Correlating the indicators

To make these considerations more precise we correlated the patterns of both the segregation and attainment gaps with changes over time in GDP, private school usage, and the percentage of permanently disadvantaged pupils. We also correlated the gaps with a binary flag representing whether the year in question was before 2011 or not.

The results show that GDP change is only very weakly related to the segregation gap (between long term disadvantaged pupils and their peers), with R of -0.06, and so R-squared of less 0.004 (Table 14.1). As already illustrated, the drop in the segregation gap cannot be explained by economic factors, once these have been controlled for by focusing on long-term disadvantaged pupils (Chapter 11).

The other three possible confounding variables are much more strongly related to the segregation of long-term disadvantaged pupils (R-squared of between 0.44 and 0.59). When there are more disadvantaged pupils, the level of SES segregation in state-funded schools declines markedly, as expected. This shows that even the results for the more stable long-term disadvantaged group are somewhat susceptible to economic and related changes. This issue is addressed in the final part of this chapter. Nevertheless, the segregation gap is noticeably lower during the Pupil Premium era.

GDP change is slightly more strongly related to the KS2 attainment gap than to segregation, with R-squared of 0.04 (R of 0.20 in Table 14.2). As expected, when the economy improves, the attainment gap is larger. However, the impact for these long-term disadvantaged pupils is minor. When there are more pupils in private schools (and so not part of the gap calculation), the attainment gap declines, again as expected (see above). This is presumably because the marginal private

TABLE 14.1 Correlations (R) between the long-term disadvantaged segregation gap, and economic indicators and the Pupil Premium

	GDP annual change	% pupils in private schools	% long-term disadvantaged pupils	Pupil Premium era flag
Long-term FSM Segregation gap	−0.06	−0.71	−0.77	−0.66

TABLE 14.2 Correlations (R) between the long-term disadvantaged KS2 attainment gap, and economic indicators and the Pupil Premium

	GDP annual change	% pupils in private schools	% long-term disadvantaged pupils	Pupil Premium era flag
Long-term FSM attainment gap	0.20	−0.32	−0.53	−0.66

school pupils have somewhat higher attainment, and so taking them out of the gap calculation makes the remaining state-funded pupils appear closer on average. As with segregation, the Pupil Premium era is associated with a substantially lower attainment gap ($R = -0.66$, R-squared = 0.44).

However, these possible predictors or confounds are themselves correlated with each other, and it is important to consider the potential impact of Pupil Premium net of all of them combined. So we use them all together in multivariate analyses.

Modelling the gaps

Key Stage 2

The next stage in the analysis is a simple regression model, used to predict/explain the national KS2 attainment gaps 2006 to 2019, using the economic indicators above as predictors, along with a flag representing the Pupil Premium era or not. It is possible to consider the net potential impact of Pupil Premium funding by looking at economic changes first in the model.

Table 14.3 shows that it is possible to explain almost 75% of the variation in the attainment gap using only three economic indicators, and the Pupil Premium flag, and that the vast majority of that explanation comes from knowledge of whether any year was after 2010 or not. Put another way, the attainment gap for the relatively stable group of long-term disadvantaged pupils is slightly affected by economic conditions, but once accounted for the best single predictor (by far) of the attainment gap in any year is whether it is during or before the Pupil Premium era.

Table 14.4 shows the coefficients for all four predictors in the model. All other things being equal, having fewer pupils in the private sector is associated with an apparent increase in the attainment gap, as predicted by Gorard et al. (2019),

TABLE 14.3 Strength of model predicting KS2 attainment over time

Step	R	R-squared
1. Economic indicators	0.34	0.12
2. Whether in Pupil Premium era	0.86	0.74

TABLE 14.4 Coefficients for model predicting KS2 attainment over time

Coefficients	Standardised
GPD change	+0.34
Percentage of long-term FSM-eligible pupils	−0.25
Percentage of pupils in private schools	−0.82
Pupil Premium era flag	−1.40

because those on the margins of private schools will tend to have higher than average attainment. In any year where most of these marginal private school students are in state-funded schools they are included in the NPD gap calculation and so the apparent gap is higher, whereas if they are removed from the calculation the gap is lower. When the economy is better, the gap grows slightly, and also when there are slightly fewer long-term disadvantaged pupils, as there would be when the economy was better.

The Pupil Premium era flag has the largest predictive coefficient, and more importantly produces by far the largest increase in R-squared. This is not a test of causal influence, and there are many other variables that we might wish to include in the model, but it is clear that something quite remarkable has happened since the advent of Pupil Premium, for the KS2 attainment gap.

Key Stage 4

A similar model was created for attainment at KS4. This is weaker (lower R-squared at each step) than the KS2 model (Table 14.5), as expected given the more mixed historical pattern of the attainment gap as KS4. However, in all other respects the model is the same as for KS1. Knowledge of whether the year was in the Pupil Premium era or not still adds 16 percentage points to the R-squared.

Table 14.6 is similar to the correlations in Table 14.2. When there are more pupils in private schools, the apparent attainment gap at KS4 goes down. The variable for the Pupil Premium era is still substantial (negative because the Pupil Premium era is coded as 1), suggesting that net of economic factors the Pupil Premium is still linked to an improvement in the attainment gap.

TABLE 14.5 Strength of two step model predicting the KS4 attainment gap for long-term disadvantaged pupils and their peers

Step	R	R-squared
1. Economic indicators	0.43	0.19
2. Whether in Pupil Premium era	0.59	0.35

TABLE 14.6 Standardised coefficients for model predicting the KS4 attainment gap for long-term disadvantaged pupils and their peers

Coefficients	Standardised
GPD change	+0.21
Percentage of long-term FSM-eligible pupils	−0.27
Percentage of pupils in private schools	−0.46
Pupil Premium era flag	−0.57

Predicting the "official" attainment gap

For comparison, Tables 14.7 and 14.8 show the results for the same kind of multiple regression model, but with the gap defined in terms of pupils ever being eligible for FSM (rather than always being eligible) during their five years in secondary school. This is important because this EverFSM value is how the official attainment gap is computed.

The resulting model is much stronger (higher R-squared) overall than for the long-term disadvantaged gap, but the variation in the attainment gap here is <u>only</u> explained by economic factors (Table 14.7). The Pupil Premium is completely irrelevant here (the R value remains the same when this flag value is added to the model). This shows starkly one of the dangers of the official attainment gap. It seems to be entirely associated with economic factors and is, according to this model, absolutely nothing to do with the actions of schools in response to their extra funding or indeed anything to do with education at all. The official attainment gap is therefore merely a disguised economic indicator.

This is then reflected in the coefficients (Table 14.8). The value for the Pupil Premium era is negligible, while the values for all other possible predictors are much higher than in the models above. There is a very real danger that the official attainment is based solely on non-educational changes over time, and that this is not realised or understood by policy-makers and other bodies such as think tanks, Ofsted and research organisations. Any practice or policy recommendations based on these misleading results will be unwarranted. Again it seems, schools and regions are being unfairly praised or blamed for variations in figures that are not under their control to influence.

TABLE 14.7 Strength of two step model predicting the official KS4 attainment gap for ever disadvantaged pupils and their peers

Step	R	R-squared
1. Economic indicators	0.84	0.71
2. Whether in Pupil Premium era	0.84	0.71

TABLE 14.8 Standardised coefficients for model predicting the official KS4 attainment gap for ever disadvantaged pupils and their peers

Coefficients	Standardised
GPD change	0.46
Percentage of pupils FSM-eligible for 5 years	1.03
Percentage of pupils in private schools	1.21
Pupil Premium era flag	0.05

Conclusion

The models presented in this chapter suggest that changes in the segregation and attainment gaps for temporarily or short-term disadvantaged pupils, of the kind used in official versions of the attainment gap, are created entirely by economic and other non-educational factors. Such figures are therefore very misleading, and should not be used for policy or practice purposes.

However, the models here also suggest that any improvements in the segregation and attainment gaps for long-term disadvantaged pupils are <u>not</u> largely the product of economic changes, annual differences in the proportion of long-term disadvantaged pupils, or of patterns of attendance at private schools. But they are linked, *ceteris paribus*, to the Pupil Premium era. If this link is a causal one, meaning that the Pupil Premium funding can play a role in reducing the gaps, how is this money best used by schools?

References

DfE (2020) *Schools, pupils and their characteristics*, https://explore-education-statistics.service.gov.uk/find-statistics/school-pupils-and-their-characteristics

Gorard, S. (2018) *Education policy: Evidence of equity and effectiveness*, Bristol, Policy Press.

Gorard, S., Siddiqui, N. and See, B.H. (2019) The difficulties of judging what difference the Pupil Premium has made to school intakes and outcomes in England, *Research Papers in Education*, 36, 3, 355–379.

CONCLUSION

15

WHAT HAVE WE LEARNT, AND WHAT ARE THE NEXT TASKS?

Introduction

This book is a compilation of research on the social and educational value of the use of monetary policies to improve attendance and attainment at school. There is considerable evidence, from this book and beyond, that financial investments in education can reap benefits, especially for students from more disadvantaged families. This is true of improving attendance in countries where attendance is far from 100%, and/or where the participation of girls is considerably lower. Money in the form of additional grants to schools, like the Pupil Premium in England, can also help reduce socio-economic segregation between schools and the poverty attainment gap, at least at primary school age. Of course, almost any educational intervention, policy or programme involves financial expenditure in some way. This book has looked at some of the ways that money can be best used to improve school outcomes, drawing on worldwide examples, and evidence from prior studies judged to be methodologically strong. These studies also helped to identify what has not worked well, and this is important because it provides guidance on where not to waste limited resources.

In Chapter 2, we outlined some of the main factors that may drive the poverty attainment gap, focussing on those that can be altered most easily in the short to medium term, and those which are the remit of schools and schooling. And we made the point there that this does not imply acceptance of poverty itself, but that the elimination of poverty itself is not a task that education is especially suited to, in the short to medium term. Nor did we suggest that the poverty attainment gap

DOI: 10.4324/9781003287353-21

could ever be entirely eliminated. More realistically, in order to <u>reduce</u> the gap through education we proposed considering:

- Improving access, enrolment in, and attendance at school
- Limiting the level of between-school SES, ethnic and other segregation
- Increasing the supply and deployment of well-prepared teachers
- Enhancing the range of activities and interactions in schools and classrooms
- And deciding on the best bets for using money to address all of the above

Having presented a wealth of evidence on these issues from our structured reviews, secondary analyses and primary fieldwork, we are now in a position to summarise what is known, and suggest what the implications might be for policy and practice. The good news is that schools can make a difference, to individuals and to closing the poverty attainment gap. But for this to happen, policy-makers and practitioners need more help in using good evidence on how to do so.

Encouraging school enrolment and attendance

It is clear that money can make a difference. In less developed schooling systems, money helps to create new or extra school places which will tend to benefit the poorest, often rural, children who would otherwise not have the opportunity to attend school. Money can then be used to improve school infrastructure, resources, and student transportation. So, one quick and simple way to address the poverty attainment gap is to ensure that all children have a free place at a nearby school. Money is needed to build and open new schools, and to provide more school places, where these are not yet universal. This helps to reduce the gap in opportunities and outcomes created by family poverty.

Once there are sufficient school places within reach of all families, schooling should be free at the point of delivery, easy to access, and compulsory. There is further evidence that offering incentives for school attendance has promising results. Monetary incentives to compensate for loss of income through school attendance is also an effective way to increase enrolment and participation in school, presumably as a temporary measure in less developed systems. Provision in kind like transport to school, or meals at school, and the removal of fees, can all encourage attendance. Feeding children at school, free, may have lifelong benefits even in developed systems such as Sweden or Finland (Lundborg and Rooth 2021). These approaches are most likely to encourage the attendance of students from poorer families. These are especially important for girls in developing countries, and for disadvantaged students everywhere, even in more developed countries. This kind of funding is best provided directly to students or families – not to schools, areas, or teachers – as an incentive for attendance, conditional on appropriately full attendance.

Schools can then provide practical, safe environments where learning can happen under the supervision and care of trained teachers and other staff members. Schools can share the burden of responsibility for child development with parents.

Our evidence from Pakistan and India shows that in the absence of school, learning can be hindered, and that poorer parents do not always prioritise their children's education over more basic economic needs (Chapter 5). In more developed school systems, near-universal school attendance has been achieved, and this has changed and, in some cases, reversed previous patterns of social inequality, with girls now getting higher attainment than boys at school, on average, and the results for pupils from different ethnic groups converging in attainment, for example.

Encouraging desegregation

Once school systems are more developed, and there are free local places for all, attention can turn to the nature of each school intake. An even distribution of disadvantage between schools makes the whole school system fairer, and allows individual schools to focus their energy where it is most needed (see Chapter 2). There is also worldwide evidence that average attainment is higher in the most mixed school systems. This kind of desegregation of socio-economic disadvantage between schools has many societal, individual and educational benefits, and so should be a priority once there are enough places for all in any school system. It will also tend to be linked to ethnic and other forms of desegregation.

This means that all schools should be open access (rather than selective in any way), and as similar as possible in structure and process across the system. School places should not be rigidly allocated in terms of nearby housing, lest the schools then reflect any local residential segregation by SES, ethnicity, or related student characteristics. School desegregation by SES may also involve the temporary use of bussing to school, or the use of lotteries to decide over-subscribed places at any school.

Money can play an important further role in equalising the nature of school intakes. Our large-scale analysis of Pupil Premium funding in England shows that money provided for schools as an incentive/recompense for taking disadvantaged students, and allowing them to prioritise such students, is linked to a reduction in the extent to which these potentially harder-to-teach students are clustered in specific schools, or types of schools.

Since the introduction of Pupil Premium in England in 2011, the clustering of long-term disadvantaged pupils in schools has declined, for all age groups. It is relatively easy to envisage how allocating money like Pupil Premium funding to schools on the basis of their disadvantaged pupil intakes would make such pupils less unattractive to schools in general, and so could reduce the historic clustering of such pupils in specific under-subscribed schools. Also, because schools can now use disadvantage as a positive criterion for allocating contested school places, the funding could have had an almost immediate (and continuing) impact on school intakes, both directly and by reducing any unconscious bias against potentially harder-to-teach pupils.

The national drop in segregation is most obvious in Years 1 and 7, which is where Pupil Premium would be initially expected to make the most difference.

This shift can neither be explained by economic or legal changes nor by a reduction in the diversity of schooling, substantial changes to admissions arrangements, or the abolition of selection by faith or ability (Gorard 2018). Pupil Premium funding is currently the best explanation for the improvement, which suggests that the policy should be continued for the time being in England, and that similar schemes could be rolled out in more developed systems elsewhere on the basis of this evidence.

As stated, one reason an over-subscribed school might be reluctant to offer places to poorer children (even if unconsciously) is that, on average, they could be harder to teach. The extra funding given to schools as Pupil Premium can be used to implement evidence based catch-up programmes or pay for the cost of extra staff time in supporting poorer children (see below). This is what makes the policy clever – it is both an incentive to desegregate, and a way of funding programmes to reduce the poverty gap. How is the latter addressed?

Reducing the attainment gap

Having free places at equivalent schools for every child, ensuring that every child attends, and discouraging any form of needless segregation between schools, are the basic elements of a good school system. They will encourage overall levels of attainment and minimise any differences in attainment outcomes. Going further than these basic elements involves consideration of how funding is spent by schools, and what happens in classrooms at school, and so depends on the priorities and decisions of local authorities, teaching staff and school leads. These considerations need to be guided by the best available evidence-syntheses (that take the quality of each study into account). We cannot provide a full account here, but readers can refer to the many reviews we have conducted that are cited and described in this book, and in our previous work. We focus more here on our newer evidence, especially from the recent work in England.

Implications from Pupil Premium for policy

There has been a marked drop in the attainment gap at KS1 in England, since Pupil Premium funding was introduced. There was the beginning of a reduction in the attainment gap at KS2, and the gap is still lower than historically. The picture at KS4 is more mixed. The attainment gap dropped and then began to grow again from 2014 onwards, linked to changes in difficulty, scoring, and value-added scores. It seems that the Pupil Premium policy may be being contradicted by other governmental interventions. Overall, we can say that the Pupil Premium seems to have worked for long-term disadvantaged pupils at primary age. They are less clustered in schools, have better KS1 scores, and somewhat better KS2 scores than before 2011.

There is a clear relationship between the attainment gap and the poverty segregation gap. It has not been proven whether these two are causally related, or in which direction, or whether they are mutually reinforcing. However, the most likely link is that a less segregated school system will tend to have smaller poverty attainment gaps. Therefore, any society should keep operating to reduce between school segregation by poverty, by any means, including using something like Pupil Premium funding when allocating resources (note this does not necessarily mean more funding, rather more calibrated use of whatever funding is available). This may then assist in reducing the attainment gap in the longer term. But meanwhile, more attention needs to be paid by policy-makers to ensure that other policies for assessment do not interfere with the worthwhile drive towards a lower attainment gap.

Areas of England like the North East, the West Midlands and London, with the greatest proportion of long-term disadvantaged pupils, tend to have the lowest attainment gaps and show the greatest improvement over time. Poverty segregation between schools is lower and declining in the areas of most long-term disadvantage, matched by lower attainment gaps in these areas as well. Policy-makers need to understand that areas like the West Midlands and North East of England, which have been criticised by the inspection regime Ofsted and others for apparently failing their students, are actually getting better results than many other areas, for equivalent long-term disadvantaged students. Policy-makers and too many other commentators are being misled, by ignoring the prevalence of long-term disadvantage and the consequent challenges for schools, into believing that the local schools in poorer areas are somehow failing their pupils in a way that is not happening in the South East or South West. This wrong diagnosis will inevitably lead to the wrong policy solutions. If there are lessons to be learned about how to deploy Pupil Premium funding, and so improve life chances for poorer children, these poorer regions are the areas that policy-makers and other commentators should include in their search for advice (rather than inappropriately denigrating them).

Similarly, the apparently low poverty attainment gap in some London boroughs is, as we have shown, almost entirely an artefact of the number of residents attending private schools, and so being left out of the official attainment gap calculation. There are boroughs where a third or more of local children do not attend state schools. Any area of England would appear to have a low attainment gap if a third of the local children, selected from the highest attaining and richest families, were omitted from the attainment gap calculation there. Again, policy-makers and others are being misled. It is certain that some good work is going on in London to help reduce the poverty attainment, but it is not clear that this is any better than, or should be a role model for, similar work going on in Birmingham or Middlesbrough for example.

Some commentators have been saying that the Pupil Premium is not always being used properly by schools, or is otherwise not being effective. They have called for the money to be used for general school funds (Allen 2018, Morris and Dobson 2020), or to recruit, develop and retain teachers (Staufenberg 2019). In the absence of evidence of the effectiveness of these alternative uses for Pupil Premium funds, it would make sense to assume for the present that Pupil Premium should be retained in something like its current form, perhaps with a greater focus on KS1 (see below), and calibrated to increase funding for the long-term disadvantaged. This is not the same as just giving extra money to schools, which prior studies have suggested is less effective, because the funding must be used for the purposes intended. The government created a parallel programme, including the Education Endowment Foundation (EEF), to provide guidance to schools on how best to spend the funds. The Pupil Premium policy also differs from one based on giving money to poorer families on condition that their children attend school (Baird et al. 2011, de Janvry et al. 2006, Morley and Coady 2003), or to regions, as with the Opportunity Areas (DfE 2018) or Excellence in Cities policies in England, and it differs from a policy based on extra funding for schools themselves that is not tied to their intake, such as the original Specialist Schools and then the Academies programme (Gorard 2005).

There have been suggestions that the UK government, as the contribution of the Lib Dems in the Coalition diminished, became less interested in the attainment gap, than they were when Pupil Premium started, and more interested in structural reforms like academisation (Whittaker 2021). If so, the government is being supported in this by other commentators suggesting that Pupil Premium has not worked, or that the funding could be better used otherwise. However, the policy is worth pursuing for a few more cohorts at least, and then evaluating robustly again. The age cohort that arrived at school in 2011 is still in school at time of writing. In policy terms, the Pupil Premium is quite young.

Use of Pupil Premium funding or similar

In terms of how funding is actually used in schools, over and above its incentive value, more work is needed to ensure that any interventions, programmes and practices used in schools are evidence-led. It is not likely that the mere existence of Pupil Premium funding would produce a reduction in the poverty attainment gap. Of course, the funding might be partly effective simply by drawing attention to the gap. But it will more likely work by providing money for resources to address the gap. Schools are increasingly encouraged to ensure that the programmes they invest this extra funding in are "backed by evidence" (Schools Week 2021). However, there are still disputes over what "backed by evidence" means (presumably robust, replicated, transferrable evidence), and it still seems that many schools are instead looking for "evidence" to deploy in support what they want to do anyway (Gorard et al. 2020). There is limited but growing evidence of what has worked to improve the average attainment of poorer children. We need more of this robust evidence, and much more and better research on how to get that evidence into use most appropriately.

Why has the same clear improvement as seen in the segregation gap not also occurred with the attainment gap for older students, and as it did at KS1 in primary schools? It may be that the improvements in primary schools need longer to feed through the system before manifesting themselves in improved KS4 outcomes. However, the changes to the nature of KS4 assessment from 2014 onwards have not helped. This is not to say that the changes were wrong. But it is not clear that their clash with the Pupil Premium objectives was ever considered and accepted as a necessary cost by policy-makers.

However, another possible explanation is the relative lack of evidence on how to use Pupil Premium funding at KS4 level. At the time of writing, the EEF had reported complete evaluations of 120 distinct interventions, of which 17 were listed as "promising". Promising here means that the evaluation succeeded, the results are deemed trustworthy, and that the intervention was reported as having benefits for pupil attainment. This 10% to 15% of positive outcomes for otherwise plausible (i.e. with equipoise) approaches is to be expected. Of the 120 approaches trialled, 80 (67%) were for early years or primary phases. Of the 17 promising approaches, 12 were for the primary phase (71%). This means that schools and networks seeking evidence on how best they might use their Pupil Premium funding have a much greater number of promising interventions if they teach younger children. This may be part of the reason why the attainment gap has reduced more, in the Pupil Premium era, at KS1 and even at KS2 than KS4.

In any case, as discussed in Chapter 8, not all schools and teachers in England appreciate the advantages of using robust evidence when planning programmes and conducting interventions in schools. Many might see the need to explain their use of Pupil Premium funding as a burden rather than as a condition of funding. And they might only go through the motions of using it for purportedly evidence-led improvement to satisfy Ofsted or the DfE. Of course, it is not clear that Ofsted or the DfE understand properly what it means for actions to be evidence-led (as suggested by some of their own research programmes and claims). And, evidence on how best to promote attainment should only be one of the factors used in such decisions, along with context and intentions (Gemmink et al. 2021). But evidence should be used. Unfortunately, as we pointed out in Gorard et al. (2020), schools might be putting links to research evidence on their websites to support actions that they had already decided on, rather than as a genuine part of the decision itself. This kind of cherry-picking and box ticking seems to be common, and is perhaps even worse in policy-making (Gorard 2020).

How can we encourage the use of evidence-led approaches?

Over the last 30 years, governments and funders worldwide have sought to improve the quality of evidence produced by publicly-funded research. Understanding of effective interventions to inform education policy/practice has improved since the creation of the US Institute of Education Sciences, the Education Endowment Foundation (EEF) and other initiatives. There has also been considerable progress in methods of summarising and synthesising research results, with the work of the Campbell Collaboration, What Works Centres and others. Evidence of what worked, or not, is increasingly available for the first time.

As this body of more robust evidence on how to improve the attainment gap grows, a linked problem is becoming clearer. There is, as yet, no equivalently robust research on how to get high quality substantive evidence to be taken up and used appropriately by the majority of schools and teachers. The small amount of pioneering work that has been done in education so far has shown no impact (Gorard 2020, Gorard et al. 2020). It is crucial that attempts to narrow the poverty attainment gap, and deploy the funds available worldwide, are actually based on the best available evidence. How are users like school leads and local politicians supposed to judge the quality of research?

There are several published protocols for judging the robustness of a research finding. Some are intended for the users of research, like That's a Claim (https://thatsaclaim.org/). Some, like the Weight of Evidence framework from the EPPI Centre, are more for researchers who want to judge a body of work consisting of many individual studies (Gough 2007). Some, like the security ratings used by the EEF, are intended for use when judging the quality of an individual study based on a randomised control trial or similar (https://educationendowmentfoundation.org.uk/help/projects/the-eef-security-rating/). Others, like the Maryland Scientific Methods Scale, are like that of the EEF in being concerned with what works, and like the EPPI Centre version in being used to judge systematic reviews of evidence (Madaleno and Waights n.d.). In Chapter 3 of this book we presented a simple sieve for use when judging the trustworthiness of single studies, as explained in more detail in Gorard (2021).

All of these processes have a similar purpose, and there is considerable overlap between them, as would be expected. The idea is to provide tools, checklists or guidelines to help others to judge whether a study or a body of evidence is trustworthy, in the sense that its findings could be used ethically, and with a reasonable expectation that this evidence-led use would be effective (a best "bet").

Applying such a process for judging the quality of research, it becomes apparent that much publicly available research is very weak (for examples see Chapter 3 onwards). It is often inadequately described, using poor designs (or no design at all), mis-represented, overly technical, and/or flawed, including the use of inappropriate techniques like significance testing with non-randomised cases. Even worse, when bodies of research are synthesised to try and present an overall result, this is usually done with no consideration of the quality of the research being synthesised. This is clear in the meta-analyses of meta-analyses in the EEF Teaching and Learning Toolkit, in Hattie's (2008) "Visible Learning", and many similar attempts. The problems with these are described in more detail in Gorard (2018). Averaging "effect" sizes from very different studies - perhaps involving different outcomes, different age students, or different sampling processes, and ignoring issues such as the amount of missing data – is very dangerous and can yield very misleading summaries.

As an example, Hattie and Timperley (2007) reported a hyper-analysis of enhanced feedback based on synthesising the results of 74 meta-analyses that totalled 4,157 individual studies (reporting 5,755 different effect sizes). They did so without re-examining the original studies themselves or appraising their quality or appropriateness to be combined in this way. The results of Hattie and Timperley (2007) were heavily influenced by the prior meta-analysis by Kluger and DeNisi (1996) because they said it was 'the most systematic' and 'included studies that had at least a control group, measured performance, and included at least 10 participants'. This sounds good until the implications are realised. Other meta-analyses among the 74 therefore included studies with no control group, fewer than 10 cases, and/or did not measure performance!

When we conducted a review of enhanced feedback, we used the sieve approach described in Chapter 3. We ignored all of the single studies rated 0, and focused only on studies with primary age mainstream students. We found 19 studies of at least 1 🔒, and the majority of these (14) were only 1🔒. Of these 14 tiny weak studies, 11 (or 79%) reported positive findings (Gorard et al. 2017). If these are included in a synthesis without a quality rating (as is usual) this poor research would skew the overall result towards positive. Of the other five studies, three were considered 2🔒, of which only one was positive and two were negative about the use of enhanced feedback. The final two were considered 3 or 4🔒 (the strongest), of which one was positive and one negative. When quality is taken into account the picture for enhanced feedback is far less rosy than had been painted by prior reviews. Our point here is not about feedback itself, which is only used as an example, but about how untrustworthy most summaries of existing research can be. This has to change.

What should money not be spend on?

We have reviewed a considerable body of evidence on how to improve school outcomes (e.g. See et al. 2020). There is increasing evidence on school, family and classroom interventions/resources that can help reduce the attainment gap (Sharples et al. 2011, Gorard et al. 2017, See and Gorard 2020). There is an even larger body of evidence on plausible-sounding ideas that do not seem to work. And there remains a large number of plausible approaches whose impact is unclear because they have not been properly tested. We will only mention a few of these ideas here, concerning things that did not work or have not been tested. Given scarce and limited educational resources, these are approaches that money should not be spent on at present, while there are more evidence-led approaches available.

Parental engagement, for example, has been shown to be closely associated with children's learning and children's attainment (e.g. EEF 2021). Evidence from developing countries suggests that financial incentives given to parents can improve children's school attendance (Akresh et al., 2013, Cardoso and Souza 2004). Some studies even suggest that cash incentives given directly to disadvantaged children, instead of parents, can improve their school attendance and attainment (Alam et al., 2011, Sharma 2010). But intervening to enhance parental engagement in children's learning and school life has not yet been demonstrated to be a clear causal factor in equalising the academic outcomes of disadvantaged children. Therefore, funding programmes to support parental involvement for disadvantaged children are not a promising use of money if the main objective is improvement in student attainment (See and Gorard 2015a, 2015b; See et al. 2021a). This may seem counterintuitive, but most research on parental engagement fails to find evidence of effects, mainly because those parents who are most in need of support are the least likely to take part, or most likely to drop out.

The situation is similar for many ideas, such as the concept of family "cultural capital", which is often used by academics and government as an explanation for social inequalities in school and later-life outcomes. There is little evidence that engagement in highbrow cultural activities by itself, or enhancing so-called cultural capital, makes a positive difference in attainment outcomes (Stopforth and Gayle 2022). This is because a large majority of relevant studies are only correlational in design (or worse), so are unable to control for unobserved or confounding factors.

There are many examples like these, where an association is too often mistaken for causation. Positive attitudes to education, high aspirations, good "behaviour", and a positive self-concept are strongly associated with educational attainment at school. Correlational studies, however, do not and cannot indicate the direction of any causation. For example, is it high aspirations and a positive attitude that lead to better performance at school, or is it that students who perform well develop high aspirations and a positive attitude? If it is the former, then raising aspirations and attitude should improve attainment. Structured reviews of evidence suggest that this either does not work or has not been tested properly (e.g. Gorard 2012).

Similarly, engagement in uniformed activities like Scouting, and in youth social action like litter-clearing, shows some promise in assisting wider school outcomes such as self-esteem and team-work. But they are less promising for attainment outcomes (Siddiqui et al. 2019). The same could be said for extra-curricular activities in general (Kravchenko and Nygård 2022).

As a final example, just because successful schools invest heavily in IT or Edtech does not necessarily mean that technology is the cause of the success (See et al. 2021a, 2021b). The overall evidence on the use of technology in schools is not promising, despite what advocates might claim (Gorard et al. 2016, Evans and Acosta 2020). There are still many unknowns and many caveats with regards to the use of educational technology.

In fact, many popular approaches reported by others as most promising in improving the attainment of disadvantaged pupils (including current favourites like metacognition) are not nearly as clear once the quality of the evidence is taken into account. The evidence and the findings presented in this book do not always support popular beliefs. This is because the evidence we have collected has been carefully calibrated and filtered in terms of its trustworthiness, a process which is largely missing in most previous reviews.

Final word

The good news is that school attendance has increased, and the attainment gap has decreased in the areas of India and Pakistan in our study. National segregation and the long-term poverty attainment gap in England have declined over time and across regions, mostly in a way that can be associated specifically with the post-2011

Pupil Premium era. This has happened in all regions, and for students recognised as having a special educational need or disability, and for major ethnic groups. If the improvements noted can be (at least partly) attributed to the Pupil Premium funding policy then there are also implications for school funding in other countries faced with similar issues. Given a choice between providing incentives for teachers, families or students, general funding for schools, and the kind of targeted resource represented by Pupil Premium funding, education systems should prefer the latter on the basis of the overall evidence. The funding must be tied to school intakes (following students if they move) and not to schools or areas, and its use must be exclusively for the most promising evidence-led resources and interventions. This use would have to be audited better than it is now, in order to make the payments conditional on coherent evidence use.

References

Akresh, R., de Walque, D. and Kazianga, H. (2013) Cash transfers and child schooling: evidence from a randomized evaluation of the role of conditionality, *World Bank Policy Research Working Paper* 6340.

Alam, A., Baez, J. and Del Carpio, X. (2011) Does cash for school influence young women's behavior in the longer term? Evidence from Pakistan, *Evidence from Pakistan (May 1, 2011). World Bank Policy Research Working Paper* 5669.

Allen, R. (2018) *The pupil premium is not working (part III): Can within-classroom inequalities ever be closed?* https://rebeccaallen.co.uk/tag/pupil-premium/

Baird, S., McIntosh, C. and Özler, B. (2011) Cash or condition? Evidence from a cash transfer experiment, *The Quarterly Journal of Economics*, 126, 4, 1709–1753.

Cardoso, E. and Souza, A.P. (2004). The impact of cash transfers on child labor and school attendance in Brazil, Microsoft Word - 1cardoso-souza_nov03.doc (psu.edu).

De Janvry, A., Finan, F., Sadoulet, E. and Vakis, R. (2006) Can conditional cash transfer programs serve as safety nets in keeping children at school and from working when exposed to shocks?. *Journal of Development Economics*, 79, 2, 349–373.

DfE (2018) *Opportunity Area Programme*, https://www.gov.uk/government/publications/opportunity-area-programme-research-and-analysis

Education Endowment Foundation (2021) *Parental engagement*, Parental engagement | Education Endowment Foundation | EEF.

Evans, D. and Acosta, A. (2020) Education in Africa: What are we learning?, *Journal of African Economies*, 30, 1, 13–54.

Gemmink, M., Fokkens-Bruinsma, M., Pauw, L. and van Veen, K. (2021) How contextual factors influence teachers' pedagogical practices, *Educational Research*, https://doi.org/10.1080/00131881.2021.1983452.

Gorard, S. (2005) Academies as the 'future of schooling': is this an evidence-based policy?, *Journal of Education Policy*, 20, 3, 369–377.

Gorard, S. (2012) Querying the causal role of attitudes in educational attainment, *ISRN Education*, 2012, Article ID 501589, 13 pages, https://doi.org/10.5402/2012/501589

Gorard, S. (2018) *Education policy: Evidence of equity and effectiveness.* Bristol: Policy Press.

Gorard, S. (2020) *Getting evidence into education: Evaluating the routes to policy and practice*, London: Routledge.

Gorard, S. (2021) *How to make sense of statistics: Everything you need to know about using numbers in social science.* London: SAGE.

Gorard, S., See, BH and Morris, R. (2016) *The most effective approaches to teaching in primary schools*, Saarbrucken: Lambert Academic Publishing.

Gorard, S., See, B.H. and Siddiqui, N. (2017) *The trials of evidence-based education: The promises, opportunities and problems of trials in education*. London: Routledge.

Gorard, S., See, B.H. and Siddiqui, N. (2020) What is the evidence on the best way to get evidence into use in education? *Review of Education*, 8, 2, 570–610.

Gough, D. (2007) Weight of Evidence: a framework for the appraisal of the quality and relevance of evidence, *Research Papers in Education*, 22, 2, 213–228, https://doi.org/10.1080/02671520701296189

Hattie, J. (2008) *Visible learning*, London: Routledge.

Hattie, J. and Timperley, H. (2007) The power of feedback, *Review of Educational Research*, 77, 1, 81–112.

Kluger, A.N. and DeNisi, A. (1996) The effects of feedback interventions on performance: A historical review, a meta-analysis, and a preliminary feedback intervention theory. *Psychological Bulletin*, *119*(2), 254.

Kravchenko, Z. and Nygård, O. (2022) Extracurricular activities and educational outcomes: evidence from high-performing schools in St Petersburg, Russia, *International Studies in Sociology of Education*, https://doi.org/10.1080/09620214.2021.2014933

Lundborg, P. and Rooth, D. (2021) *Swedish school lunch reform, nutrition, and lifetime income | VOX, CEPR Policy Portal (voxeu.org)*, Swedish school lunch reform, nutrition, and lifetime income | VOX, CEPR Policy Portal (voxeu.org).

Madaleno, M. and Waights, S. (n.d.) *Guide to scoring methods using the Maryland Scientific Methods Scale*, https://whatworksgrowth.org/public/files/Scoring-Guide.pdf

Morley, S. and Coady, D. (2003) *From social assistance to social development: Targeted education subsidies in developing countries*, Peterson Institute Press: All Books.

Morris, R. and Dobson, G. (2020) Spending the pupil premium: What influences leaders' decision-making?, *Educational Management Administration and Leadership*, 1741143220905062.

Schools Week (2021) Schools face new checks to ensure pupil premium spending 'backed by evidence', *Schools Week*, 31/3/2021, Pupil premium: Schools told spending must be 'backed by evidence' (schoolsweek.co.uk).

See, B.H. and Gorard, S. (2015a) The role of parents in young people's education - a causal study, *Oxford Review of Education*, 41, 3, 346–366, https://doi.org/10.1080/03054985.2015.1031648

See, BH and Gorard, S. (2015b) Does intervening to enhance parental involvement in education lead to better academic results for children? An extended review, *Journal of Children's Services*, 10, 3, 252–264, https://doi.org/10.1108/JCS-02-2015-0008

See, B.H. and Gorard, S. (2020) Effective classroom instructions for primary literacy? A critical review of causal evidence, *International Journal of Educational Research*, 102, https://www.sciencedirect.com/science/article/pii/S0883035519317719?dgcid=coauthor

See, B.H., Gorard, S., Siddiqui, N., El Soufi, N., Lu, B. and Dong, L. (2021a) A systematic review of technology-mediated parental engagement on student outcomes, *Educational Research and Evaluation*, Full article: A systematic review of the impact of technology-mediated parental engagement on student outcomes (tandfonline.com).

See, B.H., Gorard, S., Lu, B., Dong, L. and Siddiqui, N. (2021b) Is technology always helpful?: A critical review of the use of education technology in supporting formative assessment in schools, *Research Papers in Education*, https://doi.org/10.1080/02671522.2021.1907778

Sharma, D. (2010) *Incentives for academic achievement: An experimental study* No. 320-2016-10418, 10.22004/ag.econ.61032.

Sharples, J., Slavin, R., Chambers, B. and Sharp, C. (2011) *Effective classroom strategies for closing the gap in educational achievement for children and young people living in poverty, including white working-class boys*, Centre for Excellence and Outcomes in Children and Young People's Services, Closing the Gap.pdf (york.ac.uk).

Siddiqui, N., Gorard, S. and See, B.H. (2019) Can learning beyond the classroom impact on social responsibility and attainment? An evaluation of the Children's University youth social action programme, *Studies in Educational Evaluation*, 61, 74–82.

Staufenberg, J. (2019) Re-focus pupil premium on teacher retention and CPD, say MPs, *Schools Week*, 21/2/19, https://schoolsweek.co.uk/re-focus-pupil-premium-on-teacher-retention-and-cpd-say-mps/

Stopforth, S. and Gayle, V. (2022) Parental social class and GCSE attainment: Re-reading the role of 'cultural capital', *British Journal of Sociology of Education*, https://doi.org/10.1080/01425692.2022.2045185

Whittaker, F. (2021) Narrowing attainment gap stopped being 'main focus' of DfE in 2015, says former permanent secretary, *Schools Week*, 5/3/21, https://schoolsweek.co.uk/narrowing-attainment-gap-stopped-being-main-focus-of-dfe-in-2015-says-former-permanent-secretary/

INDEX